Red Modernism

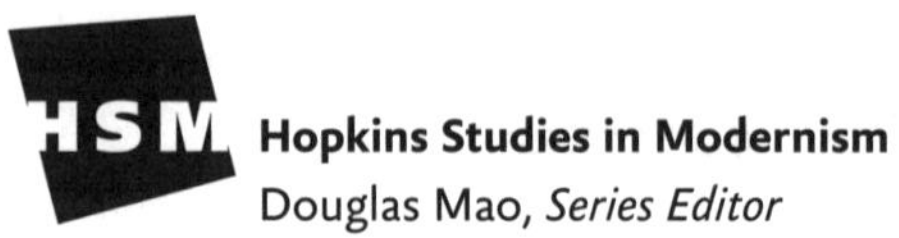
HSM
Hopkins Studies in Modernism
Douglas Mao, *Series Editor*

Red Modernism

American Poetry and the Spirit of Communism

Mark Steven

Johns Hopkins University Press
Baltimore

Printed in the United States of America on acid-free paper
9 8 7 6 5 4 3 2 1

Johns Hopkins University Press
2715 North Charles Street
Baltimore, Maryland 21218-4363
www.press.jhu.edu

Library of Congress Cataloging-in-Publication Data

Names: Steven, Mark, author.
Title: Red modernism : American poetry and the spirit of communism / Mark Steven.
Description: Baltimore, Maryland : Johns Hopkins University Press, 2017. | Series: Hopkins studies in modernism | Includes bibliographical references and index.
Identifiers: LCCN 2017003427 | ISBN 9781421423579 (hardcover) | ISBN 9781421423586 (electronic) | ISBN 142142357X (hardcover)
Subjects: LCSH: American poetry—20th century—History and criticism. | Modernism (Literature)—United States. | Communism and literature. | BISAC: LITERARY CRITICISM / Semiotics & Theory. | POETRY / American / General. | POLITICAL SCIENCE / Political Ideologies / Communism & Socialism.
Classification: LCC PS310.M57 .S745 2017 | DDC 811/.509112—dc23
LC record available at https://lccn.loc.gov/2017003427

A catalog record for this book is available from the British Library.

Johns Hopkins University Press uses environmentally friendly book materials, including recycled text paper that is composed of at least 30 percent post-consumer waste, whenever possible.

Contents

Acknowledgments

I am enormously grateful to the team at Johns Hopkins University Press, without whose collective labor the book in your hands would not exist. Douglas Mao is the most generous and attentive reader. His suggestions remade the manuscript for the better, and his goodwill has been a sustaining force. Working with Matthew McAdam and Catherine Goldstead has been a pleasure. Julia Ridley Smith sharpened my prose and saved me from countless errors. The anonymous reader contributed some excellent recommendations, especially on distinguishing between socialism and communism.

The now extinct Centre for Modernism Studies in Australia was the principal site of this book's long gestation. A thousand thanks are due to Julian Murphet, who guided this project through its initial phases as doctoral research. Julian has been a source of both razor-sharp criticism and comradely enthusiasm. He's a fierce interlocutor, and I owe a good deal of what I know about literature to his influence. Similar thanks are due to Sean Pryor. The generosity of Sean's intellect knows no bounds, and neither does his knowledge of poetry. This work also benefits from ongoing conversation with Kristin Grogan and Alex Howard and from the critical wisdom of Ruth Jennison and Chris Nealon. Everyone mentioned here read versions of the manuscript at various stages of incompletion.

Materially, this book owes much to the Faculty of Arts and Social Sciences at the University of New South Wales. Three years of relatively uninterrupted research were made possible by two scholarships. The Faculty also paid for two trips to the United States, where I enjoyed digging through poetry archives in New Haven, Austin, and Buffalo. I have to thank James Donald and Andrew Schultz for appointing me as a Research Fellow, which allowed for the manuscript's final stages of revision. Since that appointment, Helen Groth and George Kouvaros have been able guides through the weird trapeze act that is academia. Thank you, too, to Mary de Rachewiltz for permission to quote from unpublished material by Ezra Pound.

As with all long projects, this one overlapped with endings as well as beginnings. I am sorry that my dad, Bob Steven, cannot read this book (or at least shelve it with some pride) because he died before its completion. Dad's politics were pretty much indefensible, and he only knew one poem. The poem was called "Fleas," and it went like this: "Adam had'm." I'd like to think his loving recitations of these immortal five syllables (the title always preceded the rhyme) somehow evolved into my enthusiasm for both poetry and communism, perhaps by instilling an unconscious sense that even the simplest prosody might contain the utopian alternative to a world in which Adam must suffer his fleas.

Finally, this book is dedicated to Kate and Finn Montague. If it is true that family now serves as the last bastion of primitive communism—as a necessary safeguard against the isolating depredations of a universal market—then it is with these two that I have found truth. Kate embodies immense strength and Finn ceaseless wonder. This book is for them.

Red Modernism

1 Introduction

Modernism's Communism

The Real Movement

In 1917, a blinding flash of revolutionary energy lit up against the night sky of modernity's global territories. Capitalism's outcroppings were illuminated in all their jagged unevenness. Economic shock resounded across the earth's surface. Fallout irradiated every species of political discourse. And, by the end of October, a red sun had surfaced over Moscow. For Leon Trotsky, the Russian Revolution's most perspicacious historian and one of its more committed advocates, this event marked the beginning of an epic: "The working class of the world has seized from its enemies the most impregnable fortress—the former Czarist empire. With this stronghold as its base, it is uniting its forces for the final and decisive battle."[1] Almost three decades before economic negation could give way to thermonuclear antagonism, the Russian Revolution had already inaugurated the principal dissension that would characterize the short twentieth century. It fulfilled an antagonistic prophecy that had always been intrinsic to the definition of communism. Many years earlier, in 1845, Karl Marx and Friedrich Engels had described communism as the forcible suppression and subsequent supersession of capitalism. "We call communism," they wrote, "the *real* movement which abolishes the present state of things."[2] That abolition, which amounts to nothing less than the comprehensive annihilation of capitalism's relations of production, would be sanctioned by the promise of a new sociality, "an association, in which the free development of each is the condition for the free development of all."[3] In Russia, this association became a real possibility. Capitalism had been leveled. Socialism took hold. Communism was to follow. "To the Russian working class and its battle-tempered Communist Party belongs the honor of making the beginning," enthused Trotsky.

"By its October Revolution the Russian proletariat not only swung open the Kremlin doors for the representatives of the international proletariat but also lodged the cornerstone in the edifice of the Third International."[4] Elsewhere across the globe, and especially in the United States of America, the utopian soundings of this new sociality would resonate in overtone and dissonance with the inborn utopianism of what we now call modernism.

This book is about modernism and communism. It provides a new account of modernism in the United States by opening up a hitherto underexplored domain in the political history of avant-garde literature, especially avant-garde poetry. Its intention is to amplify that resonance between the universal idea of communism, the revolutionary socialist state, and the American modernist poem. It does so by showing that numerous major concerns held by avant-garde poetry during the period often described as modernism were variously responsive to the politics, ideology, science, utopianism, militancy, and overall spirit of communism. My aim is to demonstrate that modernist literary production defined itself in relation to communism to an extent that requires any serious historical account of modernism to reckon with that contemporaneous phenomenon. By "communism" and "communist," I mean a modern political ideology forged by figures like Marx, Engels, Lenin, Trotsky, Stalin, Mao Zedong, and Fidel Castro, as well as the motivation for a practical politics that once found powerful expression through state socialism in and after the Russian Revolution. Those other interrelated terms, "modernism" and "avant-garde," will acquire more specific meanings later and in process, but for now we can settle with provisional definitions of "modernism" as a period in cultural and aesthetic history defined by the uneven economic developments of industrial capitalism, and of "avant-garde" as the path-breaking artistic practices that responded to those developments and eventually helped solidify modernism into an ideology. Working with those terms, this introductory chapter sketches a theory of modernism and communism, addressing the highly mediated relationship between avant-gardes and vanguards, issuing some preliminary definitions, setting out methodological qualifications, and summarizing the historical conjuncture in which modernism was formed. It also contains a handful of illustrations taken from several poets who are not at the forefront of the following chapters, which comprise detailed engagements with three of the most recognizable modernists in poetry: Ezra Pound, William Carlos Williams, and Louis Zukofsky.

The subsequent chapters are designed to show the interplay between communism and a limited number of literary works that attest to those writers' sense and deployment of poetry. The strategy for reading poetry here coheres with Walter Benjamin's directive for all politically committed aesthetic criticism: because "the correct political tendency of a work includes its literary quality, because it includes its literary tendency, we can now formulate this more precisely by saying that this literary tendency can consist either in progress or in regression in literary technique."[5] In order to make good on the real distance between literature and politics, between aesthetic creation and the destruction of capital, between modernism and communism, the claims made by this chapter and the chapters to follow are all wagered on the hypothesis that the politics of art is invariably a matter of aesthetic production, or what Benjamin calls the quality, tendency, and technique of literature. Any literary engagement with communism must be mediated by and simultaneously make its presence felt within the material substance of literature—by and within the complex interplay of language, sound, and image. As Jacques Rancière stipulates, in a similar vein to Benjamin, "'politics of literature' means that literature 'does' politics as literature—that there is a specific link between politics as a definite way of doing and literature as a definite practice of writing."[6] Bearing all of this in mind, our engagements with Pound, Williams, and Zukofsky, as well as with a handful of other poets, take the shape of historically embedded readings, which attend first and foremost to the specifically literary strategies through which communism finds itself mediated into lines of modernist verse. In other words, the primary interest here is in those procedures whereby political content and revolutionary context become entangled with literary form: with questions of diction, meter, rhythm, syntax, tone, and so on. But our focus is not nearly as myopic as that makes it sound. The subsequent chapters also use their favored literary works as an occasion to map the relationships between modernism, communism, and numerous other occurrences of historical and poetic interest. For instance, the chapter on Pound discusses his investments in large-scale industry, in radio, and in militarization; the chapter on Williams discusses his latent romanticism, his theories of the imagination, his evolving sense of poetic portraiture, and his late-career interest in economics; and the chapter on Zukofsky, the poet most readily identifiable with communism, rereads his poetry as a type of science fiction, underscoring its affections for interstellar exploration and cybernetic technology.

There is a loosely geographical logic to the way these chapters have been ordered and arranged. We begin with Pound because his cosmopolitanism put him in much closer proximity to the Russian Revolution and the USSR than the other two poets, even though they were generally more sympathetic to communism's ideology. During the 1910s, Pound was conscious of inhabiting the England described by Marx half a century earlier as the epicenter of global capitalism. From Paris during the early 1920s, he heard firsthand accounts of the Russian Revolution. And, during World War II, he was deeply embedded in the far Right of a European culture that was militarily cleaving between the forces of communism and those of fascism. All of this positioned Pound as a kind of geopolitical lightning rod—in his own words, one of "the antennae of the race"[7]—receiving communist signals and relaying them back through the conductive substance of modernism. The chapters on Williams and Zukofsky return us to American soil. The argument about Williams evolves through that poet's nativist and regional sense of modernism, to describe how the Russian Revolution and the USSR actively shaped his thinking about class in the USA and specifically in New Jersey, and goes on to examine his late absorption of Marx-inflected economics, if not actual Marxism. The argument about Zukofsky emphasizes the geographical and ideological distance between the USA and the USSR. Specifically, it begins with Zukofsky's perception of the radical differences between the American and Soviet contexts, and it explores the utopianism that results from his electrifying attempts to connect the two. After these three case studies, a brief epilogue proposes summary conclusions about the relationships between modernism and communism more generally before gesturing to an ongoing narrative of both in the ascent of postmodernism. That epilogue looks to a moment when the story of Lenin, Trotsky, and Stalin's Russia is eclipsed by Mao's China and Castro's Cuba, two socialist states that would enter into the political unconscious of postmodern poetry.

Pound, Williams, and Zukofsky all enjoyed exceptionally long careers, collectively spanning modernism in literature and the pre–Cold War years of state socialism in the USSR (at least up until Nikita Khrushchev succeeded Stalin as general secretary in 1953). But the duration of these poets' literary careers notwithstanding, their names have become close to synonymous with modernism in poetry in a way that lends heuristic and polemical value to their privileged positions here as case studies. These poets are our focus because of the enormous influence they are understood to have exerted over the development of modernist poetry in America and because of the critical familiarity that influence has afforded them. But rather than implicitly endorse the myth of a monumental modernism, my intention is to reexamine already familiar episodes from the development of modernist poetry precisely because of that familiarity. The point here is to demonstrate the active presence of communism in poems where, despite the critical attention from which they have already benefited, it has somehow been overlooked or underplayed. Communism has received more critical attention in Zukofsky's writing than it has in the writing of the other two, of course, but still there are more ways to appreciate how communism seized hold of his unique aesthetic. In sum, my reading within a set of poets and poems whose claim to modernism is relatively uncontroversial is a tactical maneuver, designed to focus critical attention on elements of poetry that might have been engaged with or responsive to communism without having to make at length the case that the poems are indeed modernist. These poets and their poems are modernist, in short, because they actively respond to the cultural logics of modernity; because they register the process of modernization as incomplete, uneven, and contested; and because they use all of that to imagine a noncapitalist future. That there is a good deal of consensus on what makes each of these poets modernist will therefore maximize the critical dividends of an argument that seeks to demonstrate, through these particular bodies of work, the transformative role of communism within modernism. But another reason for settling with these three poets is that they all wrote their major works within one very specific genre: the modern epic.

Epic and Totality: Forms of History

There is, for Alain Badiou, "an essential link between poetry and communism," which resides in the fact that, "as the poem gives its inventions to language and as language is given to all, the material world and the world of thought must be given integrally to all, becoming no longer the property of a few but the common good of humanity as a whole." In this view, poetry and communism belong together, finding common cause in a shared antipathy to private property, looking toward the one utopian destiny independent of place and time. He insists further that the one genre in which this communitarian association is bound to play out is the epic. "The communists' poem," he argues, "is first the epic of the heroism of the proletarians."[8] Though putting too much faith in Badiou's abstractly formalist argument would lead to an undesirably ahistorical essentialism, here I want to modify its hypothesis and formulate a materialist theory about communism and the epic. What Badiou is really interested in is the classical epic, derived from the models of Homer and Virgil, not because of that genre's totalizing aspirations but because of its emphasis on the heroism of struggle. But that genre, in its unadulterated and ancient form, has been outmoded by history and has evolved into what Franco Moretti describes as the modern epic, or "world text," a form that nevertheless bears traces of the classical epic in its textual genetics. According to Moretti, the modern epic claims for itself the representation of totality as orchestrated by the economic integration of the globe under capitalism, "combined development: where historically non-homogenous social and symbolic forms, often originating in quite disparate places, coexist in a confined space."[9] When, during the modernist period, the epic found itself drawn into engagements with the Russian Revolution and with the founding of the USSR, it did so primarily because that event fundamentally shifted the parameters of global development, instantiating a viable alternative to capitalism and doing so from within one of capitalism's economically underdeveloped enclaves, thus restructuring the world that was to be absorbed by world texts.

To cite only the most familiar example of this genre—which, as it happens, is not a poem but a work of prose—perhaps that sense of totalization is why Leopold Bloom, in a narrative event written in August 1920 but set on June 16, 1904, delivers a utopian manifesto trimmed with communist injunctions and bound up in socialist conceptualization.

> I stand for the reform of municipal morals and the plain ten commandments. New worlds for old. Union of all, jew, moslem and gentile. Three acres and a cow for all children of nature. Saloon motor hearses. Compulsory manual labour for all. All parks open to the public day and night. Electric dishscrubbers. Tuberculosis, lunacy, war and mendicancy must now cease. General amnesty, weekly carnival with masked licence, bonuses for all, esperanto the universal language with universal brotherhood. No more patriotism of barspongers and dropsical impostors. Free money, free rent, free love and a free lay church in a free lay state.[10]

Although not all of Bloom's social vision is directly related to communism and while his manifesto reads more like a satire on utopianism than its serious articulation, these words nevertheless mark an obvious incursion of communist thought into the modern epic's high-water mark of aesthetic attainment. This outburst speaks to so much more than the fiery form taken by Bloom's reformist liberalism, and it does so because the thinking totalizes. "Revolution," as Joshua Clover tells it, "is a total thought, a thought of the totality; they are necessarily entangled. Reform, repair, regime change, recuperation," by contrast, "all of these are the politics of the partial, of isolating specific problems as if they admitted of independent solution."[11] On that score, Bloom is indeed thinking more like a communist revolutionary than a liberal reformer. His seemingly hyperbolic phrases echo popular conceptions of socialist economics; the circumambient desire for positive universalism in opposition to national chauvinism finds its historical adjunct in the Comintern; the use of machines instead of humans for labor is, in its affirmative as opposed to exploitative conception, a socialist aspiration; and, importantly, the seemingly indiscriminate coupling and negation of scientific, psychological, geopolitical, and economic ills is cognate to any revolution's totalizing ambition. More overtly responsive to communism than all of that, however, Bloom also decries the unnamed industrialists of Dublin's Nighttown, using not only the rhetoric of Marxism but a direct allusion to one of communism's founding documents. "Machines is their cry, their chimera, their panacea," he intones. "Laboursaving apparatuses, supplanters, bugbears, manufactured monsters for mutual murder, hideous hobgoblins produced by a horde of capitalistic lusts upon our prostituted labour."[12] As is well known, the first English translation of *The Communist Manifesto* said nothing about stalking specters but instead referred to its eponymous ideology as a "frightful hobgoblin" sprung from the recently industrialized forces of production.[13] Bloom, it would seem, senses his place not only within the world system but also as the modern embodiment of an ancient genre, the epic hero now facing off against the monstrosity of capital itself, and thus he finds himself preternaturally and presciently drawn to communism.

If, as Moretti avers, one of the characteristic features of modern epics is that they "reveal a kind of antagonism between the noun and the adjective: a discrepancy between the totalizing will of the epic and the subdivided reality of the modern world," communism may well have contributed to the further modernization of the genre, given that it instigated one of history's most insurmountable subdivisions. That is one of the ancillary lessons of C. D. Blanton's work on what he calls "epic negation," a dialectical form that deploys evidentiary documents and metonymic allusions to intimate the force and flux of history without ever claiming to encapsulate historical totality as such. The refreshing novelty of Blanton's argument—which has its roots in G. W. Hegel and Georg Lukács, as well as Moretti—is its critically belated hardwiring of modernism's insurrection in verse to history's parallel revolution, which took place in Russia after 1917. For instance, Blanton provides us with a strong account of T. S. Eliot's late-career appeals to Marxist thought, showing how a modified sense of dialectical materialism underwrote Eliot's evolving idea of culture and how it informed the metonymy of fragmentation in some of his poems. "For what Eliot discovers most fundamentally in Marxist thought," argues Blanton, "is the need to account systematically for the entirety of bourgeois culture, not merely to resist a few of its aspects but rather to grasp the interpenetration or even identity of all of its aspects at once."[14]

Looking earlier, however, we can see clearly how the force of revolution infiltrates Eliot's most recognizably epic poem, an exemplarily self-negating work of literature that, in Blanton's words, "chronicles the formation of modernist critical thought in real time, both absorbing and propounding its largest contradictions."[15] With the publication of *The Waste Land,* in 1922, one of the major events in poetic modernism entered into uneasy alignment with historical communism, to which it may well have been guided by the totalizing drive of its chosen genre. Here, as in "The Second Coming" by W. B. Yeats, referential engagement with political history is obscured by dense figuration and religious mysticism. Nevertheless, in the poem's fifth and final section, modernism and communism are drawn together as though magnetically by a concern for the historical process Eliot's ironic endnote disparages as "the decay of eastern Europe," a process that sends its "hooded hordes swarming" out westward "over endless plains" and "over the mountains."[16] These lines are glossed with a quotation from Herman Hesse on Eastern Europe, which strengthens a potential association with the Russian Revolution. "Already half Europe," the note has been translated, "already at least half of Eastern Europe, is on the road to Chaos, drives drunken in holy madness along the abyss and sings the while, sings drunk and hymnlike as Dmitri Karamazov sang."[17] Though it might seem overreaching to suggest that communism helped shape the poem's sense of European geography, thereby transforming this modern epic's totalizing worldview, that is precisely the suggestion its author would make five years later. "For the Russian Revolution has made men conscious of the position of Western Europe," recalled Eliot in 1927. "And this awareness seems to be giving rise to a new European consciousness. It is a hopeful sign."[18]

As we shall see, Pound, Williams, and Zukofsky understood the Russian Revolution as an augury not just for poetics but also for life under capital, and so they responded to it as part of the historical totality in ways that forced transformation in the means of poetic composition. That said, if there is another poet who writes of communism in the epic mode, surely that poet is Muriel Rukeyser. As Jenny Goodman has rightly maintained, "Rukeyser successfully reworks epic conventions to compose a narrative of national redemption in which women become shapers of myth and history."[19] My sense, however, is that Rukeyser reworks these conventions without necessarily writing modern epics or without committing to that genre's totalizing aspirations. Instead, her brilliance stems from the way she infuses lyric and dramatic verse with epic tropes and tones so as to equip individual experience with collective and communizing affect. That is what we encounter, for instance, in an early poem concerned with the Scottsboro Trial of 1931. It opens by locating revolutionary potential within a historical climate defined by ideological circumscription and conservative foreclosure. For Rukeyser, the trial is an expression of "eternal death of the soul and the body in murder or despair," which will persist, we are told, "until the thoughtful rebel may triumph everywhere." But the revenants of this quasi-Nietzschean "eternal death" also manifest through epic katabasis, when the guilty verdict invokes a spectral army of "sweet generous rebels," whose collective presence amounts to a source of political strength. Once the guilty verdict is delivered, when "the mythic lips of justice open, and speak," the reaction is purely and irreducibly epic.

> Hammers and sickles are carried in a wave of strength, fire-tipped,
> swinging passionately ninefold to a shore.
> Answer the black-thrown Negro face of the lynched, the flat
>   forehead knotted,
> the eyes showing a wild iris, the mouth a welter of blood,
> answer the broken shoulders and these twisted arms.
> John Brown, Nat Turner, Toussaint stand in this courtroom
> Dred Scott wrestles for freedom there in the dark corner
> all our celebrated shambles are repeated here: now again
> Sacco and Vanzetti walk to a chair, to the straps and rivets
> and the switch spitting death and Massachusetts' will.[20]

The first two lines transpose a vision of the protesting communists, amassed under "fire-tipped" banners, out of Scottsboro, Alabama, and onto the "shore" of an ancient battleground. Epic affect inhabits the African Americans who now stand prosecuted and whose martyred bodies have amassed behind the proper noun "Negro." The epic genre writes itself upon the nine boys' collective body, on "the flat forehead knotted," in "the eyes showing a wild iris," and in "the mouth a welter of blood," as the "black-thrown" heroes of revolutionary struggle, the warrior souls of John Brown, Nat Turner, Toussaint Louverture, and Dred Scott, manifest alongside it. This is a moment of defeat, to be sure, but even in defeat the collective stands affirmed. Only through the collective does communism escape or exceed its "celebrated shambles" to obtain a conciliatory "wave of strength," and in this poem the collective is distinctly epic. Not content to draw strength from the living combatants of a bannered army, the heroic body now stands shoulder to shoulder with the immortal shades of its political prehistory.

And yet, what makes these lines from Rukeyser epic (in the ancient as opposed to the modern sense) is their affectionate predisposition toward a heroically embattled communism, to a kind of political subjectivity that finds antecedent in Homer and Virgil. While Rukeyser's subsequent poetry would reach for totality, here in its explicitly communist mode we encounter something else: communism as personal experience, as an affectively charged way of being, operating aside from the material determinations of political economy. What I want to argue, inversely, is that the specifically modern epic, with its purchase on fractured or negated totalities, is the one genre predisposed by its historical circumstances to engagements with communism irrespective of personal experience. In other words, my interest is in the way certain literary forms, specifically the modern epic, incline their authors to engage with particular content, regardless of those authors' political commitment. Badiou, by contrast, settles exclusively with poets committed to communism—namely, César Vallejo, Pablo Neruda, and Bertolt Brecht—and whose commitment is given straightforward articulation. This, the hypothesis of generically encoded necessity, is reason to critically favor the three most prominent epic poets of the modernist period as opposed to affirmatively communist poets who then use the epic genre in pursuit of political writing. And even if, in the following chapters, totality is not always addressed by name, the questions it motivates are pursued through an abiding concern with that insurmountable division between two economic systems and their respective states. That is to say, communism as it is encountered here has less to do with Badiou's philosophical formalism and more to do with the determinations of political economy. Pound, Williams, and Zukofsky all compose verse that spans the tectonic rift between communism and capitalism, between the USSR and the USA, and thereby totalizes into one form the principal economic as well as a significant geopolitical antagonism of their historical moment. The modern epic's totalizing impulse is at its most pronounced in these works when they apprehend the absolutely adversarial relationship between two modes of production and two different kinds of state. Aesthetic reactivity to that relationship—not a staid configuration but the ever-changing stuff of history, of two very possible world-historical paths—is what makes these poems not just modernist but also definitively avant-garde.

Avant-Garde and Vanguard, Specters and Hobgoblins

It will be advantageous here to rehistoricize the concept of the avant-garde within its revolutionary conjuncture and to emphasize the avant-garde's coherence with social antagonism and revolutionary commitment. We already know that the Russian Revolution and its global repercussions occupied the same temporal coordinates as avant-garde modernism in the United States—that these two occurrences ran on parallel timelines. Indeed, the present argument takes hold of poetry from within the historical simultaneity of modernism in American literature and the geopolitical sequences initiated by Russia's exemplarily communist event. We also know that, since Peter Bürger popularized the argument back in 1974, it has become a critical commonplace that the term "avant-garde" derives from a military vocabulary and that, during the period of modernism, the historical avant-garde was primarily associated with the political discourse of communism.[21] As Matei Calinescu summarizes, "since the early 1890s, but especially after the 1917 October Revolution in Russia, and with increasing emphasis during the whole Stalin era, the term avant-garde came to be almost automatically associated with the idea of the monolithic Communist party. That was true not only for the Soviet Union but for Marxist-Leninist orthodoxy all over the world. Because of the role it played in the Marxist-Leninist-Stalinist political idiom, the term developed, for the adherents of that doctrine, such highly reverent connotations that its use in other contexts would almost have been regarded as blasphemy." Calinescu clarifies that the avant-garde is reducible to neither communism nor modernism, though it nonetheless designates, possibly within modernism, an artistic ally for communist revolution. That alliance owes itself to a shared enemy. "The most prominent students of the avant-garde," he insists, "tend to agree that its appearance is historically connected with the moment when some socially 'alienated' artists felt the need to disrupt and completely overthrow the whole bourgeois system of values, with all its philistine pretensions to universality."[22] Of course, and whether it was mere posturing or not, that avant-garde desire for complete overthrow was simultaneously articulated and committed to action by communism's living embodiment in the USSR. "It is still necessary," declared Lenin in 1917, "to suppress the bourgeoisie and crush their resistance."[23] However, as Raymond Williams reminds us, the political coordination of the avant-gardes, in their rabidly anti-bourgeois stance, has always been fissiparous: "The new art could find its place either in a new social order or in a culturally transformed but otherwise persistent and recuperated old order."[24] Reaction and revolution are equally probable when it comes to avant-gardes, and in the second and third decades of the twentieth century, we witness both. But what about avant-gardes in the United States, which never really had an "old order" to begin with, or at least not in the culturally dominant way that Britain and Europe did, and which never stood a serious chance of crushing and suppressing the bourgeoisie, as was the case in Russia?

If "bourgeois" (in the nontechnical sense used by Calinescu) refers to a set of values embodied by a particular class, one of the most contextually important of which is its predilection for socially expressive consumption, perhaps we need to modify our sense of what it is that both aesthetic avant-gardes and political vanguards oppose in the period of modernism and specifically in the United States, where bourgeois culture was undergoing considerable transformations in the emergent hegemony of Fordism. Christopher Nealon describes those changes in his excellent account of modernist poems from the 1930s, in which he demonstrates that the interregnum between world wars was defined, politically and economically, by "an ever-expanding, and ever-intensifying, process of consumption that linked political personhood to commodity activity," and which thereby dispersed the bourgeois culture of consumption into the broader paradigm of capitalism. For an avant-garde to react against this historical expression of the bourgeoisie is to therefore engage capitalism as an entire mode of production, or at least to engage one of its most prominent superstructural articulations, a fact that became widely apparent in relation to communism: "That this interwar conjunction of the political and economic problems and strategies was specifically capitalist is made clear by reactions to the emergence, after 1917, of a noncapitalist world centered on Soviet Russia, whose seeming immunity to the ups and downs of the business cycle in the 1920s and 1930s led both to strident anticommunism and to social-democratic compromises between labor and capital in the United States and Europe alike."[25] It is thus that the vanguards and the avant-gardes from the modernist period find their otherwise different energies combined in opposition not only to the bourgeois class or culture but also to capitalism as a system of systems. By pursuing a similar line about avant-garde poetry in the 1930s, Ruth Jennison helps us square the relationship between communism and modernism. In her analysis, the modernist period was defined by two historical events, "bound together by their opposition," whose centripetal energy fuses modernism's unstable social materiality out of a supercharged communism and an unstable capitalism. "The twentieth century's most visible of capitalist crises—the global Great Depression of the 1930s and the socialist revolution conducted against the system of exploitation as a whole—combine and clash in a global, antagonistic unity."[26] Building on the allegorical intimations of Calinescu and Williams, the critical lesson I want to distill from the materialist work of Nealon and Jennison is that, because of its opposition to capitalism, avant-garde modernism in the United States is haunted at every turn by the communist specter that was first named in 1848 and which aggressively materialized in October 1917.

That specter—or hobgoblin, as it was for Bloom and the earliest translators of Marx and Engels—is what we encounter in the most unlikely of places, where writing that would otherwise have existed at a peaceable remove from political ideology found itself drawn inexorably into the gravitational field of communism. To cite only the most celebrated of these outwardly apolitical avant-garde poets, it was not until Gertrude Stein set out to write a book about the United States, published in 1936, that she felt the need to engage with communism, and there she would imply that her verse was antagonized by its historical presence. Here Stein attempts to reconcile a cultural history of the nation with its natural landscape in one long prose poem, and in doing so she produces this line of integration:

> What is the relation of communism individualism propaganda to human nature what is the relation of it to the human mind or is there none. There is a human mind oh yes there is one. Is there any relation to it in communism individualism or propaganda and has all that only to do with human nature, has it has it, remember about tears and age and memory and swallows flying and birds which always sing the same thing to any one but not to themselves they the birds have tears but no memory.[27]

Stein diverts from or perhaps even answers the question of communism and humanity with recourse to a series of bird images, which by contrast to the disembodied political concepts of "communism individualism propaganda" seem all the more organic and perhaps even naturally beautiful. The human mind is said to manifest not through those concepts but instead through the lyric imagination, which is bound up in the intense personal experience of "tears and age and memory," so that communist ideology and a self-conscious lyricism deflect away from one another. The deflection suggests that, for Stein, there can be no positive relation between political thought and humanity as she understands it, and that poetry—which is both described and enacted in the rhyming assonance of "birds which always sing the same thing"—aligns with humanity at the cost of any sort of meaningful engagement with communism. "Communism," to be sure, is coupled with "individualism" and "propaganda," which together form a triumvirate of ungainly-sounding terms unlike the consistently shorter and sonically pleasing words that surround them. And this forceful separation between communism and humanism, working on levels of both content and form, is maintained elsewhere. Later, Stein describes a subjectivity that "cannot listen to the human mind," which, the text insists, therefore belongs to "a communist. A communist and individualist a propagandist a politician cannot listen to the human mind, a business man can and anybody who can sit and write can he listen to the human mind." Of course, these lines were written at a significant remove from both the ideals and the actualities of communism. To equate communism with all individualism and all propaganda is willfully reductive and even contradictory, not to mention just plain wrong, but to then oppose the "communist" to the "business man," a clichéd embodiment of capital, is to betray sensitivity to the economic enmity within which that opposition obtains and to choose sides therein. In other words, this writing finds itself compelled to self-define, as avant-garde poetry, in relation to and emphatically against communism. Capitalism mediates between communism and the poem, but this time it produces an entirely negative reaction, which momentarily redirects Stein's poetry into the generic realm of sentimental beauty whose birdlife serves as a clarifying double to her own prosody.

But the communist specter is not exclusive to avant-garde poetry. A provisional argument can be made that the more narrative arts realized, in their various structural impulses, how they too would find kinship with communism. The agitprop posters of El Lissitzky and Kazimir Malevich, the world-historical murals of Diego Rivera, the revolutionary symphonies of Shostakovich, the balletic choreography of Kasyan Goleizovsky, Eisensteinian montage and Vertovian Kino-Glaz, Brechtian stagecraft, Piscator's epic theater, Rodchenko's monochromes—all of these artistic achievements, which retroactively group together as avant-garde modernism, were deeply and openly indebted to the idea of communism and to the actuality of socialism in Russia. As for narrative production at an ostensible remove from that actuality, Fredric Jameson has interpreted modernism's renovation of literary character as an allegory for "the transformation of the world itself, and therefore of what is called revolution," the historical phenomenon exemplified by communist politics.[28] Keeping within a strictly American frame of reference, that revolutionary character lives and breathes in numerous works of narrative art spread across multiple media. In the novel, we have the terrorist insurgents of Henry James's late fiction, the historical persons who populate John Dos Passos's and John Steinbeck's sprawling chronicles of working-class struggle, and the heroes of any given proletarian novel from the period, but perhaps most famous are those characters in the semi-autobiographical tales of Mike Gold, Jack Conroy, and Tillie Olsen. The Provincetown Players drew together revolutionaries and dramatists to produce an avant-garde theater that found its greatest success under the direction of Eugene O'Neill. Hollywood, while not necessarily avant-garde, served to deliver the most popular of all the narrative arts; numerous films of the period either include communist characters or plot their action in relation to the Russian Revolution. A playful sampling includes some well-known moments in film history. D. W Griffith used the French Revolution as an allegorical caution against the swelling tides of Bolshevism. Cecil B. DeMille did much the same with his blockbuster Bible stories. The great ape, King Kong, was not only the gloriously monumental embodiment of proletarian revolution, but his ascent of the Manhattan skyscraper is virtually identical to an award-winning sketch of Lenin's statue atop the unrealized Palace of the Soviets in Moscow. When Greta Garbo first laughed for the cameras, she did so as a special envoy sent to Paris on official business from the Soviet Union. And when Charlie Chaplin speaks at last, in the final minutes of his satire on fascism, he does so in language whose every syllable has been infused with the unmistakable rhetoric of communism.[29] Avant-garde or not, the centrality of these texts to our understanding of a specifically American modernism brings with it the ideological import of communism; flanking poetry, which is our singular focus, modernist texts in prose, theater, and film variously attest to the presence of communism in the historical atmosphere and the aesthetic regime.

Descending from this more theoretical vantage and into the real of literature, the chapters that follow are a consolidated attempt, in league with a number of well-known propositions made along comparable lines, to push the analogies between avant-garde and vanguard a step further and to gauge the real outcome of modernism's determinant relationship with communism. That said, although our interest is in the effect of communism on modernism, we should remain alert to the fact that this relationship contains some degree of reciprocity, with the socialist regime in Russia integrating avant-garde aesthetics into its propaganda and modeling elements of its statecraft on artistic design. This, for Boris Groys, is the structural correlate of communism's economic regulation. "When the entire economic, social, and everyday life of the nation was totally subordinated to a single planning authority commissioned to regulate, harmonize, and create a single whole out of even the most minute details, this authority," he argues, "was transformed into a kind of artist whose material was the entire world."[30] Like Groys, Susan Buck-Morss is acutely sensitive to how the socialist state attempted to incorporate avant-garde art for the perpetuation of a political vanguard: "Lenin immediately articulated this revolution even in terms of cosmological temporality, situating the October Revolution within world history, and in his Plan for Monumental Propaganda he sought to secure this vision of a particular historical trajectory with the help of art."[31] While the aesthetic dimensions of the socialist state are not our primary focus, to realize that communism also sought to absorb modernism into its own program, even if only doing so in fits and starts, establishes an understanding of their relationship as already reciprocal. By accounting for the opposite determination, the transposition of forms from communist politics into modernist aesthetics, I want us to think in new ways about avant-garde modernism as the collaborative other to communism, a term that now requires more detailed explanation.

Keywords: Communism, Socialism, Capitalism

In essence, "communism" means developing humankind's productive forces free of capitalism's class relations and to such an extent that production will satisfy the material needs of absolutely everyone. The closely related concept "socialism" is the strategy for transitioning out of capitalism to what Marx calls the "higher phase of communist society."[32] And "capitalism," the negative referent of those first two terms, is a social order structured around the antagonism between two irreconcilable classes, one of which works while the other accumulates the value of that work. These three politico-economic terms—"communism," "socialism," and "capitalism"—are best explained in conjunction. The founding premise of socialism is that it is both possible and desirable to eradicate capitalism's relations of production in pursuit of a sociality predicated on economic cooperation, as opposed to exploitation. To do so, however, will require the tactical seizure of state power, which will be used to crush the armed forces of counterrevolution while establishing the postcapitalist economy. Lenin is particularly lucid and singularly influential on the role of socialism and of the socialist state in an intermediary stage between capitalism and communism. "The transition from capitalism to communism is certainly bound to yield a tremendous abundance and variety of political forms," he says, "but the essence will inevitably be the same: *the dictatorship of the proletariat.*" According to Lenin, the dictatorship of the proletariat, a socialist reversal of capitalism's relations of production, will lead to the eventual abolition of those relations and, with that abolition, the hard-won actualization of stateless communism. "The possibility of this destruction," or so Lenin described the eventual eradication of the bureaucratic apparatus, "is guaranteed by the fact that socialism will shorten the working day, will raise the people to a new life, will create such conditions for the majority of the population as will enable everybody, without exception, to perform 'state functions,' and this will lead to the complete withering away of every form of state in general."[33] From capitalism to socialism, from socialism to communism: this stagist model of history is what informed political action in Russia after 1917, with its revolutionary implementation of state socialism directed toward the end goal of a communist utopia.

Even though these conceptions will mutate in their material applications and political adaptations through history, with communism and socialism typically being conflated into one entity, and while they regularly enter literature in admixture with various other forces, the idea of communism as a mutually beneficial association between working men and women, to be achieved after the socialist abolition of capitalism, is retained here because its adventure comprises one of the great untold narratives in the story of modernism. An unavoidable part of that narrative is the USSR's failure to produce communism and the gradual separation of the socialist state's policies from the political beliefs with which it was created. Even though enthusiasm for the idea of communism outlived enthusiasm for the USSR, decline in the latter nonetheless meant that avant-gardes lost their principal means of imagining communism as the direct consequence of a living socialist precursor and therefore as an immediate historical probability. There are several reasons for this waning of enthusiasm. These include the USSR's "Socialism in One Country" policy, first proposed by Stalin in 1924, which contradicted a founding premise of communism by shifting the parameters of political aspiration back from global revolution to focus on internal strengthening of the Soviet state. Other reasons are the Left's defeat in the Spanish Republic in 1939, the Nazi-Soviet Pact later that year, and, most emphatically, revelations of the show trials, mass murders, and other horrors of Stalinism. "Irresoluteness before the individual peasant enterprises, distrust of large plans, defence of a minimum tempo, neglect of international problems," wrote Trotsky in 1937—all of this shaded the very essence of Stalin's policies.[34] However, acknowledging these frequently catastrophic shortfalls as historical fact is not to endorse the all-too-prevalent morality tale of lapsed judgment, according to which modernism's poetic engagements with communism would only amount to brief flirtations punctually thwarted by revelation of communism's irreducible "truth," a brutal totalitarianism dressed up in egalitarian ideals. Rather, it is to concede the real distance between socialism and communism, and then between the reality and the rhetoric of the USSR, which had undeniably widened over time as the socialist state failed to produce communism. As we shall see, the poets themselves were highly attuned to these distinctions.

In 1945, for instance, Wallace Stevens composed a poem that explicitly references the historical personage of the Russian Revolution and, in its shifting tonalities, potentially intimates the scission between communism and socialism—or, more specifically, between a sense of utopian futurity and its stalled realization in the state. This poem, "Description Without Place," includes a glimpse of the historical and philosophical preconditions that gave rise to the Russian Revolution, and it connects them up with the lyricism of Stevens's own established poetic.

> Lenin on a bench beside a lake disturbed
> The swans. He was not the man for swans.
>
> The slouch of his body and his look were not
> In suavest keeping. The shoes, the clothes, the hat
>
> Suited the decadence of those silences,
> In which he sat. All chariots were drowned. The swans
>
> Moved on the buried water where they lay.
> Lenin took bread from his pocket, scattered it—
>
> The swans fled outward to remoter reaches,
> As if they knew of distant beaches; and were

Dissolved. The distances of space and time
Were one and swans far off were swans to come.

The eye of Lenin kept the far-off shapes.
His mind raised up, down-drowned, the chariots.

And reaches, beaches, tomorrow's regions became
One thinking of apocalyptic legions.[35]

At first impression, this poem appears to thoroughly dehistoricize its historical content by installing the subjective paragon of communism beside a lake, where that figure, now just a man or even a romantic symbol, attempts to feed the swans. And yet, there are reasons to argue that Stevens's poem is too referential to be a mere exercise in pure formalism. In the years preceding the Revolution, Lenin was indeed confined to a life in Switzerland, by Lake Zurich, which remained landlocked by multiple countries engaged in imperialist warfare. It was in Zurich that Lenin famously studied Hegel, Feuerbach, and Aristotle, all of whose philosophy informed the dialectic that would provide ideational ballast to his political strategies for the implementation of state socialism. That is what this poem seems to be channeling: the dialectic is mobilized, with the swans as its agents, in the folding together "of space and time," so that "swans far off were swans to come," all of which posits historical flight as emanating from the "mind" of Lenin. While that flight is sutured to those traditional avatars of poetic lyricism—the swans—the lines themselves seem to endorse the combination of lyric beauty and the idea of communism with a series of internal and feminine rhymes ("reaches" and "beaches," "one" and "come," "regions" and "legions") that attach the language of this decadent silence to the mind of an impatient revolutionary. It is precisely when the scene goes loud, in the "disturbed" action of the swans' collective flight, that their submerged "chariots" transform into those of the "apocalyptic legions" preparing to make landfall in "tomorrow's regions." Even if this poem clearly echoes the reactionary verse of Yeats and Eliot, positing a causal line from thoughtful communist to socialist apocalypse, it nevertheless maintains a distinction between these two things, imagined at the point of their dialectical entanglement. According to Alan Filreis, who reads the poem in the context of postwar anticommunism, Lenin here "participates in the decay of purely imaginative, inconsequential rumination" by attempting, "even in his reduced state, to control 'the far-off shapes' and to transform a harmless, local poetic observation of receding swans into advancing, transregional 'apocalyptic legions.'" In other words, the thesis of this passage could be that "the revolutionary imagination itself eschews a specific sense of time and place in order to do its exclusively forward-looking work—work done nonetheless in the name of history."[36] What we encounter, then, is a vision in which an idea or ideal is torpedoed by history—a vision in which communism spoils in its transposition through socialist actuality, becoming the bureaucratic-military machine.

"Surely," Stevens would muse several years after the publication of this poem, "the diffusion of communism exhibits imagination on its most momentous scale."[37] If that sentiment, which privileges the idea of communism over the actuality of socialism, remains oblique because obscured by Stevens's complex and overarching irony, it enjoys much clearer articulation in the work of Pound, Williams, and Zukofsky. What the ideologically divergent writing of these three poets shares is not just a commitment to the epic or an avant-garde disposition but also a unique appreciation for that frequently overlooked distinction between communism and socialism. They were all attuned to the problem of transitioning from socialism to communism, and to that problem's historical ramifications both in and out of the USSR. While this problem is glimpsed retroactively and thus conclusively in Stevens's lyric from 1945, for Pound, Williams, and Zukofsky it becomes gradually visible in real time, doing so precisely because of that commitment to the epic, which in all three cases necessitates sustained attention to historical totality during a period of decades when that distinction was making itself widely known. And yet, as we are going to see, for the three poets examined here, communism evolved through an unstable historical sequence and as a multifaceted, interpretable ideology. Rather than adhering to a coherent or predictable narrative—be that an apparent teleology or the rise and fall of the socialist state under Lenin and Stalin—communism meant vastly different things when considered from different perspectives and at different times. In short, the political beliefs of each poet modified over time and in response to the rapid development of reality, with the contexts of communism's reception becoming just as important as the thing itself. Pound's thinking and writing about communism in fascist Italy were vastly different from those of Williams, whose view of politics was filtered through the radical history of New Jersey, and from those of Zukofsky, whose outlook was shaped by a perceived distance between his ancestral homeland, Lithuania, and his actual home in Manhattan. All things considered, this book's approach to the evolution of three distinct bodies of poetry as they transition between various political positions is designed to make obvious that American poetry has been engaged with, if not the entire breadth of communist thought, then at least a multitude of its historically specific and popular variants.

Here, however, it should also be clarified that Lenin's view of the socialist state need not be adapted into an immutable and iron law of its own, which might well affirm the state form and socialist realpolitik as the supreme models of anti-capitalism, but neither should this view be understood as a mere failure of theoretical aptitude. The state is—for Lenin in 1917 as much as it remains today—necessarily contested terrain for any sort of revolutionary politics geared toward the establishment of communism. "If we do not think that the state should remain in the hands that it is in," Jodi Dean has written, "then we lapse into the politics of the beautiful moment when we fail to factor it into our political perspective."[38] Once again, political economy asserts itself as integral to the modern epic, to the avant-garde, and as a distinguishing factor among poets. Pound, Williams, and Zukofsky all understood communism not as an ahistorical abstraction or formalist ideal, not as "the beautiful moment" of Lenin by Lake Zurich, but as the result of material processes, both economic and political, to which the state would be of central importance. That is to say, during the second, third, and fourth decades of the twentieth century, state socialism appeared as a practical necessity, a weapon against capitalism. Even then, however, its realization would become increasingly undesirable, whereas communism lived on as something yet to be established: an immortal idea wanting for content, alive to the immemorial utopian currents of thought itself.

Always Mediate!

One of the great temptations for dialectical criticism is to use structural homology as a means of resolving different forms into a synthetic absolute—to exploit the logic of what Louis Althusser once called "expressive causality." If, for instance, a modernist avant-garde and a communist revolution were found to be analogous, the task of the critic would be to demonstrate how these otherwise autonomous phenomena might be assailable together because they are temporally or formally analogous. As an interpretive method, this approach can be dangerously reductive in its adherence to what Hegel once cautioned against as "monochrome formalism," the kind of thinking that repeats the same interpretive formula in relation to everything it encounters and thereby approaches all things as abstract.[39] In this instance, either the revolution would be approached as if it were an avant-garde, or the avant-garde as if it were a revolution, because the two share similarities, irrespective of that insurmountable difference between political and aesthetic forms. With each category assimilating into its opposite, a literary history that accedes to this temptation might conclude that modernism, with its various aesthetic ruptures and antibourgeois postulates, is the aesthetic ideology in which all avant-gardes are revolutionary and therefore communist. We have already encountered this kind of argument with Badiou, but it is just as prevalent within the more specialist discourse of modernist studies.

For instance, in a pioneering book published in 2006, Martin Puchner has produced such an argument, comparing aesthetic and political manifestos based on the theoretical misconception that, within this genre, it is the manifestos' "form, not their particular complaints and demands, that articulates most succinctly the desires and hopes, maneuvers and strategies of modernity: to create points of no return; to make history; to fashion the future."[40] Slavoj Žižek is particularly keen to disabuse us of any overinvestment in this kind of thinking and makes his point with reference to a particularly appurtenant anecdote. "The encounter between Leninist politics and modernist art (exemplified in the fantasy of Lenin meeting Dadaists in the Cabaret Voltaire in Zurich) cannot structurally take place; more radically," he insists, "revolutionary politics and revolutionary art move in different temporalities—although they are linked, they are two sides of the same phenomenon which, precisely as two sides, can never meet."[41] Or, as Eric Hobsbawm is surely right to emphasize, as a materialist historian, even though the shared temporality of political vanguards and artistic avant-gardes might suggest their affiliation, the suggestion alone cannot constitute sufficient conditions to suppose a unitary circuit between them. "There is no necessary or logical connection between the two phenomena," he says, "since the assumption that what is revolutionary in the arts must also be revolutionary in politics is based on a semantic muddle."[42] That is to say, even if modernism and communism were intimately associated, a final synthesis of the two into a single, unitary phenomenon—or, in this case, a single, abstracted form—would simply be a mystification.

A properly materialist account of modernism and communism begins here, in the affirmation of their asymptotic relationship as an incontrovertible fact. Understanding that modernist literature and communist politics can only relate by way of parallax, with each phenomenon occurring semi-autonomously from the other, is methodologically necessary for a compelling account of modernism's communism. Bearing that in mind, the present undertaking recovers the details of modernism's connection to communism without converting either category into an abstracted reflection of the other. The goal is to account for literary modernism as related and responsive but ultimately irreducible to communism. The historical simultaneities and structural analogies shared by modernism and communism will more fruitfully serve as mediations, connective pathways between the double helix of politics and art, orchestrating transferences between these two autonomous phenomena without neglecting the irreconcilable differences between them. In other words, I want to insist methodologically on the necessity of mediation: a dialectical third term that facilitates the adaption of critical analysis from one level or instance to another, or the establishment of what the economists might call a "lateral field of causality" between seemingly disparate entities.[43] While mediation has enjoyed significant and polemical attention in materialist theory, Jameson's illustrious account is the one best suited to the present undertaking. In his explanation, mediation announces itself as "the classical dialectical term for the establishment of relationships between, say, the formal analysis of a work of art and its social ground, or between the internal dynamics of the political state and its economic base." As a critical method, mediation is in itself a durable form of anti-capitalist thinking. As Jameson notes, mediation is not only "a device of the analyst" but also used to overcome the division between regions in social life, and in such a capacity it doubles as a psychical counterforce to the reifying divisibility of life under capital. In short, it allows us to apprehend the otherwise inaccessible force and flux of totality: "Such momentary reunification would remain purely symbolic, a mere methodological fiction, were it not understood that social life is in its fundamental reality one and indivisible, a seamless web, a single inconceivable and transindividual process, in which there is no need to invent ways of linking language events and social upheavals or economic contradictions because on that level they were never separate from one another."[44] In that sense, the present strategy for reading accords with the universalizing aspirations of its poetic and political subject matter —communism, to be sure, is the realization of that entanglement, the "seamless web" of totality itself, as inalienable social substance. Here, at the level of method, the medium is indeed the message.

While there will be context-specific mediations between particular moments in the evolution of modernist poetry and various types of communist matter, at this point I want to emphasize three circumambient or fundamental mediations that pertain to the book as a whole. To that end, the remainder of this introduction summarizes those mediations and illustrates them, using a handful of politically committed poems. With these examples, however, engagements with communism derive as much from the genre of poem as from the authors' personal experience and political commitment. That these illustrative poems are all lyrics suggests they will also be, in contradistinction to the epic, both subjective and instantaneous. As such, these poems are structured by communism in ways different from those associated with the epic. In the lyric, we should expect responses to communism to take shape as though from within a single speaking consciousness and from a particular instant in space and time. In the epic, that consciousness is more dispersed, and so communism might be grasped there from multiple perspectives or from an evolving perspective. Because the lyric is composed with this personal orientation, it is all the more likely to articulate politics in such a way that we hear a distinct political accent in the shifting cadences of its speech. While that means these poems are not as well placed to grasp anything like historical totality, they nevertheless offer clarifying insights into moments of political apprehension as subjectively decisive, when the work of mediation is laid bare.

First Mediation: Labor's Obstinacy

During modernism's flourishing, one historical contradiction above all generated the conditions of possibility for an essential mediation between American letters and Russian politics: namely, the rapid intensification of that generalized conflict between labor and capital. Specifically, labor's realization as the structural opposition to capital took shape via a politics of tactical obstinacy, to borrow a term from Alexander Kluge and Oskar Negt, which found a powerful ally in the socialist state.[45] The Red Scare of 1919 was the product of a genuine fear that labor in the United States was going to follow Russia into socialism. The fear was well advised, given that, after 1917, Lenin, Trotsky, and the other Bolsheviks were openly declaring their intentions of worldwide revolution, the possibility of which now seemed more real than ever. As Lenin indicated in 1918, "The American workers will not follow the bourgeoisie. They will be with us, for civil war against the bourgeoisie. The whole history of the world and of the American labor movement strengthens my conviction that this is so."[46] While the Red Terror was being reported and condemned in newspapers across the United

States, various unions and labor organizations were identifying or being identified with the Russians and preparing for a year of industrial action: "Altogether during 1919 there would be 3,600 strikes in the US, involving more than four million workers—for which it was all too easy, and convenient, to blame Bolshevik agitators."[47] The presence of obstinate labor within American poetry predates the Russian Revolution and the formation of the USSR. However, after 1917 labor found itself catalyzed anew by the real possibility of revolution. For instance, an early poem by Carl Sandburg, written in 1916, begins with a metaphysical landscape. Its speaker observes the "blue haze and red crag" of mountains, is amazed at "endless tide manoeuvres," pauses beneath "the stars on the prairie," and is said to be always "full of thoughts." But the speaker knows he cannot reside here, because the poem belongs not to that elevated inscape but to the social reality that grounds it: "And then one day I got a true look at the Poor, millions of the Poor, patient and toiling; more patient than crags, tides, and stars; innumerable, patient as the darkness of night—and all broke, humble ruins of nations."[48] This is a moment of demystification, an epiphany made flesh, in which the truth of social contradiction makes itself known—when "the Poor," a multitude whose anonymity here has everything to do with their stated innumerability, assert a presence more concrete and more real than any of the images the speaker might otherwise imagine. This interest in the nation's immense reserves of labor power would, after the Russian Revolution, see its object reorganize under the banners of communism. The supposed patience manifestly wears thin.

Lola Ridge composed this incendiary address as early as 1920.

> They think they have tamed you, workers—
> Beaten you to a tool
> To scoop up hot honor
> Till it be cool—
> But out of the passion of the red frontiers
> A great flower trembles and burns and glows
> And each of its petals is a people.[49]

The first four lines echo Marx's account of capitalist ontology as a chiasmus wherein humans become objects and objects take on a life of their own. Contracted as variable capital, the worker is degraded to the status of an inhuman "tool," whereas the product of his labor, the commodity, absorbs his humanity (what this poem refers to as "honor"), which coagulates into the sellable object. In striking opposition to this grim reality, communism presents itself as the quintessence of life: a living, blossoming flower, prospering in "the passion of red frontiers," whose constituent workers all retain their singular petal-like integrity. Other poets worked harder to represent the devastation of labor under capital—perhaps the best poem to do this is Rukeyser's "Book of the Dead" from 1938—but the juxtaposition of labor under communism and labor under capitalism finds exemplary treatment here in Ridge.

In 1934, Richard Wright concluded a long poem by prophesying the activation of labor's revolutionary consciousness, uniting black and white workers in class solidarity against capital.

> I am black and I have seen black hands
> Raised in fists of revolt, side by side with the white fists
> Of white workers,
> And some day—and it is only this which sustains me—
> Some day there shall be millions and millions of them,
> On some red day in a burst of fists on a new horizon![50]

This poem presents a single black subject's vision of the world and his imagination of a utopian future. It relates the revolutionary blackness of its speaker to the revolutionary class of white workers. Their common "revolt" brings them "side by side," thus projecting a future of interracial harmony but also a future contingent upon the kind of solidarity promised only by communism. So it is that the shared destiny of black and white is necessarily "red," with which the metonym of "hands" becomes that of "fists." It was a vision that did not last. When the USSR abandoned its progressive policies on race and agreed to the Hitler-Stalin Pact, the probability implied by "some day" and "some red day" became an apparent impossibility. Wright, along with Ralph Ellison and Chester Himes, would later abandon this enthusiasm for the USSR.

One year later, in 1935, this poem by Lorine Niedecker used a beachside setting and a unique visual arrangement to decry capital and affirm communism.

> No retiring summer stroke
> not the dangerous parasol
> on the following sands,
> no earth under fire flood lava forecast,

not the pop play of tax, borrow or inflate
but the radiant, tight energy
boring from within
communizing fear
into strike,
work.[51]

Work without end, with no foreseeable reprieve, as the scorched beach-scape of both finance capital and the leisure class (punned together in "the pop play of tax, borrow or inflate") solidifies like cooling "lava," into which no "dangerous parasol" can be driven. The first word of the first four lines modulates on negation, rhyming and repeating "no," "not," and "on," before the poem introduces a new sound that also negates: "but," which alliterates that negation with the activity conveyed by the subsequent "boring." With the introduction of communism, a "radiant, tight energy," the poem changes sound and, with each line narrower than the one above it, becomes the tip of that parasol, sharpening into a monosyllabic point. The shape of this poem is an American answer to El Lissitzky's Red Wedge, which is here ready to "strike" against the hard-baked ground of capital. That word "strike" should be read for its polysemy; like "pop" and "inflate," it describes both a beachside activity and an economic or political operation—the strike, famously affirmed by Rosa Luxemburg as central to any sort of revolutionary politics. "The mass strike," she had written in 1906, "is the first natural, impulsive form of every great revolutionary struggle of the proletariat and the more highly developed the antagonism is between capital and labour, the more effective and decisive must mass strikes become."[52] Here, at the parasol's tip, its sharpest point, we find ourselves back with the labor force whose revolutionary potential has been named in the lines from Ridge and Wright.

While anticommunism's internal manifestation only intensified that pre-existing antipathy between capital and the organization of labor, externally, socialist states were seen as a serious threat to economic imperialism, which in the twentieth century constituted the new kind of political rule: "Instead of aiming for territorial expansion along the lines of old empires, US military interventions abroad were primarily aimed at preventing the closure of particular places or whole regions of the globe to capital accumulation."[53] If 1919 was the year in which these two interrelated fears, of the communist influence over American workers and of an aggressively anti-capitalist state in the USSR, first coincided to marshal an explicitly anticommunist culture, these fears would come to a head with the "red decade" in the 1930s.[54] Here is Michael Denning's summary of this conjuncture: "The years of depression and war saw a prolonged 'war of position' between political forces trying to conserve the existing structures of society and the forces of opposition, who were trying to create a new historical bloc, a new balance of forces." Indeed, the coincidence of these events resulted in the mainstream media, elected statesmen, business owners, and self-appointed patriots together developing a bloodily hostile obsession with the quasi-socialist organizations whose members were sought out and systematically assaulted or executed. If avant-garde modernism is theoretically anti-capitalist, then modernist poetry in America was drawn into determining relationships with communism by way of capital's antithesis, namely, labor, which at that point in history identified communism as the greatest living ally to itself. "If," writes Denning, "the metaphor of the front suggests a place where contending forces meet, the complementary metaphor of the conjuncture suggests the time of the battle."[55]

What is less apparent in those poems from Sandburg, Ridge, Wright, and Niedecker, then, is the violent antagonism with which communism and communists were met when capital retaliated against labor. But other poets knew and wrote about this too. To cite just one example, Kenneth Fearing accounts for the extirpation of communists with an aesthetic that has been accurately described as "Marxist noir," a subgeneric peculiarity that recasts technological shock and economic unevenness within the hard-boiled settings of pulp fiction.[56] In these lines, from a poem published in 1935, communist commitment correlates with mortal imperilment.

> Nevertheless, we know; as every turn is measured; as
>   every unavoidable risk is known;
> as nevertheless, the flesh grows old, dies, dies in its
>   only life, is gone;
> the reflection goes from the mirror; as the shadow, of
>   even a Communist, is gone from the wall;
> as nevertheless, the current is thrown and the wheels
>   revolve; and nevertheless, as the word is
>   spoken and the wheat grows tall and the ships
>   sail on—[57]

The repeated word "nevertheless" maintains the fatalism that introduces each of these four overlapping vignettes. Taken as a whole, these lines depict the experience of capitalism in 1930s America. From the perspective of labor, "every turn is measured" and "every unavoidable risk is known," and there is no alternative to the economically circumscribed cycle of exploitation, depredation, and death. It is a situation from which the spectral figure of the communist—here, a proper noun—has abruptly and mysteriously "gone," as though to emphasize the structural foreclosure of anything antithetical to the iron law of the market. In the absence of communism, capital continues to produce and circulate its commodities: "the wheat grows tall and the ships sail on." These are granted more vitality than the dying flesh that surrounds them, whose subsistence ("only life") has been relegated to a mere supporting role for the market. The technological metaphor, "the current is thrown," not only gives expression to the mechanized sphere of production and circulation but also conjures up a specific event in the cultural history of the Popular Front that feeds into the already chilling intensity of these lines. It is, of course, an allusion to Nicola Sacco and Bartolomeo Vanzetti, two left-wing radicals who were unjustly executed in 1927, despite mass protests led by communists.[58]

Second Mediation: The Socialist State

After 1917, the world came to know what Bruno Bosteels calls "the actuality of communism," namely, the means by which communism finds "inscription in a concrete body, the collective flesh and thought of an internationalist political subjectivity."[59] Even if socialist stagism is neither the ideal nor the only means of building communism, in the years after the Russian Revolution it was indeed the socialist state that embodied "the real movement" whose ambition was to abolish capitalism the world over. Although that abolition was ultimately unrealized, we can nevertheless identify a widespread belief in the socialist state's capacity for transformation operating in multiple poems, many of which lovingly idealize an imagined Russia. This, to be sure, is what Steven Lee has described as the ineluctable allure of Moscow during the 1920s and 1930s, its "magical, even religious significance for many minority and non-Western artists and writers," to whose number we might add the socially marginalized in general.[60]

That attraction is what we encounter, for instance, when in 1932 H. H. Lewis enthusiastically confirmed the political commitment of his verse.

> I'm always thinking of Russia
> I can't keep her out of my head

I don't give a damn for Uncle Sham.
I'm a left wing radical Red.[61]

These lines are intentionally uncomplicated, and much of their pleasure arises from what Cary Nelson describes as the third line's "wilfully childish pun," which levels its charge against the national personification of the American government.[62] The internal rhymes of that third line, as well as the end rhymes of the second and fourth line, make this resemble that most playful of forms, the limerick, which endorses a willful simplicity. If the alliterations between "Russia," "radical," and "red" sonically register a coherent political through-line for the poem, the form itself is an effect of the speaker's class alignment, insofar as Lewis sought to compose verse in the vernacular language of American workers, placing his poetry and its speaker in direct confrontation with its social and literary situation. "This isn't Auden or Spender," writes William Carlos Williams. "This is a Missouri farmhand, first cousin to a mule, at one dollar a day. If Lewis' subject matter should distress some readers, it's about time they learned what makes their fruits and vegetables come to ripeness for them—and what kind of thoughts their cultivation breeds in a man of revolutionary inheritance."[63]

While, like Lewis, most American poets observed communism from afar, as a distinctly Russian or European phenomenon, and while some immersed themselves in its local manifestations through the Popular Front, several others bridged the geopolitical divide by traveling from the United States to the Soviet Union with the express purpose of experiencing the new social order firsthand. Langston Hughes visited the USSR in 1932 and composed several poems about his experience with and within the socialist state. These include a friendly address to a personified revolution ("You're the very best friend," he tells it, " I ever had"[64]) and, from the perspective of the postcapitalist émigré, this excited farewell to conservative dogmatism:

Kings, generals, robbers, and killers—
Even to the Tsar and the Cossacks,
Even to Rockefeller's Church,
Even to THE SATURDAY EVENING POST.
GOODBYE, CHRIST
Goodbye,
Christ Jesus Lord God Jehova,
Beat it on away from here now.
Make way for a new guy with no religion at all—

A real guy named
Marx Communist Lenin Peasant Stalin Worker ME—
I said, ME![65]

"The poetic voice that Hughes creates," writes James Smethurst on the poet's shifting aesthetic through the 1930s, "is not that of the individual narratorial consciousness, but of a simultaneously unitary and multiple urban community."[66] This verse, so free and open with its expostulatory rhythm and its capitalized, shouted emphases, simulates the demotic voice, meshing an African American idiom with the Soviet possibility. The first sentence, stretched across four lines, nominates the fixtures of prerevolutionary Russia and of capitalist America, readily associating the superannuated embodiments of Russian absolutism with "Rockefeller's Church," an institute that conceals the enormous wealth of the Rockefeller family with the ideological mask of organized religion. Given that these lines were penned in the USSR, it is likely that their dismissal of the church stemmed from the Bolsheviks' punitive suppression of organized religion, which Lenin and Stalin both assumed was serving as a front for the residual powers of absolutism. In the late 1920s the Soviet regime suspended all church activities, from charity to procession, with the singular exception of closed religious services: "Enthusiastic Komsomols and activists from the League of the Militant Godless engaged in acts of iconoclasm and vandalism, whilst church bells were melted down and valuables confiscated."[67] In the cultural space formerly occupied by religion, which has been cleared away by revolution, the poem asserts the primacy of a "new" and "real guy," who speaks the American lingo but identifies with the figureheads of the USSR, which are delivered as proper nouns on a line of their own, culminating in the speaker's resounding, pronominal identification with all of them. But this overwhelmingly positive identification was not to be shared by all poets who visited the USSR.

Though he was certainly not a minority figure like Lewis or Hughes, E. E. Cummings traveled to the USSR in 1935. Cummings was initially enthusiastic about communism, writing pro-communist poems and letters of endorsement immediately after the Russian Revolution and throughout the 1920s. But what he encountered in the USSR, under the rulership of Stalin, ultimately crushed that enthusiasm. As he would write to Pound, about a decade later, "It is all very well and to view it in theory, but unless a theory works for the betterment of the human race and one sees HOW IT WORKS by ACTUAL LIVING, it is no good."[68] One particularly crude and ostensibly simple poem, written that year, is an expedient indicator of Cummings's reaction against the socialists' attempts to implement communism through extreme measures.

kumrads die because they're told)
kumrads die before they're old
(kumrads aren't afraid to die
kumrads don't
and kumrads won't
believe in life)and death knows whie

(all good kumrads you can tell
by their altruistic smell
moscow pipes good kumrads dance)
kumrads enjoy
s.freud knows whoy
the hope that you may mess your pance

every kumrad is a bit
of quite unmitigated hate
(travelling in a futile groove
god knows why)
and so do i
(because they are afraid to love[69]

What makes these lines critically interesting is the way that communism, even as the poet seeks to distance himself from it, registers on the poem's technical apparatus. The first sextain reconfigures the self-sacrificial heroism of socialists as little more than the mindless commitment to a death cult. Its predictable, masculine rhymes ("told" and "old," "don't" and "won't," "die" and "whie") require that each line terminate in accordance with preceding terminations, as though these lines and their subjects, the willing "kumrads," have all been ordered to that end. It is thus that the rhyme scheme harmonizes with the unquestioning fatalism the poem describes as the defining feature of all "kumrads." The fatalism of the first sextain is then referred to in the second, in the line "moscow pipes good kumrads dance," which also nominates the fatalistic effect sustained by this isomorphic rhyme scheme. The controlling force of "moscow" is then compared with psychical development, suggesting that each "kumrad" is not just politically but also psychically susceptible to his or her own "altruistic smell" and to a "hope that you may mess your pance." The irony does not pass unnoticed. As Cummings was probably aware, "s.freud" famously emphasized the association between money and anal eroticism, between gold and feces, which can be extrapolated into a determinant relationship between the accumulation of capital and the kind of excremental uncleanliness described here.[70] Finally, the third sextain appears to maintain the rhyme scheme of the first two, but there are some differences that amount to its relaxation: the rhyme between "bit" and "hate" is broken by incompatible vowel sounds, and the rhyme between "groove" and "love" requires preposterous mispronunciation. There is an argument to be made that this final sextain's departure from the determining fixity of rhyme and its notable omission of a final clinching parenthesis reflect the belated introduction of the poem's speaking "i" and the concept of "love," neither of which want to be constrained by the communism this poem seeks to reject. Unlike the communists who travel "in a futile groove," perhaps figured here by the constrictive and almost colonic parentheses, the poem's speaker expects a kind of individuated freedom. Even though these lines rely on a conflation of the totalitarian state with its inhabitants and ideologies, and a conflation that is evidently influenced by an American sense of individualism, their technical density is first and foremost an index to the poet's understanding of the difference between the American and Soviet states, as underscored by capital.

Third Mediation: Technology

Our third mediation resides in a more speculative argument, which posits that the poets themselves discovered and developed an unstable analogy between poetic technique and manufacture technology—that they sensed a kinship between their images and their end-stops and their rhymes, on the one hand, and the machinery of industrial production, on the other. "Art," writes Theodor Adorno, "is modern when, by its mode of experience and as the expression of the crisis of experience, it absorbs what industrialization has developed under the given relations of production." That modern art's technological inflow predisposes it toward communism is particularly true of the historical avant-gardes, which materialize in what Adorno accurately describes as "an age in which the real possibility of utopia—that given the level of productive forces the earth could here and now be paradise—converges with the possibility of total catastrophe." My hypothesis for this third mediation is that, by using literary technique to distinguish between itself and the extant conditions of production or even its own social content, poetry generates "an image that is not a copy of the event but a cipher of its potential." The historical name of this potential is surely communism—a utopian mode of production that, by way of world-historical irony, only becomes a probable reality once the "productive forces" of capitalism have evolved to such an extent that they threaten history with the "total catastrophe" of absolute subsumption.[71]

This mediation is not an attempt to suggest that extraliterary technological matter leads directly to specific formal innovations or that literary technique successfully mimics industrial technology. Rather, the relationship between technique and technology is defined by a kind of pathos. While the poets themselves were exploring this relationship, it remains irreducible that literary technique will only ever correspond to industrial technology in the loosest possible sense. David Trotter's media-historical use of the term "cool" might help make this point. For him, this term describes the human subject's conscious occupation of the "slack" between technological materiality and codified information, between machines and their messages: "Cool demonstrates that the alignment between technique and technology that has been the premise of both industrialism and postindustrialism need not be precise, or complete. Technique, in short, can be diverted, momentarily, as it slackens or slacks off." In this view, literary or cultural technique reframes itself "not (only) as obedience to the laws of nature and their social enforcement, but as a 'reflection upon those laws.'"[72] That is what we encounter with this third mediation—not a strict alignment or determination but a reflexively "slack" relationship, which animates form as well as, and sometimes even primarily, a poem's theme, topic, and content. While this might still seem densely theoretical, insecure in its relationship to the texts, the following comparison between two well-known examples taken from outside of American literature should help concretize the operations of a specifically technological mediation.

It might be obvious enough that Vladimir Mayakovsky's wonderment at the seemingly infinite potential of socialist technology is more receptive to communism than F. T. Marinetti's libidinal embrace of capitalism's military-industrial complex, even though both find expression through an array of techniques classifiable as futurism, perhaps the most technologically obsessed strand of avant-garde modernism. There is, to be sure, a fundamental ideological difference between the futurism of Mayakovsky and the futurism of Marinetti: whereas the former aimed to innovate a poetry that would capture something of capitalism's utopian alternative in communism as it had been made possible by socialism, the latter's innovations consistently allied his poetry with the probable future of capitalist progress as it accelerated headlong into fascism. While that differentiation between the two goes too far to be useful for this particular demonstration, here we can nevertheless confirm that both poets engineered a similar break with their social and literary situations, and because of this they both found themselves associated with communism. While Mayakovsky used futurism to endorse communism, Marinetti explicitly defined his futurism against it, as its competition, doing so with the irony of all fascist ideologies, precisely by using communism's rhetorical means.[73] By aiming to be contemporaneous with or incorporate a historical situation that it can never fully abide, and to present a vision of the future, a poem is not necessarily guaranteed a positive relationship with communism. Rather, it enters the historical space of utopianism—which, during the time of modernism, was dominantly occupied by a socialist state aspiring for communism. As the old structuralist argument might have it, literary style serves as "a projected solution, on the aesthetic or imaginary level, to a genuinely contradictory situation in the concrete world of everyday social life."[74] If this is true, we need not overstate how helpful a really existing socialism was to that imaginary resolution.

Like those two futurists, our three poets—Pound, Williams, and Zukofsky—are all linked by a shared fascination with the meaning of technology as it is torn between capitalist ideology and utopian potential. This is yet one more reason why our focus in this study is primarily on the modern epic. Epic poems, with their matchless polyphony, are exemplarily capable of agglomerating multiple other forms within themselves, and in modernism those forms frequently bear a technological inflection. It is here, within the modern epic, that poetry's adaptive responses to the first machine age find a literary space in which to combine and comingle, to project critical visions of the present and utopian visions of the future that are variously shaped by communism. That is what we can see in the evolution of Pound's vortex-images relative to industrial turbines, in his emulations of radio voice, and in his satire on the weapons trade. We can also see it in the transformation of Williams's poetic line, which responds to the reifying technologies of the cultural industry, in the photomechanical development of his literary portraiture, and in his belated discovery of economics as a means of understanding geographical scale. And, finally, we can see it in the way Zukofsky identifies his verse explicitly with the USSR's newly liberated means of production, propelling his poetry into the space of a science fiction equally interested in extraterrestrial exploration and cybernetic advancement. In all of these cases, poetic technique forces distance between the actualities of technology under capitalism and its utopian potential, always doing so from within the inclusive space of the modern epic.

Traveling through the channels established by these three mediations—predicated on labor, geopolitics, and technology—the various forms of communism coursed outward from revolutionary Russia to infuse the wellsprings of modernist literary production in the United States. There it would find a destination in avant-garde and artistic culture more generally, by way of journals and magazines and manifestoes, to be given new expression in the aesthetic substance of literature. Within this context, the modern epic attempted to grasp the vast field of operations in which capitalism and communism rival one another as two parts of historical totality. Simultaneously, the distance between vanguards and avant-gardes would diminish as the two were drawn together in the activation of a generic predisposition: the calling forth of avant-garde literature's inherent political potentiality, which preternaturally responds to the socialist state with its communist aspirations as though the two are long-lost twins. What this study hopes for, then, is to simultaneously confirm and expand upon T. J. Clark's remarkable conjecture that modernism "sensed socialism was its shadow—that it too was engaged in a desperate, and probably futile, struggle to imagine modernity otherwise."[75] But of course, all of this only proves meaningful provided it can be convincingly demonstrated to have impressed itself on the texts themselves and that the poems did indeed gaze upon their socialist shadow, which is precisely what we are now going to see in the epic verse of Pound, Williams, and Zukofsky.

2 Ezra Pound

Factive Revolution

The Lenin Era

Ezra Pound paraphrases Vladimir Lenin in the final completed volume of *The Cantos.* "Aesopian language (under censorship)," reads Pound's version of Lenin's statement, "where I wrote 'Japan' you may read 'Russia.'" These words are lifted from the 1917 preface to *Imperialism, the Highest Stage of Capitalism*. Although the preface was belatedly added from Petrograd between the February and October Revolutions, the body of that book was completed in 1916, in Zurich, where Lenin remained in exile. "This pamphlet," claimed Lenin, "was written with an eye to the tsarist censorship," which required its author to develop his critique "with extreme caution, by hints, in an allegorical language," a language whose attentive readers "will easily substitute Russia for Japan." The twentieth century's foremost communist intelligence thus found itself encrypted in the very grain of written prose, as a literary style or mythic language, where it took shape not in covert propaganda but in what Lenin explained as an "exclusively theoretical, specifically economic analysis of facts." Lenin's avowed respect for the economy as a principal force of history is one of the reasons why his book would have appealed to Pound, a poet who insisted that he could not see how "anyone save a sap-head can now think he knows any history until he understands economics." More significantly for our present purposes, however, there is also a strong chance Pound identified with Lenin's awareness that this kind of writing requires an adequate presentational method: a technical procedure for the literary capture or even the literary encryption of economic formulae and of the invisible forces they exert. In this sense, Lenin's preface complements Pound's barely less familiar definition of his favored poetic genre. "An epic is a poem including history," claimed Pound, and by "history" he primarily means economics.[1]

The Cantos contain numerous references to Russia, as well as several descriptions of the Russian Revolution and of the national and international operations of the USSR. But, in keeping with the quotation from Lenin, much of that has been sublimated into the language itself. Indeed, this chapter accounts for Pound's specifically literary engagement with Lenin and the Russian Revolution, which he wrote about during the early 1920s, and for his engagement with the USSR under the rule of Joseph Stalin, which he wrote about through the 1930s and 1940s. My principal goal is to establish the significance of those two figures and what they represent within Pound's evolving epic. While those engagements necessarily post-date 1917, it nevertheless remains possible to identify some considerable intersections between Pound's early poetry and the thinking that informed Lenin's critique of capitalism, which derived from the economic writings of Karl Marx. This is not to contradict scholars like William M. Chace, for whom Pound's "implicit understanding" of the communist critique of capitalism "could hardly be hammered into anything resembling a Marxist dialectic," not least because Pound's insistence upon economic volition is almost entirely at odds with Marxism's logic of class struggle.[2] While it almost goes without saying here that Marx was never the dominant economic figure in Pound's congregation of sources and interlocutors, just as Lenin was not Pound's favored politician, the effect of Marx's critique of capitalism and of Lenin's political being remain highly visible in the poetry and worth study on their own terms.

This chapter therefore begins by reconstructing some of the political conceptions Pound held before and during his 1915 commencement of the poem that would occupy him for the majority of his life. The argument is that at least one aspect of communism—namely, a critique of capitalism expressed in the economic writings of Marx and the inheritors of Marx's legacy—infiltrated the aesthetic program that informed Pound's poetry when he first started work on *The Cantos*. Having established this preliminary fact, the chapter offers several new readings of key episodes from Pound's epic in light of Marx and Marxism, as well as a new understanding of his epic method in relation to communism and socialism. "Not the least part of the miracle of Lenin," wrote Pound in 1933, "was his emergence from a lot of blurry and blitery German ideology."[3] Building upon Pound's early encounters with precisely that ideology, we are then able to map the evolution of

Pound's epic not only against the rise of the socialist state under Lenin's leadership but also within historical totality as described by Marx.

Vortex. Marx.

Pound's transition out of short poetry and into the epic was supervened by vorticism, an avant-garde program whose aesthetic ideology simultaneously emphasized and abjured its own materiality.[4] As Miranda B. Hickman explains, vorticism, "having set the gold standard in the arts both through its dynamism and intelligence about form, created a powerful forcefield in Pound's thought," which then "drove his formal commitments in *The Cantos;* shaped his cultural hermeneutic; and in the 1930s, significantly guided his response to Mussolini's Italy."[5] The economic and mechanical metaphors are important here, because it is through historically peculiar expressions of industrial technology that Marx's economics first entered Pound's thought. That is to say, the relationship between communism's economic critique of capitalism and Pound's vorticism is not a simple dualism. Instead, a separate force in which Marx and Pound were mutually invested mediates between their political and aesthetic ideologies. This mediator is the evolution of industrial technology under capitalism and, more specifically, the mechanized regime in England through the nineteenth and early twentieth centuries. While vorticism took shape as an avant-garde in London during the second decade of the twentieth century, that movement would inhabit the cultural and economic terrain charted by Marx approximately half a century earlier. In the preface to *Capital,* Marx tells us that in this book he examines "the capitalist mode of production, and the conditions of production and exchange corresponding to that mode," and that this object of study is peculiar to its location. "Up to the present time," he says, "their classic ground is England. That is the reason why England is used as the chief illustration in the development of my theoretical ideas."[6] For Marx, England was the privileged site for a communist critique of capitalism, and for Pound it would be the home to vorticism. As I want to show here, these two things are meaningfully related.

"Vortex. Pound." is a manifesto published in the 1914 edition of Wyndham Lewis's *Blast.* In it, the eponymous author explains this avant-garde movement as a technical matter of poetics.

> The Vorticist will use only the primary media of his art.
>
> The primary pigment of poetry is the IMAGE.

> The Vorticist will not allow the primary expression of any concept or emotion to drag itself out into mimicry.
>
> In painting Kandinski, Picasso.
>
> In poetry this by, "H. D."
>
> Whirl up sea—
> Whirl your pointed pines,
> Splash your great pines
> On our rocks,
> Hurl your green over us,
> Cover us with your pools of fir.[7]

Vortices present themselves when an artwork asserts its own medium and when that medium is simultaneously energized as an artwork. This statement might sound like a tautology, but the point is that vorticism stands for the materialization of art through objective media, which is precisely why it has mostly been celebrated in painting and sculpture, those more physically material or "plastic" forms. In poetry, however, because words are chiefly symbolic and therefore an abstract medium, the "primary pigment" cannot materialize in any simple way, and so, for Pound, it is not words but the images they produce that constitute the poet's medium. The vorticist poet will thus rely on the image to restage the immateriality of poetic art, for no literary image can ever be a medium in the strictly materialist sense of that term. Because of this felt immateriality, vorticist poetry is said to enter a paradoxical nonspace from which it cannot be assimilated back into that material substrate comprising either the other arts or the material exigencies of its historical context. Or, in more familiar terms, vorticism means a kind of aesthetic autonomy. While this explanation remains highly theoretical, my hope is that an understanding of vorticist technique will solidify through looking closely at Pound's exemplary text, quoted from H. D., as well as some of his own poems.

Given the overwhelming presence of vortices in the poetry of William Blake and Stéphane Mallarmé (to cite only the foremost examples), we might query why Pound settles with the relatively unremarkable "Oread" to illustrate this new conceptualization of literary technique. H. D.'s poem is defined by an image of the tempestuous ocean doubled with that of woodland. The repetition of "whirl" abstracts its verbal energy from the "sea" and transfers it to the repeated noun "pines," which completes the movement with a rhymed verb, "hurl," enclosing the poem's speaking "our" within the vortex. What should be taken away from this example is that Pound's ideal image is both hydrous and circular—that it is exemplified by the evanescent patterns of a whirlpool. Indeed, an overview of Pound's oeuvre would verify that he privileges the imagistic maelstrom and its whirling transubstantiation of liquid into what Hugh Kenner refers to as the "patterned integrity" and "patterned energy" of the vortex.[8] But why, of all things, should the whirlpool serve as the favored image of vorticism in poetry, the form in which literature stages its own immateriality?

Pound's verse contributions to the same issue of *Blast* were markedly less inspired than his manifesto. As Lewis would recall many years later, "at this distance it is difficult to believe, but I thought of the inclusion of poems by Pound etc. in 'Blast' as compromising. I wanted a battering ram that was all of one metal."[9] One of the reasons the poems failed to impress is that, while adopting the rhetoric of vorticism, they did not achieve the formal abstraction or the emphatic immateriality that Pound's manifesto set out for vorticist poetry. Even though the poems are variously interested in media, they do not deliver the image their manifesto proposed as the poet's medium or primary pigment. Instead, we encounter a nominal assemblage or the "mimicry" of various media that might produce a "whirl" without any one poem ever "whirling" of its own volition, as the lines from "Oread" do. And yet, Julian Murphet is surely right to identify the formative value of these poems in relation to Pound's epic strategy, arguing that they constitute "the first appearance in Pound's oeuvre of a method that would come to typify the *Cantos,* the transformation of the space of the poem from lyric purity into a cluttered multimedial zone of interaction."[10] Formative though they are, these poems cannot live up to the formal standard set by H. D. or to the stipulations of Pound's own manifesto precisely because they have been so densely "cluttered," and not only with other media. These poems are also shot through with some typically execrable ideologemes ("Let us SPIT upon those who fawn on the JEWS and their money"), as well as glimpses of an industrial landscape ("We speak of burnished lakes/and of dry air, as clear as metal").[11] Pound's epic impulse wanted to break free of the lyric so as to include history, to think politically and economically, and here that desire appears to be working itself out as an aesthetic contradiction.

The nearest these verse contributions come to a properly vorticist "whirl" is in the opening quatrain of a poem that would later be republished alongside the lines from H. D. and Pound's interview with Russian literary critic, Zinaida Vengerova: "The lateral vibrations caress me,/They leap and caress me,/They work pathetically in my favor,/They seek my financial good.[12] "Lateral vibration" is a technical term that refers to the destabilizing transfer of kinetic energy through rotational machinery and into a mechanical shaft. In all four lines the speaker of this poem submits to those active forces. The anaphoric pronoun "they" turns the "lateral vibrations" of the first line into a proximate matrix whose centripetal energies pass through the speaker, the poem's mechanized "me," conjoining it with the realm of "financial good." While these lines successfully situate the "patterned integrity" and "patterned energy" of vorticism within its historical present, equating poetry with the industrial environment of finance capitalism, where they disappoint is in their attempt to militate against that setting and preserve a kind of literary autonomy by use of subjectivist complaint. Decrying machines or capitalism as merely "pathetic" is disingenuous and ultimately mitigates the poem's otherwise productive identification with the vorticist energies it senses operating within the mode of production. The poem's complaint, which is much less persuasive than the satires Pound would develop later in his career, forces a humanist distinction between these lines and the technology they represent. While H. D. had a certain "lyric purity" on her side that allowed for her vortex to present itself as a natural image, Pound, by contrast, wants to abstract a similar image from capitalism's urban milieu, a setting that has inexorably foreclosed on what he might describe as the "Wordsworthian, false-pastoral" landscapes of lyricism.[13] Taking shape between these lines and their accompanying manifesto, the formal challenge for poetic vorticism is therefore to produce an image out of the mode of production and its technologies, but one that abstracts from the historical present and approaches immateriality. The strategies by which Pound met this challenge can be found in his contemporaneous engagement with economics and how that engagement redirected him away from questions of aesthetic autonomy and ultimately toward the politically committed stylistics of Marx.

A Bastardized Marxism

Prior to his 1914 formulation of the vortex, Pound worked as a columnist for the political magazine *New Age,* where his frequently scathing tirades about semi-industrial London entered into dialogue with criticism that was informed by and indebted to the ideas of Marx. Wallace Martin has provided a useful explanation of the magazine's ideological positions under the editorship of A. R. Orage, who published close to three hundred of Pound's columns. "As the first Socialist weekly in London," writes Martin, "it recorded the tactical history of a crucial phase in the relations between Socialists and the newly created Labour Party."[14] While the magazine's theoretical prehistory points up an engagement with Marx, its localized accent on parliamentary and labor politics would guide a transformation in its dominant ideology—a transformation that also impressed itself indelibly upon Pound's own thinking. As Martin accounts for it, "an increasing uneasiness regarding the theoretical basis of Socialism led Orage and many of his contributors to a rejection of its collectivist premises and, after 1912, to the elaboration of a political theory which came to be known as Guild Socialism." Many of Pound's co-contributors were themselves steeped in Marxian thought, if not its theory then at least its rhetoric. Tom Villis has described this accurately. "Indeed," he says, "much of the rhetoric of the *New Age* borrowed from the language of social revolutionary thought. Its conclusions were a kind of bastardization of the Marxist legacy."[15] This is less a criticism than it is a statement of fact. Witness, for example, Herbert Read's essay from June 1916, "Sorel, Marx, and the War," which concludes by taking Marx at his most teleological and stagist but also by replacing communism with the magazine's favored ideology: "Remember, too, that the more highly organised capitalist industry becomes, the more economically virile will be the industrial society which the guilds inherit."[16] What such "bastardization" would eventually sire was the magazine's avowal, as shared by Pound, of one economic program in particular: the Social Credit theory of C. H. Douglas, whose critiques of industrial capitalism would continue to provide impetus for Pound's appeals to Marxism.

In a short, unpublished note from many years later, "Marx and the Paddle Wheel Steamer," Pound compares the dialectical movements in Marx's thought to the turbine-like rotary movements of steamboat propellers. This comparison has its origin in Marx's own text and, to be sure, a moment in Marx's text that would echo throughout Pound's early writing. In chapter 15 of *Capital,* Marx describes industrial evolution as the intensified valorization of natural resources. "Increase in the size of the machine, and in the number of its working tools, calls for a more massive mechanism to drive it," he says, "and this mechanism requires, in order to overcome its resistance, a mightier moving power than that of man, apart from the fact that man is a very imperfect instrument for producing uniform continued motion." Under capitalism, nature is expropriated to serve as the driving mechanism for large-scale industry. But, in the early nineteenth century, horsepower was inadequately consistent to this end; wind was impossible to harness; and water "could not be increased at will, it failed at certain seasons of the year, and above all it was essentially local." In a footnote to this text, Marx names the mechanism that would soon overcome rivers, lakes, and seas to assimilate their energy for the rabidly evolving mode of production. "The modern turbine," he writes, "frees the industrial exploitation of water-power from many of its former fetters." According to Marx, this kind of industrial machinery would allow for gains in surplus value by diminishing the amount of socially necessary labor time needed to transform raw materials into useable or sellable commodities. What the invention of the turbine would mean, from the perspective of Marxism, is that a teleological space would be opened up between the mechanization of manufacturing labor and the absolute triumph of large-scale industry over its workers. "The instrument of labour," says Marx, "when it takes the form of a machine, immediately becomes a competitor of the workman himself." This narrative of unsustainable labor, its utopian counternarrative in that labor's deliverance from exploitation, and their applicability to the modern turbine will be echoed in the creation of Pound's vortex.[17]

Marx appears by name several times in the epic, in Cantos 19 and 46, and his work is quoted at length in Canto 33 and again, briefly, in Canto 47. All of that, however, postdates the material and the context we are looking at here. Though it is difficult to tell just how familiar Pound was with Marx's own text during this early period, or when he first read it, we can nonetheless hear its echoes throughout his writing. It is from within the quasi-Marxian context of the *New Age* that Pound started to think about the linguistic substrate of poetry in terms of the industrial apparatus that the magazine would critique and about which Marx had written. In 1912, for instance, Pound encouraged his readers to think of language through an assemblage of mechanical similes: "Let us imagine that words are like great hollow cones of steel of different dullness and acuteness; I say great because I want them not too easy to move; they must be of different sizes. Let us imagine them charged with a force like electricity, or, rather, radiating a force from their apexes—some radiating, some sucking in." For Pound, words themselves are cumbersome in their metallic materiality, which equips lexemes with different degrees of "dullness and acuteness," and they are simultaneously capable of carrying an imaginary and immaterial charge, "a force like electricity," which suggests analogy to the function of the image in vorticism. And, later that year, he wrote similar things about the modern poet, a figure he likens to "a sort of steam-gauge, voltameter, a set of pipes for thermometric and barometric divination." Like the words he or she moves about, the poet is another mechanical instrument, a complex machine mobilizing the less complex parts of the mechanical apparatus, which together compose the industrial organism. The relationship between the poet and his or her words is presented as one and the same with what Marx had described as the peak of industry. "All fully developed machinery," writes Marx, "consists of three essentially different parts, the motor mechanism, the transmitting mechanism, and finally the tool or working machine." To summarize, when writing for the *New Age,* Pound was thinking about industrial technology in language that is notably indebted to Marx, and, moreover, he was simultaneously learning to recognize industrial technology's impress on artistic and literary production, all of which contribute conceptual coordinates for vorticism.[18]

Two years later, in 1914, Pound reached for precisely this kind of machine imagery when writing up not only his vorticist poems (with their "lateral vibrations," a transference of energy we might now identify with the turbine) but also his manifesto. Preceding any mention of poetry, the centerpiece of "Vortex. Pound." is this:

> THE TURBINE,
>
> All experience rushes into this vortex. All the energized past, all the past that is living and worthy to live. All MOMENTUM, which is the past bearing upon us, RACE, RACE-MEMORY, instinct charging the PLACID,
>
> NON-ENERGIZED FUTURE.[19]

The turbine is a machine that literally energizes "placid" water into "whirlpools," an action analogous to how the poet generates images out of language. For Pound, "experience" does not rush into the turbine itself; rather, it passes through the turbine and is transvalued into the vortex. "For the vortex," observes Hugh Kenner, "is not the water but a patterned integrity made visible by the water."[20] This, then, is a solution to the formal challenge of vorticism: to identify poetry not with the thing itself, the industrial machine, but with the energies and patterns that machine produces. This is also why the whirlpool will hereafter become Pound's privileged image for vorticism, because it comprises the "patterned integrity" and "patterned energy" produced by the turbine without necessarily correlating poetry with machines as such. Even if there is a problem in the fact that whirlpools are predominantly natural phenomena, as in the poem by H. D., when they take place within the industrial forces of modern history, they become something quite different—currents of the machine blasting through nature.

That distinction between turbines and vortices becomes increasingly apparent if we approach Pound's manifesto via its antagonistic relationship with a competing avant-garde. When Pound insists that Italian futurists "are the CORPSES of VORTICES" and that "Marinetti is a corpse," we should hear a clear echo from Marx on the way laborers are bled dry by their machines: "By means of its conversion into an automaton, the instrument of labour confronts the labourer, during the labour-process, in the shape of capital, of dead labour, that dominates, and pumps dry, living labour-power."[21] The vortex might therefore be understood as an abstraction from or the figural estrangement of the turbine. The two are related by causality (as opposed to strict determination), but they are not to be thought of interchangeably. This is different from futurism's positivist identification with machines as machines, rather than with an abstraction of their immanence or potential. For F. T. Marinetti, humankind is and ought always be prostrate before "divine" machine-gods, described as "great turbines turned by columns of mountain water to strip animating electricity from the air." In the imagined triumph of futurism, he predicts, the turbine will become a sublime monument to its own technology: "Some of us ran to nearby waterfalls; gigantic wheels were hoisted, and turbines transformed the velocity of the waters into electromagnetic spasms that climbed up wires suspended on high poles, until they reached luminous, humming globes."[22] While Marinetti makes a fetish of the machines themselves, Pound's interest is in the energies and patterns they produce; and this, a movement away from the machine itself, is the crucial difference between vorticism and futurism. The point of vorticism, in contrast to futurism, is to harness the aesthetic energy of machinery without succumbing to its destiny as dead labor. The vortex refers to the image of a hazardously promising space between the invention of a new technology and its absolute victory over those who operate it—its unrealized utopian potential.

This potential has a social equivalent. In identifying the hypothetical value of large-scale industry while maintaining a critical distance from its implementation within capitalism, Pound seems to have expressed an understanding of the well-known communist belief that utopia will manifest through a comparable kind of material immateriality. As Terry Eagleton describes this idea, in a useful summary of what at first sounds like an insurmountable paradox: "The dialectical Marxist twist is that only materiality will release you from the dull compulsion of material. Freedom does not mean being free of determinations, but being determined in such a way as to sit transformatively loose to one's determinants."[23] This traditional interpretation of communism resonates with an aesthetic that is abstracted from its medium, like how the image might be "loose" from its determining words or how the vortex is irreducible to the turbine. While Louis Zukofsky and, eventually, William Carlos Williams both found something revolutionary in communism's approach to industry, Pound's initial interest in this Marxian critique of technology (which unlike that of Zukofsky and Williams predates the Russian Revolution) has more to do with providing a critical history of capitalism, so as to "include" that mode of production within an epic poem. And yet, as we will later see, while Pound might not have seen industry as a potential force of revolution, for him it nonetheless contained the essence of utopianism in its capacity to save workers from capitalist exploitation.

But there is a curious anachronism to Pound's machine. He was a poet famously obsessed with the "new," yet by 1914 the turbine was anything but. Lewis would recall having written the following to Marinetti: "You wops insist too much on the machine. You're always on about these driving belts, you are always exploding about internal combustion. We've had machines in England for a donkey's years, they're no novelty to us." And apropos the Russian Revolution: "The average Englishman is scarcely going to get the true Marxian kick out of turbines and cantilevers. Because in Moscow it is a matter of daily routine to stick up gigantic posters of power-plants under the nose of the gaping moujik." Like driving belts, internal combustion, and cantilevers, the turbine hearkens back to the previous century, and can even be said to solidify an ideational passage between the England of 1914 and the England of 1864, between Pound's England and Marx's. However, what this anachronism also attests to is the uneven and combined developments of capitalism and its technological extensions. England is, from an economic perspective, both 1864 and 1914 simultaneously. Perry Anderson once described London's historical doubling as the architectonic manifestation of the intersection between imperialist importation and technological underdevelopment. "Export of capital, underinvestment at home, lagging technological innovation, all mark the British economy from the last decades of the 19th century onwards," he argues: "But the huge quantitative returns of the Empire and British overseas investment masked this qualitative deterioration for a long time, and ended, inevitably, by severely exacerbating it." Or, as Pound would phrase it in a discussion of economics and the epic, "We do not all of us inhabit the same time."[24]

Waterwheels and Turbine Chunks

Marxist critique is an exceptionally practicable method by which to conceive of this unevenly developed yet economically combined situation and to represent it on the pages of an epic. Readers of Marx will be intimately familiar with a well-developed cast of staple characters, including bread, bibles, linen, shirts, and so on, all of which embody something integral to the mode of production in its developmental unevenness. According to Fredric Jameson, Marx's use of "figuration tends to emerge when the object of conceptuality is somehow unrepresentable in its structural ambiguity," and what the figure gives form to is "the possibility of different levels in this discourse, extra-economic levels, which suddenly become momentarily visible in what is at first merely a metaphorical attempt to convey the intricacies of the purely economic." Earlier it was suggested that the vortex is an abstraction from the turbine, a material image of the immaterial patterns created by that machine. Here I want to add that, as an aesthetic program, vorticism operates analogously to figuration in Marx, in that both Pound's image and Marx's figure attain their epiphenomenal energies through material preconditions to which those energies cannot be reduced. In short, the turbine and its vortex, as a machine and its energy, figure the utopian potential of large-scale industry. While Zukofsky will go on to quote from Marx's descriptions of industrial technology as the embodiment of revolutionary immanence, or what is metaphorized as "the mother of antagonism," for Pound that technology is utopian in a less revolutionary but perhaps more immediately practical way.[25]

This thought comes out clearest in one of Pound's unpublished notes on Marx, in which he describes "the improved plant," perhaps liberated from capitalism's relations of production, and how its mechanical dynamo will provide "usufruct energy" to an entire community while eventually "leaving less and less to be done by the sweat of the individual." If, however, this emphasis on improvement and the gradual lessening of exploitation is more reformist than revolutionary, elsewhere he reaches for a different and more absolute rhetoric. In another unpublished though remarkably coherent essay, "Means of Distribution Exist," he argues that capitalism has in fact produced the infrastructure and machinery with which to obviate against all scarcity, and that concealment of those means is an act of malefaction. He concludes the essay by repeating its axiomatic title in emphatic capital letters before delivering a revolutionary call to arms that resembles communist rhetoric in both tone and content. "There is," he claims, "no need of living for yet another decade under the nightmare that has damned and dominated the capitalists' world all through my lifetime." If a turbine figures the ongoing "nightmare" of modern history under capitalism, then the vortex might be a cipher of that system's liberating or liberated potential, "distributing its usufruct energy to the community as a whole," an unrealized future whose name might indeed be communism. This hypothesis, that Pound has absorbed Marx's economic thinking about industry and that for him it plays into the difference between turbines and vortices, can now be tested out against some specific episodes from within *The Cantos*.[26]

It is hardly coincidental that the first utterance of "work" in all *The Cantos* attaches itself to a paradisiacal depiction of the turbine's Iberian predecessor. Consider the ancient "vision" at the beginning of Canto 5.

> and North was Egypt,
>   the celestial Nile, blue deep,
>   cutting low barren land,
> Old men and camels
>   working the water-wheels;
> Measureless seas and stars,
> Iamblichus' light,
>   the souls ascending,
> Sparks like a partridge covey,
>   Like the "ciocco," brand struck in the game.[27]

According to Marx, the waterwheel is "the elementary form of all machinery," and in it we can observe "the antithesis between the views of the ancients and the moderns." Whereas the ancients are said to have viewed the waterwheel "as the giver of freedom to female slaves, and the bringer back of the golden age," the moderns have adapted this technology to exploitatively serve capital.[28] Pound's lines ground the waterwheel on the banks of the River Nile, in ancient Egypt, and the citations hearken back to Neoplatonist ontology. This universe is made properly infinite; its globe and cosmos are immeasurable and are together held by the philosopher's light. What the image of the waterwheel represents here is the Georgic harmony of precapitalist labor, but if that harmony is Georgic, what it lacks is the relentless drudgery that typified Virgil's paradigmatic poem, presenting something much closer to Marx's utopian vision of ancient technology enjoying its "golden age." In that vision, Marx says, "the work of girls" is performed by "nymphs" that "skip lightly over the wheels, so that the shaken axles revolve with their spokes and pull round the load of the revolving stones."[29] Something like this is implied by the punctuation in the lines from Pound. The semicolon separates earthly labor and cosmic heavens, as though to mark an abstraction away from "men," "camels," and "water-wheels," into the aesthetic space of the infinite. What we are encountering, across that semicolon, is a shift from the material to the immaterial, from nascent industry to its utopian potential: from turbine to vortex. There is a "loose" correspondence between the two, with the whirling motion suggested by the "water-wheels" corresponding with the spatial register of the verse's blazoned image of "souls ascending" as would "a partridge covey." This image alludes to Canto 18 of Dante's *Paradise,* where souls spiral upward as a vortex into which they have been admitted precisely because of their earthbound virtuousness. Back on earth, the waterwheel produces energy in its rotations, and the host of souls rotates analogously in paradise.[30] Even though this riverside's material harmony is compromised by modernity so as to fade "on the barb of time," the "measureless" vision is abstracted from its material contingency and given immortality: "always," we are told, "and the vision always."[31] This abstraction of energy from earthbound materiality and into the vortex is what in *The Cantos* shall become the cipher of noncapitalist labor, connecting up with a vast web of other space-times where work and capital are not meshed or have been forcefully pried apart. The vortex ciphers a type of work that cannot be brought under erasure by the machines that were supposed to assist and enable it but instead, as we know, worsened exploitation.

Now compare that paradisiacal vision to the second appearance of turbine technology in the epic, from Canto 22. Here Pound turns a critical eye to the capitalist's manufacturing plant in England.

> And he came in and said: Can't do it,
> Not at that price, we can't do it."
> That was in the last war, here in England,
> And he was making chunks for a turbine
> In some sort of an army plane;
> An' the inspector says: "How many rejects?"
> "What you mean, rejects?"
> And the inspector says: "How many do you get?"
> And Joe said: "We don't get *any* rejects, our . . . "

And the inspector says: "Well then of course
you can't do it."[32]

"Skilled labour counts only as simple labour intensified," says Marx of capitalism.[33] That is what we are seeing demonstrated here. Pride in labor gives way to profit, and the kind of man who once inhabited a universe of ancient work-being is now alienated from his labor. Joe's proud and possibly chauvinistic insistence on "no rejects" is a reaction to one of the sacred laws of depersonalized capitalism: a standard rate of rejection, which is built into the value of the commodity. Despite that pride in labor, Joe will always be alienated from the finished product, "some sort of army plane," whose nominal indeterminacy renders it unknown to those who engineer its essential parts. The machine itself, the turbine, is anathema to the men who created it. On one level, these lines are dealing with incomplete part-objects, a series of "chunks" from which the turbine will be assembled, thanks to some future, other labor to which these workers will not have access. It is an instance of what Pound describes via Marx as the "formal uncertainty in machines that are composite of several simple machines, or a congeries of machine of same function."[34] On another level, the turbine is a teleological figure, being made to fit "some sort of army plane," the war-machine, which would overtly accelerate the mechanical onslaught already underway in the factory. To be sure, these lines were published in 1929 and therefore postdate World War I, which introduced heavier-than-air, turbine-powered aircraft into military aviation. We discuss Pound's figuration of the military-industrial complex later, but for now we can assert that there is no trace of the vortex in these lines: no whirling, abstracted energies. There are no images at all, for that matter, only an anecdote about the futurist-sounding machine and the implication of a teleological narrative. This is a dead poetry for deadening labor, the textual registration of machines making men obsolete.

In these examples the turbine suggests itself as a figure of capitalist totality, a critical expression of capitalism's "extra-economic" dimensions, representing the integrated subsumption of work and technology. The vortex, by contrast, encodes another kind of technologized sociality: that which is not and which cannot be ensnared, exploited, and obliterated by capitalism. The turbine operates as a figure for an enslaving mode of production and its teleology, whereas the vortex is as an imagistic impress left by that technology's unrealized potential, the autonomous trace of a fossilized turbine whose material stuff has either been withered away by time or which awaits revolutionary activation. But for Pound the vortex is not just an imagistic trope related to machinery. It is also and even primarily the ordering this trope implies—an abstraction of form from the otherwise formless, a force capable of unifying historical particulars into an image that is both dynamic and coherent, and that can finally be "included" on the pages of an epic poem. "Vortices have analogous structures," insists Kenner; "events, relationships, recur in history." The vortex is a localized technique and a structuring method for Pound's epic historiography, which in Kenner's formulation reads "all phenomena as indices to some process larger than the span of lyric attention."[35] In that capacity, vorticism seeks to preserve in epic poetry those utopian space-times in which work retains its autonomy from capital or in which work and capital are seen to be actively separating from one another: Sigismondo Malatesta's Rimini, Thomas Jefferson's America, Leopold's Rome, Confucius's China, Benito Mussolini's Italy, and—most importantly for us—Lenin's Russia.

London to Moscow (via Paris)

In an essay on what she calls "Vortorussophilia," Rebecca Beasley points up the connections between vorticism and Russia, and especially between vorticism and Russia's prerevolutionary and predominantly socialist avant-garde. In her words, "Russia becomes a cipher that plays a significant role in Vorticist aesthetics, but it can only do so when detached from individual works of art."[36] Instead of pursuing connections with either pre- or post-revolutionary Russia, so far we have aimed to document the relationship between vorticism and the conceptual and critical thought that informed the Russian Revolution's chief actant, Lenin. Before encountering Lenin as a living agent of history, however, I want to shore up the relationship between Pound's epic historiography, which will soon need to engage the Russian Revolution, and the Marxist thinking we have seen in several localized expressions of the vortex, as well as in one of its conspicuous absences. To do this we return to where the chapter began, to Russia, where Lenin's preface retroactively introduces the Russian Revolution as an historical optic through which to read his text, a strictly economic critique of capitalism.

Lenin signs off on the preface with a location and date that would immediately assume world-historical significance: "Petrograd, April 26, 1917."[37] That place-name appears more than once in *The Cantos* but as the site of revolution only in these lines from Canto 27:

Refining the criterion,
Or they rose as the tops subsided;
Brumaire, Fructidor, Petrograd.
And Tovarisch lay in the wind
And the sun lay over the wind,
And three forms became in the air
And hovered about him,
                                    so that he said:
This machinery is very ancient,
                                                surely we have heard this before.
And the waves like a forest
Where the wind is weightless in the leaves,
But moving,
            so that the sound runs upon sound.[38]

Written in the mid-1920s, this is a belated (and not the poem's first) response to the revolutionary leveling of Russia, in particular to the dictatorship of the proletariat, which "rose as the tops subsided," thus completing the socialist reversal of class relations. These lines present an immaterial abstraction ("three forms became in the air"), they refer to a technology from which that abstraction remains distinct ("This machinery is very ancient"), and they consciously allude to "Oread" by H. D. ("the waves like a forest"). They are another localized instantiation of vorticism, and the utopianism of the vortex is here made to harmonize explicitly with communism or at least with a socialist revolution waged in the name of communism. But the revolution here is not exclusively Russian. Similarly to how the Russian word for "comrade"—namely, *tovarisch*—entered the national lexicon by way of German Marxism, Canto 27 arrives at Petrograd by way of French Revolutionary history, about which Marx had famously written with specific reference to the Brumaire. In Marx's view, by consciously replicating the events of the late eighteenth century, the Republican revolutionaries of 1848 ultimately revealed their own abject conservatism. His metaphor for this replication was that of a poem: "The social revolution of the nineteenth century cannot take its poetry from the past but only from the future."[39] The idea of a poetry "from the future" would have spoken to Pound's own desires for literary invention, and, in these lines from Canto 27, a conscious performance of that poetry is associated with communism. The three proper nouns, "Brumaire, Fructidor, Petrograd," collocate two months from the French

Republican Calendar with the site of the Russian Revolution. Together, all three nouns posit their revolutionary upheavals as a specifically historical sequence or a temporal unfurling.[40] The collocation of these nouns establishes a pattern between them, from which Pound abstracts an image, but more importantly they are an instance of the epic poem's historiography seizing upon the idea of revolution. While they deliver another localized expression of the vortex, they correlate that expression with the poem's architectonic, its search for abstract patterns, which we can now see is also determinately responsive to Marx's own interpretation of historical patterning. That those revolutionary ideas take shape as forms "in the air," as the immaterial things that "hovered about him," as "sound runs upon sound," should simultaneously clue us in to the specific medium through which Pound first conceptualized revolution: namely, the radio, with its electromagnetic "waves," which now brings us to the site of that revolutionary event, though without ever leaving Paris.

Radio Voice Part I: The Factive Personality

It is common knowledge that, immediately before and then during World War II, Pound made hundreds of radio broadcasts from near his residence in Rapallo, Italy, and that almost all of these enjoined allegiance to Benito Mussolini and Italy's National Fascist Party. Daniel Tiffany's work on this episode has been controversial to many of Pound's more dedicated readers, but Tiffany accurately asserts that these broadcasts constituted "the practical and theoretical horizons" of tropes and techniques first developed in the early poetry.[41] There are two important implications in Tiffany's claim. First, it implies that radiophonic technology had always been anachronistically immanent to Pound's literary writing, which is possibly why the poet eventually claimed to have foreseen radio's ascent to cultural omnipresence and to have predicted that ascent in his poetry. "I anticipated the damn thing in the first third of Cantos," Pound claims in 1940.[42] Second, for Tiffany, these thoughts on poetry and radio occupy the same interpretive space as an assumption that "fascism discovers in radio not only a technical medium that is essential to its practical dissemination, but its proper ideological medium as well."[43] To extend Tiffany's argument only slightly, the medium of radio, which has always been immanent to Pound's poetry, is also "proper" to fascism. This thinking implies that the poetry was always destined to fascism. Tiffany's interpretation, which is shared by multiple readers, would recast the early poetry as the fated precursor to the epic's subsequent realignment with fascism.[44] From this perspective, the image itself—the poet's "primary pigment," the poem's singular medium—is predestined to serve as political armament for the far Right. "If," Tiffany concludes, "we view the medium of radio as a specific political formation of the imaginary, then the imaginary (and ideological) correspondences between telegraphy and radiation, between broadcasting and radiography, must be considered germane to the poetics of the modernist Image."[45]

In contradistinction to Tiffany's argument and to arguments made along similar lines, my objective is to show how radio's relationship with fascism is, within Pound's poetry, only one side of that medium's more complex political history, the obverse of which is communism. Indeed, when Pound first started thinking seriously about radio as a medium analogically related to poetic technique, he was primarily concerned with its importance to the revolutionary advent of socialism in Russia. In Pound's view, any meaningful economic action, the kind that might pose a serious threat to the obstructions of capital, should utilize radiophonic technology. For Pound, Lenin was first to make this discovery. "Reformers," Pound would later argue, "monetary reformers who haven't even yet arrived at the concept of linotype government, can not expect to rule in a radio age. To reiterate: Lenin won by Radio."[46] Working from a biographical perspective, A. David Moody has also pointed up the connection between Lenin and the radio, which he describes as integral to the political mitosis, a division between communism and fascism, that infected Pound's writing when the poet was first establishing himself in Italy. Pound wanted to emulate Lenin and Mussolini, "the two who in our day know how to 'move' in the highest degree, who are masters of speech that goes into action," and that, for Moody, was "the condition Pound's prose aspired to in Italy—'speech that goes into action.' "[47] That goal eventually guided Pound from the page to the radio. But in what ways did this identification between radio broadcasting and political ideology impress itself upon his verse?

While "speech that goes into action" is a formal quality shared, for Pound, between Lenin, Mussolini, and the radio, it is also a precondition for the classical epic, a genre that requires certain kinds of action to gather an epos into the unity of poetic speech. Hegel provides the canonical explanation of this: "the history of a country, the development of its political life, its constitution, and its fate, may also be related as an event: but if what happens is not presented as the concrete act, the inner aim, the passion, life, and accomplishment of specific heroes whose individuality provides the *form* and the content of the whole actual occurrence, then the event exists only in the rigid independent advance of its *content* as the history of a nation or an empire." Or, as Hegel summarizes his own point, "we can derive the general rule that the particular epic event can only be given vitality in poetry if it can be fused in the closest way with a single individual"—if, to be sure, the epos acquires its shape through the totalizing actions of a hero.[48] Even though Pound's "poem including history" was never intended as an epic in this classical sense, its author nonetheless desired a hero or heroes for it to personify history.

The exordium to the *Ur-Cantos* is a riposte to Robert Browning, whose epic poem about the troubadour Sordello de Goita comprised a "whole bag of tricks" or "intaglio method" for apprehending "the modern world" in verse.[49] "But Sordello," asks the speaker of Canto 2, compressing a more detailed argument from the first Ur-Canto, "and my Sordello?"[50] Of course, Canto 1 introduces the Odyssean mask that serves as a mainstay throughout the poem, but *The Cantos* only shift their theater of operations from the world of ancient myth to include history proper when Pound alights on an individual who fulfills the role of hero, Sigismondo Malatesta, a fifteenth-century warlord from Rimini, in northeastern Italy, who occupies Cantos 8 through 11. Malatesta is the first of several men whom Pound championed throughout his career as "factive personalities," heroic individuals whose noble words are inseparable from their apparently glorious deeds. "No one has claimed that the Malatesta cantos are obscure," Pound would later recall. "They are openly volitionist, establishing, I think clearly, the effect of the factive personality, Sigismundo, an entire man."[51] To this explanation, we should add that the factive personalities are epic in much the same way Hegel describes the genre's heroes.

The technical achievement of the Malatesta Cantos is in their deployment of written documents emptied directly into the poem from a fifteenth-century "post-bag," whose contents serve as indexical proof that the heroic individual, Malatesta, once "lived and ruled."[52] The hero's governance, the social reality of his lived heroism, is therefore conjoined with a form of expression; and, in that sense, Cantos 8 through 11 present a literal manifestation of "speech that goes into action." But Malatesta's action is also important on its own terms. For Pound, Malatesta served the "magnificent commune of the Florentines" in Rimini first and foremost as a patron to the arts. His great victory, as presented in *The Cantos,* was the construction and decoration of the church of San Francesco, also known as the Tempio Malatestiano, which instituted a mutually beneficial exchange for patrons and artists. But the heroism of Malatesta can only subsist at a significant remove from the world Pound inhabited, the world to which we have seen him respond with vorticism. The contents of the "post-bag" attest to a far-flung, nearly forgotten prehistory, which Canto 11 is clear enough to show was already in decline, corrupted by capital, during Malatesta's own lifetime. This is one of the reasons why Lawrence Rainey begins his celebrated study of Pound and Malatesta by clarifying that, in Cantos 8 through 11, the poem's "monument of culture is a tomb. It commemorates death, ruin, the remains of human life."[53]

Following the introduction of Malatesta and detours through a triumvirate of economic parables (in Canto 12) and the ancient China of Confucius (Canto 13), Cantos 14 and 15 return the poem to London, a grotesque hell populated by "monopolists, obstructors of knowledge," and "obstructors of distribution."[54] The bracing juxtapositions between fifteenth-century Rimini and modern London seem to confirm Hegel's merciless relegation of the epic to earlier historical epochs, an argument that (by the nineteenth century) modernity had become so regimented that no individual could act in such a way as to submit historical totality to the unifying form of a singular personality. In that view, modern individuals are only capable of obeying the totality in which they participate, rendering them acquiescent to historical conditions. "An epic," claimed Pound in 1910, "cannot be written against the grain of its time: the prophet or the satirist may hold himself aloof from his time, or run counter to it, but the writer of epos must voice the general heart," and that genre should concern itself with "real men, whose deeds surpass all the fictitious deeds of fabled heroes."[55] What the epic required, then, was a well-nigh impossible personality capable of effecting positive change in the historical present, a living heir to Malatesta's legacy. Though Pound would eventually invest his faith in Mussolini as the embodiment of that personality, several years before the turn to fascism, another hero presented himself, stepping out from relative obscurity and onto the historical stage as a full-blooded factive personality, entering *The Cantos* where he breathed new life into its Malatestan fragments. That hero was Lenin.

Paris, 1923: Whites Flee the Red Wedge

Before we get to Lenin, it will be necessary to provide some biographical context for Pound's first encounters with the Russian Revolution and its heroic personalities. That context helps account not only for Lenin's entry into the epic but also for his association with the radio in Pound's apprehension. After departing London in 1919 and before immigrating to Italy in 1924, Pound spent most of the early 1920s in Paris. As he said in an interview for the *New York Herald* in 1921, he found "the decay of the British Empire too depressing a spectacle to witness at close range."[56] London was home to imperialist rot, certainly, but also to the depreciation of poetry. In "Hugh Selwyn Mauberley," Pound's notoriously ironic farewell to Blighty, a satirical quatrain gestures toward the political nonefficacy of verse made to entertain England's self-styled patrons of the arts: "A hook to catch the Lady Jane's attention,/A modulation toward the theatre,/Also, in the case of revolution,/A possible friend and comforter."[57] The idea that poetry would provide friendship and comfort to the bourgeoisie "in the case of revolution" is principally an index of the localized devaluing of art, but it also speaks revealingly to the poem's historical context. During the period of Pound's emigration from London to Paris, Great Britain and Western Europe had become popular sites of refuge for anti-Bolshevik Russians fleeing their native country. In Western Europe, the "white émigrés" were primarily drawn to either Berlin or Paris, and it is likely that Pound encountered them en masse in the latter, though he might also have encountered them in London. "The first wave of emigration," write Adele Barker and Bruce Grant, "had been educated in prerevolutionary Russia and carried that culture abroad with them, where they attempted to perpetuate it and transmit it to their children born in emigration and to the foreign cultures where they were now living."[58] The defeated subjects of the Russian Revolution found their equally appalling analogue, for Pound, in London's bourgeois philistines who, nothing like Malatesta, failed to provide good patronage to the arts. On this front, with the white émigrés occupying a cultural position similar to that of the London bourgeoisie, Pound had already acquired some motivation to sympathize with a shared enemy, the Bolsheviks.

Though quietly present in the lines from "Hugh Selwyn Mauberley," this diaspora would not enter Pound's poetry in any obvious way until the early 1930s, when in Canto 33 and alongside the words of Marx, Pound quotes and translates from the fictionalized memoirs of Gregori Bessedovsky, an infamously unreliable reporter of contemporary Russian history.

> avénement révolution allemande posait des problèmes nouveaux,
> routine commercial être remplacée par création de deux
> fonds or et blé destinés au proletariat victorieux (allemand)

to functionaries of legation in Berlin who are members
of the party (1923)

bureaucrat paisible, Van Tzin Vel se montra, tout à fait incap-
able d'assumer le rôle de chef d'une révolution sanguinaire.
(according to Monsieur Bessedovsky)

for ten years our (Russian) ambassadors have enquired what
theories are in fashion in Moscow and have reported their
facts to fit (idem)[59]

Comparable to redactions from Marx in the same canto, these lines posit a complication for the mediations taking place between Pound and the Russian Revolution. The realized unreliability of this anecdotal account—as suggested by the tentative attribution of "according," the apparent sensationalism of the description, the idea of "facts" made to "fit"—implies that any history of the Russian Revolution told from its own highly politicized present will exceed claims to simple objectivity, that it will be mired in partisan ideology. The lines are doubtful, maintaining a healthy skepticism toward the anecdote. Furthermore, their text derives from a moment in history to which Pound was directly exposed, an historical terrain from which he had been writing, which we encounter in a poem written from the time and place of Bessedovsky's questionable account, namely, Paris in 1923. To be sure, the French context provided a politically significant interregnum to Pound's fascination with Italy. "Life was interesting in Paris from 1921 to 1924," claimed Pound in 1933; "nobody bothered much about Italy." And one of the reasons why Italy failed to prove interesting at this time is that its political life paled in comparison to Russia, which Pound was presently hearing about from sources in Paris. "Communists took over some factories," he adds, "but couldn't dispense with credit. No one has told us whether ANY Italian communist even thought of the subject. Lenin couldn't, after all, be both in Turin and in Moscow."[60]

Revolution Frequency

Completed in 1923, Canto 16 comprises the final installation in the 1925 publication of *A Draft of XVI Cantos.* Obeying the poem's Dantean architectonic, it narrates an escape from the London underworld into the poet's more immediately purgatorial present. Its opening lines depict "the running form, naked," of William Blake, who flees the "hell mouth." There are at least two significant reasons for Blake's appearance at this decisive moment in the epic. First, Blake was a well-known progenitor of the poetic vortex, which in this episode he has almost come to resemble, "whirling his arms" in the rotary movements of the turbine, "like flaming cart-wheels." Second, that it is Blake and no other poet decrying the horror, running with "his head held backward to gaze on the evil," makes good sense. Blake was a fierce critic of industrialization, capital, and the evolution of England's "dark Satanic mills," the outcome of which we encountered in the London of vorticism and which reappears, immediately before this episode, in Cantos 14 and 15. But the lines that open Canto 16 refuse attachment to a romantic vision of the world before the advent of modern technology and large-scale industry. Instead, they are replete with mechanical and electrical imagery.[61]

Given that Pound is known to have described the radio as a galling "devil box,"[62] here we might playfully literalize that epithet and draw out a spatial metaphor from the opening image of Canto 16, which almost resembles that technology: two solid, conical objects made of "hard steel" on either side of a "mouth," and from one a "road like a slow screw's thread," all conjoined by a unitary "circuit," which conveys a singular "running form," somewhat like an electrical pulse. Though it is tempting to liken all of this to a description of the crystal radio (comprising two headphones connected by wire to a detector and tuning coil), which was the commonest available radio device during the early 1920s, we should stop short of that probably fallacious interpretation, while still confirming that this particular technology, the radio, was a dominant medium in the discourse network in which Canto 16 was composed. DIY crystal-radio kits sold particularly well in Paris between 1921 and early 1923, the years when national radio was first established, broadcasting Radio Paris from atop the Eiffel Tower. Walter Benjamin describes the advent of Radio Paris as the technological acquisition of this monument: "When the Eiffel Tower was built, it served no practical purpose of any kind; it was simply a landmark—a wonder of the world, as people say. But it was followed by the invention of radio telegraphy, and, at a stroke, the huge construction suddenly acquired a meaning. Today the Eiffel Tower is a Paris radio transmitter."[63] Indeed, it is difficult to imagine that Pound was not aware of the radio when composing Canto 16, and we might even conjecture that it unconsciously infiltrated the mechanical and electrical metaphors of the opening image. This conjecture is made all the more viable if we consider that Canto 16 was drafted in a notebook covered by an advertisement for Radio Paris.[64]

Subsequent to this opening image, Canto 16 is quick to invoke the classical epic. Having exited the London inferno and after bathing himself in acid to remove "the hell ticks," the speaker soon passes "the tree of the bough," an allusion to the golden bough of Virgil, which granted Aeneas communion with the undead shades of his fallen allies. The speaker then encounters "the heroes," Malatesta and his brother, Novello, who are stopped "by their fountains." But the poem does not linger here. "In the quiet," we are told, "one man rose from his fountain/and went off into the plain," abandoning the heroes just when the poem changes scene, transposing itself from myth into history; a shift in language signals that the poem is moving into its immediate historical context.[65] A Gallic line, "et j'entendis des voix" ("and I heard voices") introduces a series of names, which originate from World War I and the friends of Pound that war killed and maimed, before the poem's stable speaker gives way to a polyphony of unfamiliar voices, switching between French and English. These voices acquire a resonance with the mythic world of the classical epic and enunciate themselves as ghosts, but they might also be produced by modern technology. David Farley notes that much of Canto 16 is "constructed out of speech, secondhand reports, and rumor as much as it is of firsthand observation. It gives the impression of on-the-spot reporting and firsthand accounts, but its main preoccupations are in the ways that rhetoric and speech incites action and the manner in which this information is transmitted."[66] The metaphor of transmission is of the essence here, for it grasps the technological conceit underpinning the poem's dialogism. "Simplest parallel I can give," Pound would say in describing *The Cantos* one year later, "is radio where you tell who is talking by the noise they make," and surely we can say as much for the spectral voices that compete for volume in Canto 16.[67] That is what we encounter here, a kind of speech that makes sense as both epic and radio, but thus far it is a speech that lacks a unifying heroism. Even though, from Homer and Virgil onward, the battlefield has been an exemplary location for the epic poem and the emblematic site at which heroes distinguish themselves from anonymous foot soldiers, for Pound the battlefield is only a manifestation of cultural degradation and militarized stupidity. "The face gone," we read, "generation."[68] In Pound's view, the trenches of World War I blight the arts that Malatesta would have preserved and patronized.

Announcing itself from within that frontline broadcast, a new, unfamiliar voice brings Canto 16 to its concluding episode. That voice is a kind of geopolitical vulgate, speaking in English but with a thick German accent.

Dey vus a bolcheviki dere, und dey dease him
Looka vat youah Trotzsk is done, e iss
        madeh deh zhamefull beace!!
"He iss madeh de zhamefull beace, iss he?
        "He is madeh de zhamevul beace?
"A Brest-Litovsk, yess? Aint yuh herd?
        "He vinneh de vore.
"De droobs iss released vrom de eastern vront, yess?
"Un venn dey getts to deh vestern vront, iss it
        "How many getts dere?
"And dose doat getts dere iss so full off revolutions
"Venn deh vrench is come dhru, yess,
"Dey say, "Vot?" Un de posch say
        "Aint yeh heard? Say, ve got a rheffolution."[69]

The poem tunes itself to a distinctly Western European wavelength, thus signaling its own historical situation, producing a German voice speaking in English to a presumably French audience about the Russian Revolution. This accent will be lampooned by Zukofsky in the sixth part of *"A"*, but in this instance, in Canto 16, form and content are less a reaction to another poet than they are an effect of an immediate political context. The implied virtue of the "rheffolution" is made to coincide with Pound's interwar pacifism, which here is placed alongside the anecdote told by this anonymous speaker. The Bolsheviks' seizure of power allowed for "youah Trotzsk" to sign the treaty of "Brest-Litovsk," withdrawing Russia from World War I and sparing its army from further attacks, thus inaugurating what the anecdote's unknown warmongers will "dease" about as a "zhamevull beace." For the communists there was definite shame in the treaty, but that shame belonged specifically to their adversaries. "The Treaty," writes Lenin, "rendered a most useful service to humanity by exposing both imperialism's hired coolies of the pen and petty-bourgeois reactionaries," thus "opening the eyes of the millions and tens of millions of people who are downtrodden, oppressed, deceived and duped by the bourgeoisie."[70] The Russian Revolution suppresses the warfare that had consumed the owners of the names and voices to which Canto 16 has listened, extracting Russia from the unforgivable situation of total warfare. The revolution presents itself sympathetically here as a corrective to what the earlier parts of Canto 16 projected as the warring underworld of capitalism or what was, in Lenin's withering phrase, "a war to decide whether the British or German group of financial plunderers is to receive the most booty."[71] That these lines are emphatically spoken, that they capture the accent and intonations of a specific (though anonymous) voice, is reminiscent of the fact that while Lenin and Trotsky prepared an official statement of military surrender, the Central Committee resolved to notify their German adversaries by way of radio. Moreover, these lines remind us of exactly how Pound would have first encountered the Russian Revolution, if not by radio broadcast then as a series of word-of-mouth anecdotes filtering out from Moscow by way of Europe.

Socialist Kinesiology: A Trick with the Crowd

In the early 1920s, Pound read John Reed's feted account of the revolution. He met with E. E. Cummings, who at this stage was still a communist and writing poems about the communists in Paris. He enjoyed a real or imagined conversation with an English capitalist about Marx, which is described in Canto 19, where we also hear an anecdote about "Russian boys" singing their anthem "at two o'clock in the morning."[72] He also commenced correspondence with a communist poet from New York, Zukofsky, and he began to familiarize himself with the thought of Lenin and the Bolsheviks. Soon after, in 1926, he would write an inquisitive letter to the American journal *New Masses,* announcing an interest in communism.[73] Most important, we simply cannot underestimate how many anonymous verbal accounts the poet must have heard or been exposed to in Paris, one of the principal locations for white émigrés fleeing the revolution and also a well-known breeding ground for communist radicalism. For instance, Zhao Enlai and Deng Ziaoping from China and Ho Chi Minh from Vietnam all trained here with the communist youth groups during the early 1920s. But the loudest and clearest of these mediating voices, which came replete with multiple remediated sound bites of its own, was not anonymous. Rather, it belonged to the American journalist, Lincoln Steffens.

In October 1922, Pound heard Steffens deliver a talk to a small group of Parisians about his eyewitness experience of the Russian Revolution. Mary Colum, the Irish literary critic with whom Pound attended the talk, recalls their night in her autobiography. "Ezra insisted on taking us to a lecture by Lincoln Steffens on Soviet Russia, the Russia of Lenin," she writes. "The lecture seemed to me of an appalling dreariness and I hated being dragged to it. . . . But Ezra listened to it with rapt attention, his eyes glued to the speaker's face, the very type of young man in search of an ideology."[74] Surely there is some truth to this assessment, given the near instantaneous and lasting bond forged between the poet and the journalist. In Steffens's autobiography, Pound is recalled in terms that would echo the accounts of Russia: "Ezra Pound hated, and he charged, all fences in art; he incited the younger men to jump the barriers. He was a good revolutionary influence."[75] The compliment is repaid throughout *The Cantos,* in which Steffens's name appears three times, always couched by allusions to or anecdotes about his time in Russia, twice warranting the title "revolutionary."[76] But, to pause on Colum's impression of the enthused poet, it now seems clear enough that Pound was perhaps less enamored with the ideology of socialism—which did have its appeals for him, as a political and economic curative, and especially as a force that negated warfare—than with its equally revolutionary medium as channeled and embodied by the heroic individual at its center.

Walter Benn Michaels is certainly right to clarify "that Steffens' *Autobiography* wasn't published until 1931, while publication of the first thirty *Cantos* had been completed by 1930 and most of the material deriving from Steffens had actually been written several years earlier."[77] However, a version of Steffens's speech was printed in several papers to which Pound had access and which we can safely infer were ready-to-hand during the composition of Canto 16, not least because of close textual correspondences. The poem's privileging of voices reminds us that Pound initially encountered this material as speech, carried by a voice, to which he gave his spellbound attention. Steffens describes the revolutionary multitude gathering about the singular figure of Lenin: "the committee of hundreds would march off across the city, picking up other crowds to go and stand in front of the palace of the Czar's mistress, where 'a man named Lenin,' seeing them, would come out and speak. He spoke briefly, in a quiet tone of voice, so low that few could hear him. But when he had finished, those who had heard moved away; the mass closed up; the orator repeated his speech, and so for an hour or two the man named Lenin would deliver to the ever-changing masses his firm, short, quiet message."[78] Steffens also reproduces a transcription of Lenin's speech, which castigates the audience for their reluctance to go back to work and "make socialism," and because they appreciate revolutionaries who talk without committing speech to action. "But," Lenin concludes, "when the hour strikes, when you are ready to go back yourselves to work and you want a government that will go to work and not only think socialism and talk socialism and mean socialism—when you want a government that will do socialism, then—come to the Bolsheviki."[79] What Pound may well have been hearing in the "firm, short, quiet message" is the medium of the epic, or of the radio, a kind of "speech that goes into action." Lenin's speech was about action, but its delivery was in and of itself action, as manifested in the "ever-changing" movements of the "masses" that surround him. Perhaps it was in realizing this that the poet found a living hero capable of succeeding Malatesta.

Canto 16 recreates the scene and speech with a few notable modifications.

> That's the trick with a crowd,
>   Get 'em into the street and get 'em moving.
> And all the time, there were people going
> Down there, over the river.
>
>   There was a man there talking,
> To a thousand, just a short speech, and
> Then move 'em on. And he said:
> Yes, these people, they are all right, they
> Can do everything, everything except act;
> And go an' hear 'em but when they are through
> Come to the bolsheviki . . . [80]

The "man" decries speaking without acting and nominates Bolshevism as the political force that will successfully conjoin the two. But here, as in Steffens's account, the speech already is an action; its mode of delivery encourages mass movement in the swarming of crowds around a central speaker. If Lenin is indeed a factive personality capable of speech that is isomorphic with action, then it makes sense that the poem wants to distill that heroism into its own forms, translating Lenin's speech into its own delivery. While these lines describe a particular form—a factive personality or heroic speech-act—the descriptive content also resonates with the form of the poem itself. In other words, the poem aspires formally to what it has included with the historical actuality of Lenin's speech. Take, for instance, the multiple abbreviations of the pronominal "them" into the idiolectic "'em." By Pound's standards this is only a minor idiosyncrasy, but its reiteration here is nonetheless revealing. Its repetition emblematizes a consistency shared between the speech's framing description and the speech itself. This presumably spoken word appears before and after the colon that marks a transition between two modes of discourse, establishing a shared wavelength between the poem's inner and outer forms, between quotation and narration.

The absorption of Lenin's speech into poetic form highlights a key difference between the episode's two versions in Steffens and Pound: for Pound there is no mention of "a man named Lenin," and instead there is only "a man there talking." Where the proper name "Lenin" has been suppressed, the nominal absence of that personality allows an undivided attention to focus on something else. Instead of the divisive political figure, the flesh-and-blood character, we are presented with a unique style operating as form and content, speech and action, together and at once. As we see below, Pound added several proper nouns that did not appear in the original drafts of Canto 16, but in this case withholding Lenin's proper name is faithful to the idea that Lenin himself was a medium, channeling the very essence of communism, which was his "trick with a crowd." "And Lenin," writes Steffens, "personified the Bolsheviki, and his speech expressed the patience, determination, and wisdom, practical and ideal, of the small minority which won finally in October."[81] Or, as Trotsky recalls Lenin's arrival in Petrograd: "Only from that moment does the Bolshevik Party begin to speak out loud, and, what is more important, with its own voice."[82]

Bolshevism's Electric Witchcraft

What appears still to be missing from Steffens and Pound is the metaphor of electricity that routinely attends Lenin's public persona. According to Susan Buck-Morss, "although Lenin's speeches were reproduced on gramophone records for mass distribution, it was the live voice, the history-making event of its speech in present time, that carried mass-political charisma."[83] In multiple accounts, that live voice is remembered in a technological language derived from electronic or mechanical remediation. This is how Lenin is recalled in the remarkable words of Nikolai Sukhanov, a founding affiliate of the Petrograd Soviet and member of the non-Bolshevik Socialist-Revolutionaries: "I shall never forget that thunder-like speech, which startled and amazed not only me, a heretic who had accidentally dropped in, but all the true believers. I am certain that no one had expected anything of the sort. It seemed as though all the elements had risen from their abodes, and the spirit of universal destruction, knowing neither barriers nor doubts, neither human difficulties nor human calculations, was hovering around the reception-room above the heads of the bewitched disciples."[84] In the imaginative assessment of Theodor Adorno, radio voice is ghosted by "a touch of unreality and witchcraft," whose "haunting factor in radio is not the newness of the mechanical tool" but, rather, "the remnants of the pre-technical concept of authenticity haunting an art technique basically opposed to it."[85] When Pound comes to write about Lenin in a theoretical statement, against which we should read the lines from Canto 16, he makes recourse to that technological language. "The time has come when we should begin to study Lenin qualitatively and analytically, and not merely polemically," Pound would write several years later. "He never wrote a sentence that has any interest in itself, but he evolved almost a new medium, a sort of expression half way between writing and action. This," for Pound, "was a definite creation." Pound is more specific about particular media at the end of that publication, linking the electric charge of Lenin's personality with the socialists' apparent deployment of the radio. "The Bolshevik coup d'état could not have been effected without wireless," he says, "the other means of communication were sabotaged." Following hard upon this, he supplies an affirmation of the Bolsheviks leader: "LENIN is more interesting than any surviving stylist. He probably never wrote a single brilliant sentence . . . but he invented or very nearly invented a new medium, something between speech and action (language as cathode ray) which is worth any writer's study."[86] Though Pound is somewhat imprecise with this, as voice radio would not be made available until 1921, four years after the revolution, the electronic metaphors remain indicative of a collective fantasy that is immanent to Lenin, who in 1917 embodied what the state would become within five years time, after the Bolsheviks had installed loudspeakers in public and working environments. "By 1922," writes Steve Phillips, "Moscow had the most powerful broadcasting station in the world."[87] For us, those anachronistic metaphors express precisely what Pound has done with Lenin in Canto 16, presenting him as a singular medium that combines speech with act, transforming the voice into an electromagnetic surge: he is the heroic "cathode ray" of communism.

Imprecisions aside, electricity and the radio make apposite metaphors for communism because they capture the contagious energy inherent to this kind of politics, the way revolutionary affect spreads through multiple individuals to unite them as a politicized collective, a fused circuit of utopian desire. For instance, electrification is one of Trotsky's favored metaphors to describe the almost epiphenomenal charge of revolutionary intensities. Street fights, he says, "are small discharges of the accumulated electricity," and these are the terms by which he contemplated the founding of the Military-Revolutionary Committee: "There was that electric tension in the air which forebodes a coming discharge."[88] Following Lenin's speech, several more passages from Steffens's account find form in Canto 16. These passages describe a scene from Moscow in which a rumor spreads through the crowd that the Cossacks—who were supposed to support the tsarist regime—have changed sides to ally themselves with the masses. This rumor derives from the Cossacks uttering a Russian pleasantry, "pojalouista," when speaking to the crowd. According to Steffens, it was with this utterance that the masses understood that "all the soldiers were with them. So far had the sufferings of the troops at the front affected the army, the main support of the government." The episode ends with a tsarist solider being cut down by a Cossack, followed by an unattributed cry: "The revolution! The revolution is on!"[89]

Here is Pound's reconstruction of the episode:

> And when it broke, there was the crowd there,
> And the cossacks, just as always before,
> But one thing, the cossacks said:
>   "Pojalouista."
> And that got round in the crowd,
> And then a lieutenant of infantry
> Ordered 'em to fire into the crowd,
>   in the square at the end of the Nevsky,
> In front of the Moscow station,
> And they wouldn't,
> And he pulled his sword on a student for laughing,
> And killed him,
> And a cossack rode out of his squad
> On the other side of the square
> And cut down the lieutenant of infantry
> And there was the revolution . . .
>   as soon as they named it.[90]

The geographical markers, "Nevsky" and "Moscow station," were only added to a later draft of the poem, confirming that the action took place in Znamenskaya Square—later renamed the Square of the Uprising—which was important to the revolution for logistical, spatial, and symbolic reasons. The square was an unavoidable thoroughfare between Moscow's industrial suburbs and the Nevsky Prospect, and it comprised a large space with a podium-like statue in the center. That statue, the same equestrian monument destroyed in a poem by Wallace Stevens about the revolution, was "a symbol of autocracy, of its monolithic immobility and, at the same time, a reminder of the police who came to the square to defend it."[91]

But more important than the geographical location of the revolution is the way it registered for the poem. First, notice the process by which the revolution becomes an event. It remains an anonymous pronoun, "it broke," and is said to not exist until it is "named," in the past tense, "was," as "the revolution." Second, notice the process by which political allegiances are forged, through the word, "Pojalouista," which "got round the crowd," making known to the revolutionaries that the Cossacks are on their side. There is a technological analogue to be found in this word, which spreads through the crowd like an electrical pulse, connecting them as a circuit. In his comments on radio, Marshal McLuhan describes what he calls its "immediate aspect" in striking terms (which incidentally were borrowed from Pound). "The subliminal depths of radio are charged with the resonating echoes of tribal horns and antique drums," he says. "This is inherent in the very nature of this medium, with its power to turn the psyche and society into a single echo chamber."[92] With their echoing words and locutions, these lines detail a kind of historical echo chamber constitutive of the revolution and its own nominal form. Witness, too, how the primitivism of McLuhan's phrasing finds its correlative with the cultural metonym of the Cossacks, those anachronistically tradition-bound men who in this instance are said to cut down the "lieutenant of the infantry" and then, in subsequent lines, lay waste to the tsarist military. The Cossacks are an unknown quantity, exploding unpredictably from the medium's "subliminal depths," embodying its own uneven development as well as that of an immediately prerevolutionary Russia. But all of this neglects what is most interesting about these lines: their remarkable syntax, the rapid-fire parataxis chaining together a series of events by way of the anaphoric conjunction, "and," which will return us to Malatesta, from Cantos 8 through 11, and to the factive personality or epic hero as such.

Malatesta and Lenin, Us and Them

From its spectral wavelengths—through an unnamed German voice, Lenin's quiet message, and the Cossacks' whispered solidarity—right down to the naming of "revolution," the exemplary communist event articulates itself within poetry as a combination of historical speech acts that find their technological equivalent in the radio. But there is a significant scission between the radio voice and the written word, between the heroic act and the epic poem. Buck-Morss describes it this way, framing a problematic to be faced by any poet wanting to include Lenin in verse: "Mass cathexis onto one person is a powerful organizer, but it requires at least the trace of physical presence: an image, a voice, clothes worn by, objects touched by, beds occupied by the person in whom the mass's psychic energy is invested. The written word, in contrast, is decorporealized."[93] Of course, for a poet so preeminently sensitive to the specificity of his medium—the poetic image can never be the radio voice and vice versa, for each should have its own "primary pigment"—any direct emulation of this mechanical medium would be prohibited. We have already suggested that Canto 16 emulates the radio in its play of voices; however, once the poem shifts to Lenin and the Russian Revolution, those voices give way to formal consistency, and a familiar consistency at that. The litany of uniform conjunctions generates a steady polysyndeton, which imposes rhythmic order upon the sonic and social chaos it only represents as content, suggesting the inexorable advance of the revolutionaries. Political energy changes direction only with the negative conjunction "but," which in its single usage marks a political pivot, where the Cossacks shift their allegiance. This is a direct invocation of the form that was deployed to narrate the heroic activities of Malatesta. Pound first took it up in this extensive way toward the end of Canto 8, it is used almost exclusively during the first half of Canto 9, it reappears in fits and starts throughout Canto 10, and, here, it reemerges as the dominant syntax of Canto 11. In Pound's narration of the Russian Revolution, we can thus hear the echoing hoofbeats of Malatesta's troops:

> And we beat the papishes and fought
> them back through the tents
> And he came up to the dyke again
> And fought through the dyke-gate
> And it went on from dawn to sunset
> And we broke them and took their baggage[94]

The formative significance of Canto 16 is that it reacts to radio technology as mediated by the Russian Revolution and reacts to the Russian Revolution as mediated by radio technology. By echoing the presentational strategy primarily associated with Malatesta, it presents the Russian Revolution as an epic event with Lenin as its hero. The presentation is formative because, until this moment, epic events and heroic deeds had been a thing of the past. Lenin and the Bolsheviks had resurrected the possibility of the epic, a genre that (as we heard Pound define it earlier) "cannot be written against the grain of its time" and that should be concerned with "real men, whose deeds surpass all the fictitious deeds of fabled heroes."

Before leaving Canto 16 we must attend to one final detail, which ultimately differentiates between Malatesta and Lenin. In his reading of the lines that describe Malatesta's troops, Daniel Albright points out that Pound subtly introduces a first-person plural "we" into the narration, "in which the poet retains a half-anonymous, tentative presence on the fringes of the poem," and suggests that this technique would persist throughout *The Cantos.*[95] Canto 16, by contrast, emphasizes collective third-person pronouns, such as "them" and "they," which immediately distance the speaker from the historical events to which the poem bears witness. That remains the case until the final lines of Canto 16, which include its only first-person plural, and with that inclusion they retroactively impose an ordering frame on the narration that precedes them: "So we used to hear it at the opera."[96] While there are obvious parallels between the newly introduced operatic setting and the orchestration of multiple voices we have been hearing up until now, to embed the speaker, the poem's focalizing consciousness, within a group of anonymous and passive listeners invites two distinct but overlapping interpretations. Even though Pound was writing his own opera at the same time, the setting might nevertheless convey an understated satire, returning to a world whose cultural elite requires comfort and friendship "in the case of revolution," word of which now filters through as a series of anecdotal sound bites. Second and equally salient is the parallel between Lenin's medium, the means by which he speaks to a similarly anonymous assembly of passive listeners, and the function of art as a mode for propaganda. With this identifying pronoun "we," Pound seems to accept his role as an artist and not a politician, revolutionary or otherwise, and he thereby hypothetically commits his aesthetic ideology to the politicization of art. We are now ready to pursue the legacy of communism into Pound's more decisively fascist writings of the late 1930s and 1940s, in which Lenin has been succeeded by Joseph Stalin, whose ascendancy coincides with Pound forcibly distancing himself and his poetry from the USSR and forging an alliance with Mussolini and the National Fascist Party.

Worldview from a Counterfactual Consciousness

A review of the economic motivation behind Pound's fascism will strengthen our grasp of the place of communism in his later poetry. During the 1930s and 1940s, when Pound was delivering his radio broadcasts, the overriding ideology of *The Cantos* became dominantly and decisively fascist. This "hard right turn," as Alec Marsh characterizes it, takes place within the broader continuity of Pound's sustained anti-capitalism.[97] Whereas during the 1910s and 1920s, Pound maintained an economic stance in favor of the underconsumptionist theories of Douglas as punctuated by occasional appeals to other political ideologies and economic programs, including those of communism, in the 1930s he developed a belief that Italy had achieved good economic policy coherent with the Douglasite ideal of Social Credit. Pound's guiding misconception here is either that fascism had disabused Italy of capitalism or that it somehow maintained an economy that (like the ancient waterwheel in Canto 5) anachronistically predates the distinctly modern hellfire of large-scale industry. These arguments are made clearest in one of Pound's political pamphlets, *Jefferson and/or Mussolini,* which was written in 1933 but not published until 1935. "They still plough with oxen in Italy," he claims, "and they say that the sentimental foreigner with his eye for the picturesque and the classic scholar who likes to be reminded of Virgil, etc., are not at the root of it." Pound also insists that Mussolini tactically acts upon the cultural "prejudice" and "sentiment" surrounding classical Italy, so that this bucolic image of agrarian labor can find itself coupled with Mussolini's supposedly responsible deployment of large-scale industry. "He has looked over a few model factories," writes Pound; "he is all for machinery when it means machines in the open air in suitable places, as for bonifica, draining of swamps."[98]

These endorsements of Italian fascism coincided with Pound's escalating critiques of Russian socialism, which by the early 1940s he viewed as an irredeemable failure. One of the principal reasons for this newfound view was Pound's 1934 discovery of the economist Silvio Gesell, who extended Douglas's theory of Social Credit into a practicable model for stamp scrip and who openly dismissed communism and its primary mode of economic critique. As an anti-capitalist, Gesell stood for "the abolition of unearned income, of so-called surplus-value, also called interest and economic rent. The method generally proposed for this aim," he confesses, "is Communism." However, in differentiating between the communist "method" and his own, Gesell argues hyperbolically that capitalism is fortunate "to have Marx and Christ discussed as widely as possible, for Marx can never damage Capital."[99] Whereas communism might direct its energies into organized labor and socialist revolution, Gesell instead advocates monetary reform, specifically the replacement of money by work certificates. In Pound's view from 1933, which preempts his discovery of Gesell, "the Russian revolution is the end of the Marxian cycle, that is to say Marxian economics were invented in a time when labor was necessary, when a *great deal* of labour was *still* necessary, and his, Marx's, values are based on labour."[100] Then, in 1935, Pound confirmed the influence of both Douglas and Gesell on his disengagement from Marxism as a viable method for economic critique, using remarkably similar language to that he used two years earlier: "Two men have ended the Marxist era. Douglas in conceiving the cultural heritage as the greatest and chief fountain of value. Gesell in seeing that 'Marx never questioned money. He just took it for granted.'"[101] Finally, bringing this full circle, in 1936 Pound wrote to the anticommunist Russian, John Cournos, seeking to remedy the USSR's perceived misdirection: "As there is no way of getting one grain of sense into Communists outside Russia, would there be any way of inducing any Rhoosian intelligentsia to consider Douglas and Gesell? Especially Doug. as a phase of Communism suited to countries already in a higher state of technical development than their own."[102] For Pound, the Russian Revolution served as an endpoint for Marxism, which the poet claimed was overly invested in the labor theory of value; Douglas and Gesell provided preferable methods of economic critique and social change because they understood value as either cultural or monetary; and the economists from the USSR, bearing out the political legacy of Marxism, should therefore be educated in Douglasite and Gesellian economics.

By the mid-1930s, Pound saw Italy (as opposed to Russia) as the paragon of good governance, because he believed the fascist state to have successfully implemented policy in line with Douglasite and Gesellian economics. In a 1934 letter to the *Criterion,* Pound unambiguously insisted upon the implementation of stamp scrip as an historical event on the fascist calendar. Also notice how Pound's attention to Mussolini's speech resembles his depiction of Lenin in Canto 16.

> On Oct. 6th of the year current (anno XII) between 4 P.M. and 4-30 Mussolini, speaking very clearly four or five words at a time, with a pause, quite a long pause, between phrases, to let it sink in, told 40 million Italians together with auditors in the U.S.A. and the Argentine that the problem of production was solved, and that they could now turn their minds to distribution.
>
> Distribution is effected by means of small bits of paper, many of those bearing one, two and three numerals are for convenience sake carefully engraved, and are (apart from series number) exact replicas of each other as far as human skill can encompass.
>
> Other bits are part printed and partly filled in by hand.
>
> The science of distribution will progress in measure as people give more at-

> tention to these bits of paper, what they are, how they come there, and who governs their creation and transit.[103]

And one year later, in 1935, he praised the fascist realization of Social Credit.

> THE fascist revolution was FOR the preservation of certain liberties and FOR the maintenance of a certain level of culture, certain standards of living, it was NOT a refusal to come down to a level of riches or poverty, but a refusal to surrender certain immaterial prerogatives, a refusal to surrender a great slice of the cultural heritage.
>
> The "cultural heritage" as fountain of value in Douglas' economics is in process of superseding labour as fountain of values, which it WAS in the time of Marx, or at any rate was in overwhelming proportion.[104]

This seemingly deliberate misidentification of Italy as noncapitalist is largely what motivated the poet's aggressive "turn," an ideological shift made from within a sustained commitment to anti-capitalism, steering his verse away from any sort of communism and toward a fantasy of fascism. If, in addition to all of this, there is further need for confirmation that Pound misconceived of fascism as noncapitalist, he provided it with a postscript to *Jefferson and/or Mussolini,* added in 1935, two years after its initial composition and on the eve of publication. "These things being so," he reflects on the pamphlet as a whole, "is it to be supposed that Mussolini has regenerated Italy, merely for the sake of reinfecting her with the black death of the capitalist monetary system?"[105] In Pound's view, the fascists had succeeded in what the socialists should have set out for to begin with, eradicating not capitalism as a mode of production but the "black death" of its "monetary system," and Italy was not going to make the same mistake as Russia, allowing for capitalism to reenter a mode of production designed in opposition to it. "No other statement," confirms Tim Redman in his interpretation of this question, "could show so clearly just to what extent Pound's belief in fascism was based on his belief that Mussolini would implement the economic scheme Pound envisioned."[106]

While, in Pound's counterfactual vision, Italy was making headway from one triumph to the next, it is important to remember here that socialism in the USSR was only realized during an ongoing war that contributed to its own terminal reinfection by capitalism. Lenin and the Bolsheviks seized an economy during wartime (after World War I, the Russian Civil War lasted from 1918 to 1921), and that economy was already on the brink of collapse.

This situation forced the aspirations of socialism, including the abolition of private property and of the free market, up against the material exigencies of production and distribution in a time of inescapable scarcity. The immediate result of this conjuncture was "war communism," a type of socialism that required brutal policies to keep the Red Army in healthy material reserves, so as to continue defending the socialist state against the allied anti-Bolshevik forces and their aggressive White Army. Because of the constraints war communism placed on the USSR and its inhabitants, the Bolsheviks were faced with the prospect of a popular backlash. According to John Laver, it was because of this prospect that Lenin jettisoned war communism in favor of state capitalism under the New Economic Policy, which was introduced in 1921: "The NEP, with its emphasis on economic co-operation rather than coercion, its tolerance of private enterprise, and in particular the granting to peasants of the right to pay tax and keep their food supplies, marked a period of economic recovery."[107] In 1924, Joseph Stalin succeeded Lenin and soon replaced the NEP with a series of Five-Year Plans, which in turn supplanted the policy of communist internationalism with the conservative idea of "Socialism In One Country," the implementation of which proved economically catastrophic and, in time, ideologically abhorrent. The imposition of war communism, the advent of the NEP, Stalin's succession as general secretary, the Five-Year Plans, and the USSR's military support of the Spanish Republicans (against the fascist Nationals) and its role in World War II all become the focus of Pound's criticism and the grounds on which he contrasted the USSR unfavorably to Italy.

To summarize, then, Pound's fascism resulted in part from his relatively consistent anti-capitalism—from the fact that he incorrectly believed Mussolini to have eradicated capitalism in Italy, implementing instead a new kind of monetarism. Significantly for us, the emergence of this belief coincided with a dawning sense that the USSR had allowed itself to be "reinfected" by capitalism, first with Lenin's New Economic Policy and subsequently with Stalin's Five-Year Plans. As is now plain, more than coincidence relates these two things. Pound's fascism was undergirded by essentially anti-capitalist forms of political desire that, for a different subject or in a different context, might have evolved into communism. But it must also be stated categorically that his fascism always remained distinct from communism, even if both were perceived as facing off against the same economic system. Despite communism and fascism potentially serving as types of anti-capitalism, these two political programs remain incommensurate and opposed. That opposition is not just ideological or aesthetic but also, even primarily, material. Communism and fascism diverge on matters of social alliances and social hierarchy; on the structuration of the economy, the implantation of government, and the rule of law; on geopolitical conceptions of nationhood, war, and empire; and on the counterpoised emphases of collectives and the individual. In short, whereas communism posits a postcapitalist, postsocialist future, fascism, by contrast is, "capitalism in decay," as Lenin famously put it. This opposition is relevant to Pound's consistently anti-capitalist project because his eventual turn to fascism meant not only a turn away from communism, which he came to perceive as an undesirable or unsuccessful strand of anti-capitalism, but also a felt need to actively criticize the socialist state, which ironically ensured its persistence into his late and outwardly fascist poetry.

Set against the background of Pound's fascism, the remainder of this chapter explores the extent to which communism persists in the poetry composed during the 1930s and early 1940s. It demonstrates that communism lives on through a specific modality of Pound's epic, namely, its politically and aesthetically conflicted depictions of warfare. My argument here is that Pound reserved different modes of presentation for acts of warfare committed by either fascists or communists, by either Italy or the USSR, and that he did so with increasing consistency. The aesthetic operation with which we are concerned is Pound's satire, which is frequently deployed in the context of warfare and often in ways that are seemingly at odds with the circumambient form of the epic. It is significant here that Hegel posited the origins of epic poetry in the age of the Trojan War. "In the most general terms," he says, "we can cite conflict in a state of war as the situation most suited to epic." As we have seen with Malatesta and Lenin, one of the defining features and necessary preconditions of the epic is heroic action, which gives form to the totality of its historical moment and allows for that totality simultaneously to recognize itself within the acting hero. Heroic characters and their heroic actions are most likely to be encountered during war, which for Hegel "is fitted not for expression in lyric, nor for dramatic action, but above all for description in epic." Here we see what happens to the epic when warfare militates against the barest possibility of such heroism.[108]

Industry, Artillery, Satire

The kind of warfare that defined the classical epics to which Hegel refers has been superseded by history and consigned to an ancient past. We know that Georg Lukács and Franco Moretti have both addressed this point, yet it was not a literary theorist but Marx himself who best formulated the problematic faced by the writers of modern epics when it comes to warfare. In the *Grundrisse,* Marx argues that "certain economic relations such as wage labour, machinery etc. develop earlier, owing to war and in the armies etc., than in the interior of bourgeois society," and as a result the mode of production is made "especially vivid in the army." But the modernization of these relations ultimately forecloses on epic form in its classical realization: "Is Achilles possible with powder and lead? Or the Iliad with the printing press, not to mention the printing machine? Do not the song and the saga and the muse necessarily come to an end with the printer's bar, hence do not the necessary conditions of epic poetry vanish?" This newly administered totality and its resultantly nonheroic warfare was a reality to which Pound had become very much attuned and which he wrote up as satire. "There is satire in the Iliad and the Odyssey," Pound insisted in 1932. "I cannot believe that satire is in itself alien to epos." For Pound, satire had always been an integral part of the epic. But it is also worth remembering that with satire there is always going to be a political division at stake. "Someone must be the object of satire," stipulates Keston Sutherland, "and someone must suffer by its influence; and that means not simply that someone must be ridiculed or described grotesquely and with exaggeration, but that the whole work of thinking in satire will be in the interests of some real people and contrary to the interests of others." Up until the mid-1930s, Pound's satire would be used to galvanize thought against capitalism's fomenting of warfare, but later, after his fascist turn, it would be deployed almost exclusively at the expense of the USSR and her allies, in the interests of Italy. By serving as a beacon for satire, communism keeps alive that crucially modern aspect of Pound's epic poetry.[109]

Before Canto 16, Pound had two major strategies for writing poems about warfare while avoiding the ideologically and aesthetically regressive valorization of battle. The first strategy comprised adapting from precapitalist source materials that he used to reflect upon the context into which he adapted them, as well as the historical moment from which they originate. This strategy is what underwrites Kenner's insistence that the poems from *Cathay,* Pound's 1915 recreation of ancient Chinese verse, "paraphrase an elegiac war poetry nobody wrote."[110] Similar arguments can be made about "Homage to Sextus Propertius," which, according to Pound, "presents certain emotions as vital to me in 1917, faced with the infinite and ineffable imbecility of the British Empire, as they were to Propertius some centuries earlier, when faced with the infinite and ineffable imbecility of the Roman Empire."[111] The second and perhaps more radical strategy Pound used to write poems about warfare granted him direct access to his own historical present, and it was first articulated in "Hugh Selwyn Mauberley," which contained lengthy reflections on World War I. When this poem in its fourth subsection turns to warfare, it does so as the blackest of satires, working up a grim irony that delivers on tragic elegy while reflexively defusing the heroism sustained by that genre. The poem refers to "trench confessions" and to the "laughter out of dead bellies," two forms it closely resembles, whose "frankness as never before," the poem insists, was then being taken up and exploited by the agents of "usury age-old and age-thick and liars in public places."[112] These grisly images coupled with cultural diagnostics ruthlessly negate the possibility of military valor, and they do so for a good reason. "Poetry," wrote Pound in 1917, "gets out of reach of the stench, and satire is a quick-lime, or ammonia which cuts through it."[113] Here is the poem's fifth part, composed beyond the "stench" of the lines that precede it:

> There died a myriad,
> And of the best, among them,
>
> For an old bitch gone in the teeth,
> For a botched civilization,
>
> Charm, smiling at the good mouth,
> Quick eyes gone under earth's lid,
>
> For two gross of broken statues,
> For a few thousand battered books.[114]

"There's no irony here," claims Alec Marsh, "just the bitter truth."[115] And yet, it is precisely because of the previous lines' satirical "ammonia" that these can deliver their "bitter truth," because the poem has already announced itself as part of the rotten "civilization" in whose name the "myriad" and "the best" were slaughtered. According to Albright, this poem crystallized Pound's poetic maturation, marking the point at which he "ceased to write minor poetry" by convincing himself "that only a huge, indigestible poem would stick in the craw of a monstrous, all-consuming age. Into that poem," Albright is right to insist, "he would put what needed saving."[116] There, in the epic, Pound would also continue developing this satire of modern warfare, using it to cleave between the capitalist mode of production and the politics of his verse.

Recall that in Canto 16 the heroics of communism derived in part from Vladimir Lenin and Leon Trotsky disgorging the USSR from the battlefields of World War I, and that this self-preserving pacifism instigated the poem's epic account of the Revolution. Compare that account to prerevolutionary Russia's acquisition of armaments in Canto 18. Here Pound introduces one of the great villains of *The Cantos,* Sir Zenos Metevsky (based on the notorious Greek arms dealer, Sir Basil Zaharoff), as well as one of his associates, Mr. Giddings, who brags about lucrative investments in the "man-u-facture" of "war machinery" and who narrates a profitable sale made to the imperial navy in Russia. Giddings tells an anecdote about selling a "new torpedo-boat" that is "all electric" and operated by miniature "keyboard."[117] When the unnamed Russian "prince" is allowed to pilot the vessel, we are told, "he run damn slam on the breakwater," damaging its hull. Naval history confirms that this event took place in 1903, that the offending prince was Heinrich of Prussia, and that in 1904 the Imperial Russian Navy commissioned three submarines of the described class.[118] If these details are correct, Mr. Giddings must be an employee or representative of Germaniawerft, a shipbuilding company owned by a parent firm named after Friedrich Alfred Krupp, whom Pound elevated alongside Zaharoff as one of the chief culprits for war profiteering. The scenes of the Moscow uprising from Canto 16 contain depictions of real military struggle ("Guns on the top of the post-office and the palace," we read, "But none of the leaders knew it was coming"[119]), but those scenes are very different from what we encounter in Canto 18. Whereas the Bolsheviks and by extension the Red Army are depicted as the anonymous heroes of a battle worth fighting, not least because it is a revolutionary battle against capitalism and against the wars inherent within that mode of production, the Prussian aristocracy and the Russian Imperial Navy are satirically humiliated because of their collusion with capitalism and the type of warfare that mode of production facilitates. By contrast to Lincoln Steffens's telling of the Russian Revolution in Canto 16, here in Canto 18 Giddings's anecdote bathetically forecloses even the possibility of heroism. "And," Mr. Giddings gleefully informs us, "he was my gawd scared out of his panties."[120]

The Eclipse of Satirical Reason

Published in 1934, two years before the Spanish Civil War, Canto 38 presents totality in miniature: an interconnected mode of production inhabited by banks and bankers, disreputable statesmen and their various armies, in addition to arms dealers and manufacturers, most of whom first appeared two decades earlier in Cantos 14 and 15, the Hell Cantos, as well as in Canto 18. Several years earlier, Pound claimed that the only "useful research" on war and peace would be into the contemporary causes of conflict, and there he gestured toward "high pressure salesmanship of munitions" and "interested cliques, commercial, dynastic and bureaucratic" as two of the potential causes wanting future investigation.[121] Canto 38 presciently delineated these causes immediately before they gave rise to the Spanish Civil War and World War II, which together drew both the fascist and socialist states headlong into armed combat.

This delineation comes into full view when examining the inclusion of the two weapons magnates returning from Canto 18, Zaharoff and Krupp. Their formally symmetrical appearances almost bookend Canto 38 and generate some critical parallels with each other, amplifying the poem's sense of satire, from which Italy and Russia are visibly granted exemption. Zaharoff's infamous strategy of selling weaponry to opposing belligerents is depicted unambiguously (though attributed to Metevsky) in lines that have him trading with both rivals of an unnamed opposition.

> Don't buy until you can get ours.
> And he went over the border
>   and he said to the other side:
> The *other* side has more munitions. Don't buy
>   until you can get ours
> And Akers made a large profit and imported gold into England.
> Thus increasing gold imports.[122]

Geopolitical space is divided into two parallel and anonymous zones. Both "sides" of the division are presented only as abstract second-person plurals, "you," and are addressed with an identical (but for lineation) sales pitch, "Don't buy until you can get ours," so that each sovereign referent is made rhetorically parallel with the other. The enjambment of the second iteration, which splits Metevsky's injunction in two, is formally analogous to the process by which this arms dealer makes his "large profit" by dividing sales between two opposing forces and reaping a profit from the consequently escalating arms struggle. That is where we locate the satire of these lines, in the manner by which they undermine the proprietary nature of the sales pitch. While the seller insists either "side" should not purchase weaponry "until you can get ours," that pitch is made repeatedly, which divides and diminishes its value just as the sentence itself is divided between lines. Within this system of equivalence, the emphatic adjective "other" attains to the status of an economically motivated pivot that ensures the differentiation of two indefinable "sides," from whose nominal difference the arms dealer can generate his profitable sales. It is a law of diminishing returns for everyone except Metevsky. This lexical and structural parallelism of the two belligerent "sides," which are kept interchangeably anonymous, contrasts with the two proper nouns of the penultimate line—"Akers" (for which we should read "Vickers," Zaharoff's company) and "England" (where that company is based)—which together anchor this episode to an historical moment when the lived reality of warfare is subsumed by the profit margins of its investors, who divide and conquer by way of the market.

Toward the end of Canto 38 is this passage, which achieves a similar effect to the previous episode but via different means:

> Said Herr Krupp (1842): guns are a merchandise
> I approach them from the industrial end,
> I approach them from the technical side,
> 1847 orders from Paris and Egypt . . .
>   orders from the Crimea,
> Order of Pietro il Grande,
>   and a command in the Legion of Honour . . .
> 500 to St Petersburg and 300 to Napoleon Barbiche
> from Creusot. At Sadowa
>   Austria had some Krupp cannon;
>   Prussia had some Krupp cannon.
> "The Emperor ('68) is deeply in'erested in yr/ catalogue
>   and in yr. services to humanity"
>   (signed) Leboeuf.[123]

The first three lines extract weaponry from the referential context of warfare and reposition it within the nexus of capitalist accumulation. For "Herr Krupp," guns are not weaponry but "merchandise" that can be dissociated from the battlefield and approached from "the industrial end" or "the technical side." But, and this is part of the satire, the lines that follow contain nothing of industrial or technical manufacture; instead, they read like a sales ledger, with every proper name coupled with the details of an exchange. What drives the satire in these lines is their inversion of the formal operation we encountered in the previous episode, when here the anonymous "sides" are militarized states with proper names. History will remind us (as it did Pound) that these states all used their purchased weaponry to annihilate one another. If these lines read like a sales ledger, that ledger also serves as a rough timeline for wars by naming the opposing forces as regular clientele. While the line beginning with a date, 1847, nominates the year in which Krupp designed his first cannon, the remainder of that line and the line that follows gesture toward the fact that Krupp failed to sell it until touring in France and Egypt, after he had taken orders for other weaponry from the two opposing sides in the Crimean War.

Ironically, both sides decorated Krupp with honors for his nefarious salesmanship during and after that war, with the Russians presenting him with the "Order of Pietro il Grande" and the French inducting him into the "Legion of Honour." The next line, "500 to St Petersburg," presumably refers to Krupp's sale to Russia, while another armaments firm, Creusot, is retroactively introduced after sending "300 to Napoleon Barbiche," who led the allied forces against Russia. The two subsequent lines that comprise a syntactical and lexical parallel engage the Battle of Sadowa, a decisive event in the Austro-Prussian War. The battle famously obliterated both forces, which, according to these lines, were both deploying "some Krupp cannon," a piece of "merchandise" that cannot in any way, after these lines, be seen exclusively from "the industrial end" or thought about only from "the technical side." Finally, then, completing the satire by undermining Krupp's own avowal of industrial and technical fetishism is a witheringly ironic note, signed by the minister of war for Napoleon Barbiche; it confirms that Krupp's practices are inextricable from the "humanity" they annihilate.

In the structural symmetry between militarized states and the industries of militarization, Canto 38 configures itself within a transhistorical matrix of economic relations whose nodal points comprise only the suppliers of weaponry and their customers. The lines are openly satirical in the ways that have been suggested, as well as in their bracing tonal shifts. For instance, two more arms dealers, the brothers Bolhlem and Hallbach Schneider from Creusot, are described in terms that recall the London of Cantos 14 and 15, and the nightmare situation from which Russia extracts the epic in Canto 16. "Twin arse with one belly," reads the metaphor, immediately recalling "the great arse-hole" that hangs airborne above the English "hell-rot."[124] Exempt from Canto 38's satire are Stalin's Russia and Mussolini's Italy, both circa 1930. They are referred to side by side in these lines:

And they put up a watch factory outside Muscou
And the watches kept time Italian marshes
been waiting since Tiberius' time.[125]

Stalin's establishment of the First Moscow Watch Factory and Mussolini's draining of the Pontine Marshes in Central Italy were considered by Pound to be responsible modernizations that bypassed the entanglements of capital and were ordered directly by the respective heads of state. The content of these lines appear to reflect Pound's geopolitical assumptions and so his positive assessment of the two states, which he made clear in 1933: "Two countries," he describes them, "and only two have made any attempt to face modern reality."[126] What is interesting about the double exemption from capitalism is that it situates Russia and Italy within different temporalities. Italy reaches back into and preserves something of its ancient past, whereas Russia recalibrates its relation to the present. This is partly an effect of Pound misidentifying fascism as noncapitalist, whereby Social Credit's supposed victory over capitalism is allowed to endow fascism with an ancient heroic grandeur, of which communism remains wanting. Yet both are immeasurably distinct from capitalist modernity, and together they abide within the continuity of Pound's anti-capitalism. The harmony between fascism and communism does not last much longer, though, and one of the principal reasons for this is that both Italy and the USSR committed themselves to the warfare from which Canto 38 kept them separate.

In *Jefferson and/or Mussolini,* Pound also argued that the kind of arms trade satirized in Canto 38 is an exclusively capitalist enterprise: "The selling of guns and powder differs from ALL other industries in that the more you sell the greater the demand for the product. The more goes to consumer A the greater the demand of the other consumers. Hence the love, the loving and tender love of banks for munition works." These exemplarily capitalist relations are opposed to what Pound still viewed, in 1935, as the ideological correctives of either communism or fascism. "Gents who make guns like to sell 'em," he says, "such is the present state of the world, in the bourgeois demo-liberal anti-Marxian anti-fascist anti-Leninist system."[127] The presuppositions implicit in this bizarre formulation are that the "present state of the world" is "bourgeois" and "demo-liberal," and that this world rejects the lessons of Marx, Lenin, and fascism. The point here is not to align Marx, Lenin, and fascism—to be sure, these lines were written several years prior to the Molotov-Ribbentrop or Hitler-Stalin Pact between Russia and

Germany, which might have made such linkage possible—but to posit the weapons market as an exclusively capitalist phenomenon that opposes itself to these largely incompatible correctives. And yet, just one year later, the poet's politically motivated satire of military production as exclusively capitalist would be challenged by Italy's Campaign in Abyssinia, by the Spanish Civil War, and then by World War II. Not only did these events intervene against a theoretical separation of communism and fascism from warfare, but they also delivered the states that championed these ideologies into what Ernst Mandel has described as the first great war enabled by mechanized mass production, "a conveyor-belt war, the war of military Fordism."[128] This presented another challenge for Pound's historically inclusive epic—namely, how to faithfully represent communism and fascism as militarily complicit with the capitalist economy from which the poet wished to isolate them.

Fascist warfare entered *The Cantos* before the USSR's first appearance in the poem as a military force, and it did so through a vainglorious presentation for which the poem seemed to have blunted its satirical edge. Cantos 72 and 73 are a significant departure from the depiction of warfare in Canto 38. In them, we see the return to an unreconstructed mode of classical epic, wherein a picture of fascists at war is punctuated by talismanic invocations of Homer and Dante. While the term *classical epic* is perhaps too loose, here it is meant to convey the kind of form that Hegel and Marx relegated to ancient history, whose depictions of warfare we have seen undercut and foreclosed by Pound's satire. In Canto 72, the poet appeals to Italy's fascist regime via the ghosts of its dead heroes. This approach is similar to what we encountered in Canto 16, but instead of denouncing war these ghosts and their living interlocutor champion it. Its title, "Presenza," evokes the fascist soldiers' call to arms and Mussolini's attempt to revivify the fascist army, as well as the presences summoned by Dante in *The Divine Comedy.* Here the Dantean framework of the poet speaking to the ghosts of his forebears is maintained. Within this register, the spirit of Guido Cavalcanti sings the praise of a peasant girl who sacrifices herself in the name of fascism by leading a group of Allied soldiers to their bloody death in a minefield. "Che brava pupa!" writes Pound, "che brave pupetta!"[129] Patricia Cockram has argued that Pound's "celebration of aggression in art had never extended to physical violence or war; yet here, in the midst of the second vast international conflict of the century, he found himself part of a movement that glorified war."[130] Under the sign of fascism, Pound adopts the role of epic singer to record the heroic acts of armed combatants. "Go make yourself a hero again," says the speaker to Marinetti's ghost, "& leave the talking to me. / And let me explain, / sing of the eternal war between light and mud."[131] In Cantos 72 and 73, ideological intensity transmutes the form into an uncritical revival of the classical epic as distinct from the resolutely modern depiction of warfare we encountered in Canto 38. What makes these two cantos "a disastrous failure," as Peter Nicholls describes them, is not just their uncharacteristic embrace of violence but, more importantly, the fact that "Pound's attempt to identify Cavalcanti's formal bravura with the rhetoric of fascist bravado comes decisively unstuck," producing a verse whose "heroic rhetoric is clumsily out of joint with the time."[132]

Radio Voice, Part 2: Satire Reloaded

While the USSR was absent from Cantos 72 and 73, in Pound's radio broadcasts from the time of their composition he obsessively criticized Stalin and the USSR, indicating that he was continually preoccupied with that socialist state and that his thoughts had changed drastically since writing Canto 16 and even Canto 38. "Yes," he admits, "we were once young or younger, and many of us fell for the Russian Red Revolution. Because the Marxist diagnosis was pretty near right. The remedy did NOT work. AND the revolution was betrayed." He criticizes the USSR for two betrayals in particular. First, he decries the localized implementation of socialism and how that lowered the standard of living and led to state-sponsored atrocities. On this, he repeatedly cites the disastrous construction of the Baltic Canal during the first Five-Year Plan, describing its forced labor and fatally hazardous working conditions as state crime. "The auditor knows nothing of Russia until he has heard or read the reported facts of that horror," says Pound: "Until he has considered the number of lives crushed out by Stalin's system BEFORE the massing of Russia's gigantic armies in the threat to all Europe's heritage." Secondly, Pound criticizes the way Stalin would allow the Red Army to serve capitalist wars in grand military alliances against European fascism. To make this point, he refers back to tsarist Russia, characterizing it as "an immense reserve force for western imperialism." He even cites Stalin's own claim that the tsarist army once "shed its blood on imperialist fronts to safeguard the staggering profits of Anglo-French capitalists" and that it did so, he claims, with 12 million combatants. "Joe is speaking of the war that had occurred before he wrote his little brochure," adds Pound, with reference to World War I. "As to this war: some estimates give 30 million as the cost to Russia, 30 million human lives." From Pound's view, Stalin's war cannot possibly be heroic in the classical sense that he sought to channel for Cantos 72 and 73; heroic action would be thwarted by world-historic ineptitude, and the observation of such ineptitude is guided by Pound's attempt to implicate Stalin and Russia with the ruthless acquisition of materials typical of capitalism. Given that this broadcast took place in June 1943, what Pound deliberately overlooked here was the fact that those "30 million human lives" were principally lost in the defense of Leningrad against Nazi military invasion, and so to the invading forces of Italy's military ally. Despite this fact, Pound in this broadcast presents Stalin, the political leader, as simply repeating mistakes that Lenin and Trotsky once sought to redress with revolution, and Stalin's combatants, the Red Army, have collectively been reduced to ordnance "material," unwittingly waging war in the service of capital. "I disliked a year ago to see Stalin repeating the Czarist error," says Pound of Russia's joining the Allied Forces: "sacrificing millions of Russians IN THE CAUSE of the usurers."[133]

The satire that was noticeably absent from Cantos 72 and 73 persisted outside of the poetry, in the radio broadcasts, attaching itself to the USSR, whose political descent Pound caricatures as "a purely metaphysical, typically Russian crusade. As crazy as any excess of the middle ages." His broadcasts account for the sheer horror of Stalinism as well as the USSR's ideologically compromising alliance with capitalism, but in doing so they frequently turn toward satire. This approach is what we encounter in Pound's opening to a broadcast delivered on November 4, 1941. When commenting on the implementation of socialism, Pound refers to "the gap between their effective propaganda and their local failure in solving human problems," which he clarifies to mean something along the lines of history's dramatic irony: "why they did NOT make a paradise, but mostly a sweat shop—machines before men—men as material." In the same broadcast, Pound likens the military alliance between the USSR, the USA, and England as a "triangual Darby," which "leads one to look back at the forgotten incidents of their courtship." And in that ridiculous courtship, Stalin becomes "Russian Joan," whom Winston Churchill initially refused to "come and kiss" beneath "the sickle and mistletoe."[134] These satires do not just belong to Pound. Importantly, they emerge from the USSR itself, as well as from Stalin's character. For Slavoj Žižek, the transition "from the Leninism of the 20s to the Stalinism proper of the 30s is discernible even at the level of humor in the inner party debates," where officials metabolized the precariousness of their own positions with a kind of gallows humor.[135] The typical form this humor would take is satirical, juxtaposing Stalin's buffoonery and occasional clemencies to his infamous brutality.[136] My sense here is that when the poetry, ensnared by fascism, drifted away from its productively satirical approach to warfare, communism sustained that satire, keeping it alive against the aesthetically and intellectually deadening ideology of the Blackshirts. That is what we encounter in Canto 74, the first instantiation of the Pisan sequence written during Pound's incarceration in the US Army Disciplinary Training Center after his arrest by Italian Partisans in 1945. While Canto 74 is typically read by Pound's critics as a recovery of or improvement upon the poetic that seemed lost in Cantos 72 and 73,[137] here I want to demonstrate that one of the reasons for this recovery or improvement is Pound's sustained interest in communism, even and especially because he treated the USSR and Stalin as targets for satire.

. . . as Farce

Canto 74 begins with the collapse of Italian fascism after the execution of its figurehead.

> THE enormous tragedy of the dream in the peasant's bent shoulders
> Manes! Manes was tanned and stuffed,
> Thus Ben and la Clara *a Milano*
>   by the heels at Milano
> That maggots shd/ eat the dead bullock
> DIGONOS, *Δίγονος*, but the twice crucified
>   where in history will you find it?[138]

A literal interpretation of these lines' content would suggest that the peasant's "enormous tragedy" is that Mussolini and his mistress, Claretta Petacci, had been sentenced to death by firing squad and their corpses hung "by the heels at Milano," sacrificially personifying the historical abortion of a future in which that peasant might have lived in a paradisiacal state of Social Credit and stamp scrip. For Pound, this tragedy would be representative of ongoing immiseration, embodied in the specifically "bent shoulders" of the overworked laborer. The following lines elevate that "dream," a now impossible outcome of Mussolini's perceived heroism, to a status that is properly legendary by way of allusion. Mussolini and Petacci's execution is compared to that of "Manes," a prophet who was similarly condemned and crucified and whose corpse was stuffed with hay and mounted on the gates to the royal city. While the Italian Partisans are figured as "maggots," that Mussolini is "the dead bullock" on which they feast recalls the animal sacrifices made to the ancient gods. The double death of Mussolini and Petacci being shot and then hanged is made to echo the double birth of Dionysus ("DIGONOS"), whose origin is transformed by the conjunction "but" into a double crucifixion. What we encounter with these lines is Mussolini's paradigmatic insertion into a classical world with whose forms his death might be made to resonate. But to present Mussolini as an epic hero and to do so by sacralizing his death and so mythologizing the warfare that befell him occludes meaningful engagement with the distinctly modern circumstances of World War II. Because of that obstinate anachronism, of which the lines' final question seems to confirm an awareness, this opening appears in keeping with the aesthetic of Cantos 72 and 73.

But there is a different interpretation to be pursued here, one that relocates us out of tragedy and back into comedy. These lines were added only after the majority of Canto 74 had already been composed. While they send Canto 74 "on its way bristling with self-protective hostility,"[139] perhaps reframing the poetry that follows as an elegy to Mussolini, there is an argument to be made that these lines have absorbed elements from the poetry that follows them on the page but was written before them. In what ways, then, do these lines sustain the satire, Pound's witheringly ironic depiction of warfare, that had been muted for Cantos 72 and 73? An insistence upon tragedy's articulation through historical repetition recalls the famous sentence that commences *The Eighteenth Brumaire of Louis Bonaparte*. Here is how Marx's text begins: "Hegel remarks somewhere that all great world-historic facts and personages occur, as it were, twice. He has forgotten to add: the first time as tragedy, the second time as farce. Caussidière for Danton, Louis Blanc for Robespierre, the Mountain of 1848 to 1851 for the Mountain of 1793 to 1795, the Nephew for the Uncle. And the same caricature occurs in the circumstances in which the second edition of the Eighteenth Brumaire is taking place."[140] We have already heard the *Brumaire* echo in the revolutions of Canto 27, and, perhaps even confirming an association between that text and Pound's thoughts on the USSR and Stalin, in 1928 he wrote this: "No country produces two Napoleons or two Lenins in succession; so we may expect Russia to be reasonably slow in producing Utopia."[141] Read though Marx's text, the lines from Canto 74 can be taken as farcical. The "enormous tragedy" is nothing new: it has always been there, "in the peasant's bent shoulders," as a "dream" of which he was never fully conscious. It is the hard labor that blights him into a stooped posture. The events that precipitate these lines, the stringing up of Mussolini and Petacci "by the heels at Milano," do not just perpetuate that ongoing tragedy. For Pound, Mussolini instilled hope in such a dream, but in his death that hope is eradicated, returning the peasant to his tragedy. In that repetition or return, these lines modulate into the realm of farce, whose living actors are satirized as a swarm of "maggots" now consuming the sacrificial "bullock" of fascism. The object of satire here is the transmutation from fascism into its aftermath; which, for Pound, is a disgusting regression back into capitalism as we know it from Canto 14's "bog of stupidities," with its "dead maggots begetting live maggots."[142]

The lines' final question of where such an event might be found historically is immediately answered by rewriting T. S. Eliot: "yet say this to the Possum: a bang, not a whimper, / with a bang and not a whimper."[143] While Eliot said the world would end with a whimper, now, after World War II, Pound knew it had ended or would end with a bang. But this is not just the bang that concluded Canto 72, the explosion that martyred the girl and murdered the soldiers. To enact that kind of inversion of Eliot, and to frame one of Eliot's most achingly serious poems as the work of "Possum" (a pseudonym Eliot was using to publish children's books), is to reconceive of an explosive apocalypse ironically. Yet this invocation of Eliot is one of many references to a literary present with which Canto 74 appears to associate itself, including multiple nods to James Joyce, Wyndham Lewis, and E. E. Cummings. Pound singles out these three writers for a handful of reasons. First is that, for Pound, three of their works composed a spiritual trio. As he described it in 1941, "'The Apes of God,' along with 'Eimi' and 'Ulysses,' is one of at least three books that any serious reader in 1960 will most certainly have to read if he wants to get any sort of idea of what happened in Europe between one of our large wars and another." To be sure, these three books all constitute instantiations of the modern epic in relation to modern warfare. Second, all three books are, in their own ways and even if Pound failed to register them as such, works of satire. The third reason is that Cummings's book, *Eimi,* is a travelogue of his time spent in the USSR during the early 1930s and that it aided Pound's ideological distancing from that state. "And this volume," writes Pound in 1941, "is utterly indispensable to the record, meaning that in another thirty years nobody, and I mean nobody, no son of Molotoff, no grand-nephew of Stalin will be able to find out what happened in Russia during the decade without reading 'Eimi.'"[144] According to Farley, this book was important to Pound "because it described the Russian scene so accurately that it allowed Pound to feel he had travelled there himself. And, in a way, in its indictment of a system that Pound had no allegiances to anyway, *Eimi* allowed Pound to cleave closer to his own belief in the saving ideology of Italian fascism."[145] In addition to this, it meant that the USSR, as a state and a military force, would be present in Pound's thought as both a modern epic and a work of satire. "Now what do you know of Russia," Pound asked in a 1942 broadcast. "There is one record available in both American and English readers today, namely, that made by E. E. Cummings. It may be too late for you really to use it, but you want to live also tomorrow, perhaps not. At any rate, if you want to live, even today, you better read it."[146]

If Canto 74's opening has absorbed the satire of what appears after it, we encounter that satire at full amplification in this paradigmatic invocation of Stalin, who is compared to semiliterate freshmen:

> and it is (in parenthesis) doubtless
>   easier to teach them to roar like gorillas
> than to scan Φαίνεταί μοι
>   inferior gorillas
> of course, lacking the wind sack
>   and although Siki was quite observable
>   we have not yet calculated the sum gorilla + bayonet
> and there was a good man named Burr
>   descendant of Aaron during the other war
> who was amused by the British
>   but he didn't last long AND
> Corporal Casey tells me that Stalin
>   le bonhomme Staline
>   has no sense of humor (dear Koba!)[147]

In quick succession we are presented with five belligerents: the freshmen, soon to be armed for war; Siki, a Senegalese boxer; Burr, another prisoner in Pisa and the son of a veteran; Corporal Casey, one of Pound's guards; and, finally, Stalin. The thrice-repeated simian metaphor satirically frustrates these characters' relationship with the kind of military valor they would not have understood, given their inability to scan ancient Greek. Militarization is presented here via the positivistic and racially charged equation "gorilla + bayonet," which modifies the atavistic metaphor from F. W. Taylor's *Scien-*

tific Management, in which he uses it to describe the value of unskilled labor to capitalism. "This work," claims Taylor, "is so crude and elementary in its nature that the writer firmly believes that it would be possible to train an intelligent gorilla so as to become a more efficient pig-iron handler than any man can be."[148] From a comparable cell elsewhere in Italy, Antonio Gramsci would insist "that even Taylor's term 'trained gorilla' is a metaphor to indicate how far one can go in a certain direction: in any physical work, no matter how mechanical and degraded, there is a minimum of technical skill, that is, a minimum of creative intellectual activity." But the metaphor is a jarring one, as Gramsci well knew, since its function was to illuminate how "to develop the worker's mechanical side to the maximum, to sever the old psychophysical nexus of skilled professional work in which the intelligence, initiative, and imagination were required to play some role, and thus to reduce the operations of production solely to the physical aspect."[149] And in this instance, in Canto 74, that is what we encounter with the militarized personage, for these gorillas have been equipped with bayonets, but they can no longer "roar" as they were meant to. Instead, they have become "inferior gorillas," now "lacking in wind sack." Stalin is introduced as a finale to this catalogue, after the exclamatorily capitalized conjunction, and so appears to be the ultimate object of these lines' satire. The complicated tone of his appearance seems to confirm this: there is a serious contradiction between "le bonhomme Staline" and the general secretary's reported humorlessness, and the parenthetical exclamation elevates that contradiction to satire. "Koba" was Stalin's alias before the Russian Revolution, and he borrowed it from a popular novel about a Robin Hood-like hero from his native country, Georgia.[150] In these lines, however, that alias is made patronizing by the adjective that precedes it, as though to imply that humorless Stalin fails to recognize that, in his attempted heroics, he is also a source of humor. This kind of strategy is a basic tenet of good satire. In Sutherland's reading of Marx, what the "literary practice of astonishment and discipline creates and depends on is the image of the stupefied individual, which it then satirically dominates as the specimen subject of its work of theoretical diagnosis."[151] For Pound, Stalin is just like the freshmen—who are satirized "in parenthesis" just as the parenthetical words secure his satire—in that Stalin and the freshmen are both "inferior gorillas" physically trained for warfare without any real knowledge of the militaristic tradition they have entered.

Here Stalin's mismanagement of the USSR is linked directly to the movements of soldiers on the Western Front:

> and but one point needed for Stalin
> you need not, i.e. need not take over the means of production;
> money to signify work done, inside a system
> and measured and wanted
> "I have not done unnecessary manual labour"
> says the R. C. chaplain's field book
> (preparation before confession)
> squawky as larks over the death cells
> militarism progressing westward
> im Westen nichts neues
> and the Constitution in jeopardy
> and that state of things not very new either[152]

Pound's criticism of Stalin is that he commits to the postrevolutionary retention of money despite collectivizing the means of production. This could be a criticism of communist economics more generally, which are predicated on the struggle over the means of production, as opposed to Social Credit and monetary reform ("money to signify work done"). A peculiar syntax bears that criticism. The stuttering repetition "you need not, i.e. need not," is particularly damning. The "one point" for Stalin is first that he should simply desist, that he "need not" in general; then that point sharpens into a criticism of the revolutionary sequence he inherited and to which he is now central. The association between Stalin and the "chaplain's field book" is that, for Pound, Stalin's state crime was to compel extraordinary amounts of "unnecessary manual labour," which in one of the radio broadcasts Pound describes as the USSR's commitment to "sweat the hide off of labor" or "human material" in constructing the Baltic Canal.[153] That all of this might read like economic and political rhetoric is then offset by a figurative line, "squawky as larks over the death cells," which conjoins two autonomous forms with an almost self-conscious moment of poetic technique. What makes this simile so intriguing is that it gestures toward birdsong yet simultaneously retracts that gesture with the disagreeably awkward and perhaps even laughable onomatopoeia, "squawky." The simile also likens the flight patterns of the larks to the progress of "militarism," from whose "westward" movements we can deduce that it refers to the USSR. Instead of producing paradise, then, the USSR in its commitment to militarism has simply yielded a hell, at the center of which is "the death cells." This, for the Allies on the Western Front ("Im Westen") is nothing new ("nichts Neues"); that "state of things," already familiar to all in the West, has with Stalin become the reality of socialism's failure to produce communism.

Compare these depictions of Stalin, as the stupefied gorilla and the incompetent leader, to Canto 74's reference to Lenin, in which Pound tacitly compares Soviet militarism to that of ancient Greece, alluding to "the fleet at Salamis with money lent by the state to the/shipwrights." Elsewhere, Pound uses the same incident as an example of good economic policy. "The state can lend," he writes: "The fleet that was victorious at Salamis was built with money lent to the shipbuilders by the Athenian state."[154] But in Canto 74, it is glossed by Lenin's argument that investment in military technology will not assist the state.

> Tempus tacendi, tempus loquendi.
> Never inside the country to raise the standard of living
> but always abroad to increase the profits of usurers,
>   dixit Lenin,
> and gun sales lead to more gun sales
>   they do not clutter the market for gunnery
>   there is no saturation.[155]

We have already said that warfare is very different in the ancient world of the classical epic than in modern capitalist society, and we have seen that Pound is all too sensitive to the differences. Whereas Pound satirizes Stalin for his involvement in modern warfare, Lenin retains his epic heroism precisely because he rejects it. This heroism is encoded by the diction. "Tempus tacendi, tempus loquendi" was the personal motto of Malatesta, from whom Pound took his design for the factive personality, and it translates to "a time to be silent, a time to speak."[156] For the most part, the lexical choices in these lines situate warfare within capitalism by way of economic jargon: "standard of living," "profits of usurers," "gun sales," "the market," and "saturation" are all familiar as terms that anchor tropes used by Pound in his criticisms of the contemporary. What seems out of place, then, is the rare verb "dixit," the Latin word for "speaks." The fourth line, which names Lenin and includes that verb, was only added late in the composition of Canto 74 and might account for that difference, but more likely is that here we are seeing a formal repetition of the thought behind Canto 16.[157] Recall Pound's insistence that Lenin invented "almost a new medium, a sort of expression half way between writing and action," and that this new medium was, in Canto 16, the formal substrate to Lenin's heroism. Here the heroic world of Malatesta intrudes again as the Leninist speech act, and it does so in contradistinction to the future of the USSR. Indeed, Lenin's heroic action is, as it was in Canto 16, directed forcibly against capitalist warfare. This time, however, it most likely derives from Lenin's account of finance capital as mutually imbricated with the "filthy, bloody morass of bureaucratic-military institutions which subordinate everything to themselves, and suppress everything."[158] Lenin's presence is unmarked by satire because of his attempt to extract the socialist state from capitalist warfare. Though Lenin can no longer speak or act because he is long deceased, here his presence serves as a posthumous criticism, like an indelible recording of his voice, which amplifies the satire of Stalin's mute and militaristic inheritance of the communist legacy.

That historical passage from Lenin to Stalin is narrated in these lines, from near the end of Canto 74:

> But in Russia they bungled and did not apparently
> grasp the idea of work-certificate
> and started the N. E. P. with disaster
> and the immolation of men to machinery
>   and the canal work and gt/ mortality
>   (which is as may be)
> and went in for dumping in order to trouble the waters
>   in the usurers' hell-a-dice
> all of which leads to the death-cells
> each in the name of its god[159]

At the level of narrative, these lines tell us little we do not already know, but they do so with somewhat more historical specificity, presenting the USSR's current manifestation, in World War II, as the result of a historical sequence. Here the USSR's failure to "grasp the idea of a work-certificate" and implement stamp scrip is not just Stalin's failure. Instead, that failure is present as a sequence of events. The NEP, Lenin's provisional implementation of state capitalism, is presented as the incident from which the USSR's subsequent shortcomings emerged. This "disaster" is the causal factor behind "the immolation of men to machinery," "the canal work," economic "dumping," and, finally, production of "the death-cells." In these lines we see the confluence of two forms, the epic heroism associated with Lenin and the satire associated with Stalin, working in tension with each other. The sequence is narrated by way of the anaphoric conjunction familiar from the Malatesta Cantos, Canto 16, and elsewhere. But while that form might recall the heroic deeds of a factive personality, here the series of actions are catastrophically misjudged. That catastrophic misjudgment, which by Pound's estimate cost innumerable lives and failed to negate capitalism, is sarcastically termed as a "bungle," which bathetically frames the subsequent sequence as a comedy of errors. The anaphora emphasizes this by compounding the mistakes. The lexical choices are, as elsewhere in the canto, modern—that is, until we reach the Latinate "immolation," in which we should hear an echo of the classical world. In contrast to the countervailing echo of Marx's life-giving "fire of labour," which had during the 1930s become formally generative for Zukofksy, this word refers to sacrifice, and thus recalls (or preempts) the opening lines and their sacralizing of modern war. If Russian men are "immolated" to machines, then the economic policy of "dumping" is given similarly anachronistic treatment: for Russia to trade on the international market is to enter into economic hellfire, "the usurers' hell-a-dice." This phrase is difficult to interpret. That final neologism, "hell-a-dice," could be an allusion to Mallarmé and might thus be read as a comment on Russia sinking beneath the troubled "waters" and into the hell of finance capital. It could also be a pun on prejudice, and perhaps even in the legal sense of that term, so that Russia is seen as condemned to hell by the judgment of usurers. It could be an elaborate pun on "Ulysses' odyssey," recalling the Homeric hell into which the speaker of Canto 1 first sailed. Or we could even take into account that Pound first wrote "capitalists' hell-a-dice," only changing capitalists to "usurers" in a later draft, which might imply that the possessing noun is just as important.[160] Or, simply, it could refer to a gambling den, in which the capitalists and the usurers shoot dice. All of these possible readings share an emphasis on the USSR's fall into something like the mode of production from which Lenin wanted extraction and abolition. Finally, then, as "all of which leads to the death-cells," to those metonymic invocations of politicized militarism, the lines reimagine themselves and their historical content as coordinated under the ancient sign of a failed "god."

If we are now reading too much for narrative, privileging the several references to the USSR in a poetic sequence that contains many other things, that is only because doing so is needed to bring us to this point, from which we can finally observe a larger mutation in the aesthetic and its relation to communism. Unlike the two preceding cantos, which represent warfare through a coherent ideology, insular worldview, and anachronistic formalism, Canto 74 resituates warfare within the mode of production that vividly articulates through it, and to do so it utilizes the satire developed elsewhere and in the earlier poetry. Satire negates the representation of totality as a stable thing; it maintains the dynamism of historical conflict against conservative foreclosure. And communism, as manifest in the USSR, names the force that satirically brushes Pound's fascist tendency back against itself, generating a contradictory form that is unable to reconcile its political ambition with its historical content. The name of that form is modern epic, and the truth it sustains, that modern warfare is irreducibly corrupt, is soon addressed by Pound speaking to another poet, with whom we spend the next chapter: "perhaps," muses Pound near the end of Canto 78,

> only Dr Williams (Bill Carlos)
> will understand its importance . . . [161]

3 William Carlos Williams

Moscow on the Passaic

The Native Epic

Having already published three collections of verse and with plans to write both a novel and a book of American history, by the onset of the 1920s William Carlos Williams nonetheless sensed that stagnation had befallen his poetic output. He attributed this to the geographical location of his writing and a felt necessity to engage, poetically, with local life. "At thirty-eight," writes Paul Mariani, "Williams had to come face to face with the bitter realization of what it had cost to stay at home, to try and grow prize flowers in volcanic ash."[1] Rutherford, New Jersey, was neither the London of half a decade earlier, nor was it Paris, the capital of literary modernism. The township's contrasting version of cosmopolitanism involved the factories and mills in nearby Paterson and the concentration of immigrant workers these sites for unskilled labor attracted. Unlike his expatriate colleague and former classmate, Ezra Pound, whom we have seen drawing inspiration from an immersion in European modernity, Williams remained at home, working as a doctor, and it was from within these unexceptional circumstances that he charged himself with the exceptional task of creating a native American literature. As Walter Benn Michaels has shown, Williams wrote a "nativist modernism," which is defined not by an affirmation of the American locale but, rather, by a desire to identify poetry with all that is both good and bad about its indigenous setting: "Just as in nativism the goal of the American is to be American, in Williams's modernism the goal of the American poet is to produce American poetry."[2]

This chapter accounts for some of the career-long developments of Williams's poetry and how they were ultimately geared toward the composition of a modern epic. Published late in the poet's life, *Paterson* consummates that vision of a nativist American literature, and in several ways it can be seen as the culmination of technical advancements made in the poems that preceded it. In Fredric Jameson's view, this poem is the quintessence of the nativist aesthetic. For Williams, he maintains, "to define and celebrate America is at one and the same time to identify a specifically American language as such, so that the poem's form is here also its content."[3] While no completed installment of *Paterson* reached publication until 1946, when its first volume was printed as a special edition, Williams nevertheless claimed that, by 1927, "my thoughts on the general theme I wanted to treat were well along." He had also published numerous poems whose content would be assimilated into it.[4] The first parts of this chapter focus on shorter poems that predate 1946, reading them in relation to the Russian Revolution and to the USSR, although these poems are by no means epics in their own right. The chapter ends by looking exclusively at *Paterson* as a modern epic that not only absorbs but also necessitates, as though in strict observance of dialectical reason, the technical innovations made earlier in the poet's career. The goal of this chapter is to demonstrate how, in that absorption, the epic also internalizes and nurtures a version of communism to which the poetry's early innovations had responded.

Revolutionary Imagination, Part 1: Russian Ebullience

The opening wager for this chapter is that the social and aesthetic notions that cohere with Williams's concept of "imagination" respond to the Russian Revolution and that this concept might therefore secure a link between communism and the nativist aesthetic that would eventually be taken up for *Paterson.* We begin by pursuing the development of that aesthetic through Williams's 1923 collection, *Spring and All.* In its 1923 construction, this aesthetic comprises two unique forms held together in contrast, rhapsodic prose and idiomatic verse, which together reflect the poet's commitment to American language. According to Charles Bernstein's authoritative summary, the principal form in which "the question of diction" appears for all American poetry "is the insistence that a poetry of the everyday be written in American, rather than British, English," and that is precisely what we encounter here—"a development," Bernstein confirms, "most often linked to William Carlos Williams."[5] While the major achievement of *Spring and All* might be its inauguration of this language, a poetry written in American, the conceptual name Williams bestows upon his motivation for doing so is "imagination," an imprecise philosophical term employed to describe both a social bond and an object of poetry. "To refine, to clarify, to intensify that eternal moment in which we alone live there is but a single force," Williams explains in the opening pages, as a kind of dedication: "the imagination. This is its book."[6] Although the concept is vague, *Spring and All* serves as the privileged site for its development primarily because it hosts a productive interchange between prose that contains a playful conceptualization of the imagination, on the one hand, and poems that arguably formalize some of its concepts, on the other.

There is, however, disagreement between the frequently ecstatic rapture of the prose and the seemingly muted realization of its ambitions in verse. This incongruity serves a definite purpose, allowing the collection to articulate its ideals and ambitions in prose, which is frequently ironized through self-deprecation or hyperbole, and to have those ideals and ambitions coexist in dynamic as opposed to dogmatic relation to the poetry. The prose in this collection effectively siphons aesthetically undesirable though conceptually necessary material away from the verse, as though to purify the imagination of the bourgeois toxins that, for Williams, come with the kind of academically self-theorizing poetry exemplified by the work of T. S. Eliot. This is why he goes to such great lengths to explain "the cleavage" between his prose and poetry. According to Williams, "prose has to do with the fact of the emotion," whereas "poetry has to do with the dynamisation of emotion into separate form. This," he confirms, "is the force of imagination." In other words, the shifts between prose and poetry are what move from description to creation, from fact to phenomenon, and thereby promote the collection's material to the realm of the imagination. "It is," he insists, "the jump from prose to the process of imagination that is the next great leap of the intelligence—from the simulations of present experience to the facts of the imagination."[7] The humor that regularly infuses the prose accentuates this distinction, not by ironically discrediting its content but, rather, by allowing the verse to appear as independent from literary self-theorization. *Paterson* similarly makes use of these transitions between prose and poetry, and we encounter them again later, but here our interest is in the poetic realization of that guiding concept, imagination, which conjoins the two forms and their dissimilar capacities for literary expression.

Critical readings agree on the centrality of imagination to Williams's aesthetic and have explained it variously as an expression of the book's "calculated indeterminacy," of a "desire to connect art to social reality," and of a "deconstruction of metaphysics."[8] The most obvious literary context for a poetic concept of imagination is the English Romantics of the nineteenth century, for whom imagination served as a perceptive mediation between consciousness and the sublime. In Samuel Taylor Coleridge's well-known phrase, imagination is "a repetition in the finite mind of the eternal act of creation in the infinite I AM."[9] More relevant to the concept's usage here is that, since the mid-nineteenth century, imagination has gained prominence in a radically democratic breed of American romance. According to Ralph Waldo Emerson, lecturing in 1841, "America is a poem in our eyes; its ample geography dazzles the imagination, and it will not wait long for metres."[10] Though Emerson is alluded to several times throughout *Spring and All,* it is not him but Walt Whitman that Williams nominates as the preeminent example of imagination's appearance within that democratic context. "Whitman's proposals," writes Williams, "are of the same piece with the modern trend toward imaginative understanding of life. The largeness which he interprets as his identity with the least and the greatest about him, his 'democracy' represents the vigor of his imaginative life."[11] Here I want to suggest that, in addition to these English and American precedents, there is another source for this concept, one that is definitively communist.

For Karl Marx, imagination is one of the defining features of a specifically nonalienated human labor. "But what distinguishes the worst architect from the best of bees is this," reads his famous affirmation: "that the architect raises his structure in imagination before he erects it in reality. At the end of every labour-process, we get a result that already existed in the imagination of the labourer at its commencement."[12] This is how Williams, in one of the book's early poems, introduces a fictionalized farmer, "pacing through the rain among his blank fields," with "in his head/the harvest already planted."[13] After the Russian Revolution of 1917, this kind of practical imagination as realized through labor became an even more important concept for communist thought. According to Leon Trotsky, imagination was one of Vladimir Lenin's principal virtues during the establishment of the USSR. Here Trotsky interrupts a historical narrative to explain the term, in a passage that bears lengthy quotation:

> Among other necessary attributes this work required a strong creative imagination. This word may seem inadmissible at the first glance, but nevertheless it expresses exactly the essence of the thing. The human imagination may be of many kinds: the constructive engineer needs it as much as the unrestrained fiction writer. One of the most precious varieties of imagination consists in the

> ability to picture people, things, and phenomena as they are in reality, even when one has never seen them. The application and combination of the whole experience of life and theoretical equipment of a man with separate small stopping places caught in passing, their working up, fusion, and completion according to definite formulated laws of analogy, in order thereby to make clear a definite phase of human life in its whole concreteness—that is imagination, which is indispensable for a lawmaker, a government worker, and a leader in the time of revolution. The strength of Lenin lay, to a very important degree, in the strength of his realistic imagination.[14]

For Trotsky, like Marx, the imagination is a subject's capacity to conceive of the world and to mediate that conception with his or her actions. It is the force that connects projected ideals to their everyday exigencies. "The value of the imagination to the writer," claims Williams, in remarkably similar terms, "consists in its ability to make words. Its unique power is to give created forms reality, actual existence."[15] But to what extent might this imagination, a creative force turned revolutionary, have infiltrated Williams's understanding of the concept and the composition of his verse?

In the prose of *Spring and All,* Williams refers to imagination's contemporaneous expression as an effect of the Russian Revolution. "To the social, energized class," he writes, "ebullient now in Russia the particles adhere because of the force of the imagination energizing them." For Williams, then, imagination is collective, in that it energizes "particles" at the same time as it makes them "adhere" together, and for this reason imagination, as a concept, also appears analogous to communism's emphasis on the revolutionary collective. Though the material force of imagination had visibly intensified on the streets of Moscow and elsewhere in Russia, Williams also insists that the geographical exemplarity of this manifestation does not mean its exclusivity, and he does so in terms that closely resemble communist internationalism. "The study of all human activity," he adds, "is the delineation of the essence and ebb of this force, shifting from class to class and location to location." We might even hear the echo of Marx and Engels in this unconditional claim. "The history of all hitherto existing society is the history of class struggles," they write: "Freeman and slave, patrician and plebeian, lord and serf, guild-master and journeyman, in a word, oppressor and oppressed, stood in constant opposition to one another, carried on an uninterrupted, now hidden, now open fight, a fight that each time ended, either in a revolutionary reconstitution of society at large, or in the common ruin of the contending classes." The critical challenge suggested by these similarities and citations is to demonstrate that, for Williams, imagination transposes distinctly utopian energies between the content and the form of his aesthetic, between the historical engagements set forth in prose and their relationship to the verse. The literary-historical context of *Spring and All* will aid us in this regard.[16]

Spectacle and Catastrophe

Between 1917 and 1923, Williams repeatedly encountered a communist imagination "shifting" itself into the American context. For instance, Williams attended weekly meetings at Lola Ridge's apartment in Greenwich Village. "From mid-1919 till mid-1921, and then again from the end of 1924 till the end of 1926," writes Mariani, "Ridge held parties for the writers and painters and radical thinkers in that New York ambience with an attention that verged for Williams on a religious commitment."[17] Ridge, whom we encountered briefly in the introduction, was a radical leftist and an author of communist poetry. Perhaps the most notable guest to also frequent these meetings was John Reed, who had recently returned from his firsthand witnessing of the Russian Revolution. In addition to specific events such as these, communism was articulated in the cultural climate of the United States more generally, for some as the threat of cataclysm and for others, like Ridge and Reed, as a utopian promise of the highest order. Both responses, the enthusiastic and the antagonistic, seem to register when Williams narrates the importation of this particular "force of imagination," exemplarily present "in Russia," into the United States.

Russia enters the text of *Spring and All* in a way that seems to reproduce the warring affects associated with communism during the 1920s.

> Tomorrow we the people of the United States are going to Europe armed to kill every man, woman and child in the area west of the Carpathian Mountains (also east) sparing none. Imagine the sensation it will cause. First we shall kill them and then they, us. But we are careful to spare the Spanish bulls, the birds, rabbits, small deer and of course the Russians. For the Russians we shall build a bridge from edge to edge of the Atlantic—having first been at pains to slaughter all Canadians and Mexicans on this side. Then, oh then, the great feature will take place.[18]

There is a quirky humor to all of this. What could be a serious reflection on World War I (and perhaps on the involvement of the American Expeditionary Forces) is overlaid with the "careful" preservation of caricatures of European culture, from the "Carpathian mountains" through the "Spanish bulls" and including all the ridiculous-sounding fauna that live between. Preserved from destruction alongside those other caricatures are the Russians, who are singularly employed here for "the great feature," a strange spectacle inscribed as apocalyptic vision. "The bridge is to be blown up when all Russia is upon it. And why?" we are asked. "Because we love them—all."[19] The Russians are given exemplary treatment twice over. First, they are spared destruction alongside the other avatars of European culture, but then they are separated off from those avatars and destroyed in an altogether more spectacular fashion. Russia is the contradictory exception to geopolitical antagonism, appearing under the sign of love. Even in destruction Russia conveys an expression of union, as is emphasized by that dangling pronoun, "all." This singularly atavistic treatment is suggestive of the fact that Williams's poetic is predisposed from the outset, in this radical ambivalence, to experience the importation of communism both as an explosive threat and as the means of loving renewal.

The spatial coordinates of the imagination's "great feature" and of its metaphorical bridge, which links the USSR and the USA, derive not only from geopolitical history but also from the output of a competing poet, T. S. Eliot, whose major work contributed to the aesthetic devastation faced by Williams during the early 1920s. Many years later Williams described *The Waste Land* as "the great catastrophe to our letters," claiming that its publication single-handedly stunted the growth of a truly American literature. "There was heat in us, a core and a drive that was gathering headway upon the theme of a rediscovery of a primary impetus, the elementary principle of all art, in the local conditions," he would say, explaining early attempts to forge that literature: "Our work staggered to a halt for a moment under the blast of Eliot's genius which gave the poem back to the academics. We did not know how to answer him."[20] While the fraught relationship between Eliot and Williams is well known, here I want to underline two interrelated aspects of it. First, Eliot's reaction to the Russian Revolution (which we encountered in the introduction) helped motivate an engagement with that event in Williams's writing. Second, Williams's displeasure with Eliot also produced a nonacademic verse that was, in contrast to Eliot's, invested in specifically working-class speech, the kind that might be energized by communism.

The charge Williams set against Eliot had little to do with reactionary or revolutionary politics and everything to do with an avowed classicism and how the deployment of dead and foreign languages was seen to have given "the poem back to the academics." For Williams, Eliot's learning meant not just that his poems were returning verse to the stony demesne of impersonal poetics but that these poems were also taking the form away from an American culture and the imagination that Williams sought to cultivate. "I felt," writes Williams, "he had rejected America and I refused to be rejected and so my reaction was violent. I realized the responsibility I must accept. I knew he would influence all subsequent American poets and take them out of my sphere. I had envisaged a new form of poetic composition, a form for the future."[21] Williams was perfectly aware of this relational dialectic, in which the realization of his own aesthetic resulted from the determinate negation of Eliot's. "If I could say what is in my mind in Sanscrit or even Latin I would do so," writes Williams. "But I cannot. I speak for the integrity of the soul and the greatness of life's inanity; the formality of its boredom; the orthodoxy of its stupidity."[22] The positive outcome or "success" of this dialectic is the adoption of the kind of language Marianne Moore once described as "plain American which cats and dogs can read,"[23] the kind of verse in which we can detect the motivating force of imagination and behind that force the energizing presence of communism.

The first poem of *Spring and All* responds to *The Waste Land* by rewriting it in a theoretically American voice and from within a regional context. It begins,

> By the road to the contagious hospital
> under the surge of the blue
> mottled clouds driven from the
> northeast—a cold wind. Beyond, the
> waste of broad, muddy fields
> brown with dried weeds, standing and fallen
>
> patches of standing water
> the scattering of tall trees
>
> All along the road the reddish
> purplish, forked, upstanding, twiggy
> stuff of bushes and small trees
> with dead, brown leaves under them
> leafless vines—

> Lifeless in appearance, sluggish
> dazed spring approaches—[24]

While Eliot was seen as writing poetry for the academics, Williams's verse has a pronounced working-class thematic and accent. The "contagious hospital" is, for Williams, just as much a site for reproducing labor as it is the site of cultural or aesthetic rebirth. Those who "enter the new world naked" here will eventually become the working-class subjects of the poems to follow. While the destination of the poem, "the contagious hospital," might not endorse this interpretation in any straightforward way, the lines themselves do.[25] They are rough, and knowingly so. The descriptors "reddish," "purplish," and "twiggy," applied to a nondescript noun, "stuff," develop a casual diction, and the dropping of capital letters as well as the hard enjambment give these lines a breathless inarticulacy. The result of these technical decisions is idiomatic poetry. "Williams' language is necessarily uneuphonic, unmeasured, unEliotic," writes Philip Bufithis. "There is no place for such stuff in English poetry. Its reality can be seen only through the medium of American idiom. It is local—something, that is, that must be seen with other words and with a new voice."[26] The final quoted lines, claiming that the "contagious hospital" and its locale are only "lifeless in appearance" (and are therefore not truly lifeless[27]) set the tone of the lines and the poems to follow, in that they invite the reanimating force of imagination to break free of this "sluggish" daze. While the American setting obviously offers nothing in the way of reanimation, the verse, with its distant affinity to the revolutionary enthusiasm of the Bolsheviks, might provide a means of fostering the imagination denied these "contagious" masses. Hypothetically, then, we might suppose that what appears "lifeless" here is the American working class and that communism might be one of the imaginative energies the poem alludes to as capable of bringing "the profound change" that will "awaken" these newborns.

Cathedral, Movie House, Ballpark

It is necessary to see where this form directly corresponds with the thematic presence of both the Russian Revolution and the American working class, which appear together in two poems from the book. Poem 15 is ostensibly about the secularization that attends modernity. Contrasting with Eliot's reactionary vision of the same process, from which these lines borrow their operative word, the "decay" in this poem does not direct toward irredeemable destruction, or at least if it does so, that destruction is not met by authorial condemnation.

The decay of cathedrals
is efflorescent
through the phenomenal
growth of movie houses

whose catholicity is
progress since
destruction and creation
are simultaneous.[28]

The opening quatrain declares that the "decay of cathedrals" is "efflorescent," meaning that its process is creative as well as destructive. The bidirectional energy of this term "efflorescent" animates the polysemous noun "catholicity," which here refers to the decomposing "biblical rigidity" and the parallel emergence of an all-embracing universalism. The temporal conjunction "since" then prepares the poem to express this coincidence axiomatically: "destruction and creation/are simultaneous." There is a political subtext to this transformation, a passage of time in which the waning of one institution is met by the waxing of another. The reclamation of the cathedral by the movie house displaces one multitude (ruled by incense, intonation, and the altar) by another multitude (ruled by the cinema).

This replacement is precisely what we see in the poem's remaining lines:

But schism which seems
adamant is diverted
from the perpendicular
by simply rotating the object

cleaving away the root of
disaster which it
seemed to foster. Thus
the movies are a moral force

Nightly the crowds
with the closeness and
universality of sand
witness the selfspittle

which used to be drowned
in incense and intoned
over by the supple jointed
imagination of inoffensiveness

backed by biblical rigidity
made into passion plays
upon the altar
to attract the dynamic mob

whose female relative
sweeping grass Tolstoi
saw injected into
the Russian nobility[29]

Despite its Russian ending, the poem is not about movement through revolutionary modernity, as might also be inferred from its opening quatrains. Rather, it is about the oscillation between one politically lifeless situation and another. With Tolstoy's Russia and Williams's America, the poem moves from a situation that hindsight knows would someday be revolutionized to one that remains enthralled by its ideological matrices. The inclusion of Tolstoy is particularly significant, given that the last time he appeared in a poem by Williams—1914's "Peace"—he is cited as the reporter of a false and undesirable torpor, the titular "peace," which is said to result from ideological stupefaction. "It is stupid to advocate peace," writes Williams in that poem, "in order to have me work in a factory or a field or a mine or a quarry or a forest or on the sea or at a desk or on the ice or at the sea's bottom—unless I please to do these things."[30] The significance of Tolstoy here is that this kind of "peace," guaranteeing reified class relations and the compulsion of human labor, is what sustains and is sustained by the cinema's aversion of "schism" or "disaster," the name for which is revolution.

We can learn more about these lines and their revolutionary subtext by looking to the paraphrased source material: Marya Zaturenska's contributions to the April 1920 issue of *Poetry*. In the first of two poems, an immigrant speaker weeps, from her adopted home "in a strange country," to remember "the blue cathedral" of Moscow and "the singing multitude" of her friends and family therein. In the second, she muses on the peasants of a feudal village as they "dance wildly before the great lord's castle" before returning to their work as reapers. "Backs bowed," we read, "and eyes apathetic with labor." The juxtaposition of these two poems, which contain both reverent quiescence and feverish intensity, is given ideological closure by the peasants' only spoken words, which point up the source of their exploitative containment. "There is no joy in life," they will say. "Only with God is our great gladness."[31] Here we can see that these poems, which undeniably engage with the culture that eventually birthed the Russian Revolution, helped Williams conceive of and present his own situation. They both make clear how ideology functions, permeating consciousness by way of cultural institutions and thus forestalling revolution, dooming its subjects to a joyless life of hard labor. But in Russia the uncontainable desire for revolution exceeded its ideological constraints, which invites the question of how that context might differ from the United States as Williams depicts it.

Though Louis Zukofksy would suggest that, with this poem, Williams fully understood what was taking place in Soviet cinema during the 1920s, it should be insisted that these Russian energies are all channeled into a specifically American manifestation of that technology, where instead of cathedrals cinema now serves as the "moral force" of ideological containment, by preventing an "adamant" revolution and redirecting those energies into an "imagination of inoffensiveness."[32] Julian Murphet is correct to read the poem this way, attending to the specificity of cinema when used as a capitalist medium. "In America," he says, "the movies 'rotate the object' in such a way as to 'divert schism'—all those oppositions related by and intrinsic to the medium—and deliver the 'dynamic mob' over to the regulations of the commodity form. This 'moral force' is uniquely American, and it leapfrogs the revolutionary force released by the medium in Russia."[33] All that needs to be added here is that the diverted "schism" or averted "disaster" is also a paradoxical expression of the imagination. As Jameson has argued, every film contains an "ideological function" and "a more positive function," which he describes as "that dimension of even the most degraded type of mass culture which remains implicitly, and no matter how faintly, negative and critical of the social order form which, as a product and a commodity, it springs."[34] That is to say, it is with this poem that imagination really begins to resonate between two irreducibly separate contexts, the USSR and the USA, where it finds form in the favored medium of the American working class, cinema, the Hollywood iteration of which bore little resemblance to its Soviet counterpart. The revolution is present, then, but only as an unrealized undercurrent, for here the "dynamic mob" remains damp with "selfspittle" and caught up in the ideological machinery of its own intellectual degradation.

We return to the prosody of this verse in a moment, when we are equipped to compare poem 16 with another from the collection, 26, which pursues a similar theme in a remarkably similar form. If imagination finds debased revolutionary energies in the movie house, then surely it will do likewise at a baseball game, where multiple other American poets and writers, including Pound and Zukofsky, "have detailed the manner in which baseball is consumed as an entertainment commodity."[35] Like the movie house, the baseball game is a contradictory site of working-class containment and unspoken utopianism. Where "the moral force" of cinema obviates "schism" by redirecting the energies of class-consciousness into an "imagination of inoffensiveness," here those unspent and otherwise reified energies are initially stimulated by the experience of the public spectacle before resolving into a collective inertia. The poem begins,

> The crowd at the ball game
> is moved uniformly
>
> by a spirit of uselessness
> which delights them—
>
> all the exciting detail
> of the chase
>
> and the escape, the error
> the flash of genius—
>
> all to no end save beauty
> the eternal—
>
> So in detail they, the crowd,
> are beautiful[36]

Here is another collective, one that despite its apparent lassitude contains distinct revolutionary potential. This sketch is followed by the appearance of something in the crowd, "to be warned against," before that something is described. "It is alive," we are told, "venomous/ it smiles grimly/ its words cut—." But the menacing deixis of that pronoun is as close as we get to what the poem soon terms "the Revolution," whose proper name is announced as a possible designation for the active pronoun "it." And yet, the working-class "crowd," apparently stupefied before the spectacle, "smiles grimly" and laughs "permanently, serious/without thought." For Williams, there is a stunted form of imagination in this crowd, but it only shines through individuals without ever animating the mass itself. We are told that a "power" is identified not with the collective but, rather, with the "beauty" of individual "faces," and perhaps this is why the crowd is only "beautiful" when perceived "in detail." Similar to Pound, who initially deemed it impossible to account for "that sudden emotion" of encountering a succession of "faces" in the "crowd" on the Paris Metro and who finally "equated" them with "Petals on a wet, black bough," Williams seems intent on amplifying the dialectical tension between the one and the many.[37] What is aesthetically pleasing about the crowd, making it beautiful, is the faces, and yet the spectators' shared thoughtlessness upon which this beauty rests dooms them to the same stupefaction as the patrons of the cinema. As a crowd, these individuals are imbued with a force antipathetic to the "spirit of uselessness" that delights them, but here at the baseball game, as at the cinema, revolutionary force remains immanent and unrealized.

The Freedoms and Unfreedoms of Free Verse

There are multiple consistencies between the poem of the cinema and the poem of the ballpark, which together posit improbable or occluded relationships between revolutionary energy and the working class. The most obvious consistency is a thematic correlation between two expressions of political control, both of which forestall the possibility of a revolution that their forms, the cinema and the baseball game, nonetheless urge by collectivizing masses of patrons. A more formal consistency resides in the fact that both poems are composed in short, metrically uneven, unrhymed lines that don't necessarily begin with capital letters, thus producing a distinct version of free verse. Though Williams often insisted that his "gift" to modern poetry was the "variable foot," a long line usually split into a tercet and indented, with one beat read for each line of the tercet, here I want to suggest that its invention was a belated theorization enabled by these early manifestations of free verse.[38] "The rhythmic unit decided the form of my poetry," or so he would reflect years later. "When I came to the end of a rhythmic unit (not necessarily a sentence) I ended the line. The rhythmic unit was not measured by capitals at the beginning of a line or periods within the lines."[39] Walter Schott shares this assessment: "Not Ezra Pound or E. E. Cummings, but finally William Carlos Williams freed American poetry from the irons of rhyme and meter."[40] Further, if the variable foot emerged out of free verse, I also want to reflect on how that free verse performs and allegorizes the depoliticizing transformation these poems have described.

An initial temptation is to read the free verse of these two poems as a form whose enjambment allows for the synthesis of its lines and their content, thereby using prosody to allegorize the collectivizing force that permeates the mass or multitude. More likely, however, is that Williams's intention was for each line to be modulated by radically democratic speech. "The modern line must exclude no possibility of intelligent resource," he would later explain: "it cannot be great and exclude any major element of the civilization in which it exists."[41] For Williams, free verse allows for the deployment of an idiom structured conversantly as opposed to mechanically, and this idea is what would develop into the variable foot, as we can see here, from an essay by Williams on Whitman: "American verse of today must have a certain quality of freedom, must be 'free verse' in a sense. It must be new verse, in a new conscious form. But even more than that it must be free in that it is free to include all temperaments, all phases of our environment, physical as well as spiritual, mental and moral. It must be truly democratic, truly free for all—and yet it must be governed."[42] By creating space within poetry for that manifold of speech, free verse potentially democratizes (and perhaps also communizes) poetry's distribution of the sensible, shifting verse away from the academic discourse of a poet like Eliot and making it receptive to regional and working-class expression. We'll return in a moment to that final addition, about the governance of this freedom, but first there is more to say about free verse in relation to Eliot and communism.

Eliot was famously critical of free verse, and that criticism would resound with the "decay" he later sensed had taken hold in Eastern Europe after the Russian Revolution. Eliot's well-known charge is that free verse is a misnomer, that no form of verse could ever really be free. Less familiar, however, is that he was thinking about free verse in relation to Russia as early as March 1917, claiming that it did "not exist, and it is time that this preposterous fiction followed the *élan vital* and the eighty thousand Russians into oblivion."[43] Williams's remarkably similar conception of verse as dictated by rhythm seems to derive some of its motivations from the Russian site of Eliot's analogy. But one of the crucial differences here is that Eliot was writing several months before the Russian Revolution, and so his "eighty thousand Russians" were presumably those sent to their deaths on the Eastern Front. Williams, on the other hand, was consciously writing about a

Russia and Russians that had experienced the revolution, which filled their imagination with ebullience. Moreover, he cites the USSR not just as a social context but also as a literary context that helped him forge his own aesthetic. "Writing," he says, "as with certain of the modern Russians whose work I have seen, would use unoriented sounds in place of conventional words. The poem then would be completely liberated when there is identity of sound with something—perhaps the emotion."[44] It remains unclear to which "modern Russians" he is referring here, but literary-historical context and the idea of "unoriented sounds in place of conventional words" suggest that Williams is thinking of the Russian futurists, whose work had been appearing in English since 1919. What should be kept in mind, still, is Hugh Kenner's clarification that "Williams adduced such Russian precedents but didn't believe in them," whereas he really believed in a process by which words "are liberated from the usual quality of that meaning by transposition into another medium, the imagination."[45] Yet this latter belief is actually closer to what the Russians were aiming for with their experiments in verse than Williams's brief description can allow. The Russian futurists collectively strove for a poetry in which the word could be "considered a phonetic entity possessing its own ontology," which would lead to a form "rich in sound but devoid of conventional meaning," and to a literary aesthetic "organized by phonetic analogy and rhythm rather than by grammar and syntax."[46] We might speculate that this is the kind of thing Williams meant with his advocacy of transposing words into the imagination, the technique for which, in Vladimir Mayakovsky's case also, would be a kind of vernacularism as realized in free verse.

Williams did not meet Mayakovsky until 1926, when at Ridge's apartment he admired the visitor's performance for reasons similar to those given in his endorsement of the anonymous Russians in 1923. The episode is accounted for in Williams's *Autobiography,* though its position within this book's chronology suggests that it could have been one of several encounters with Russian futurism that took place between 1918 and 1920. While these dates are incorrect, the error nevertheless points up the fact that during the period immediately before composition of *Spring and All,* Williams was indeed thinking about Russian futurism in relation to poetic form. The encounter with Mayakovsky is described as follows:

> I can't remember all the names, but once, Mayakofsky, the Russian poet, appeared with his friend and manager who was wearing a particolored vest, half

> green and half white. Mayakofsky read aloud for us his "Willie the Havana Street Cleaner." A big man, he rested one foot on top of the studio table as he read. It was the perfect gesture. He had a good voice, and though no one understood a word he said, we were all impressed by the tumbling sounds and his intense seriousness. I remember there were two giggling poets of the smarter and younger generation who, while thinking him wonderful, were more, as far as I could tell, impressed by his size than anything else. The nice little "girls." For myself it sounds as might *The Odyssey* from the mouth of some impassioned Greek.[47]

Of course, when Williams refers to "unoriented sounds in place of conventional words," which is precisely the effect of hearing a foreign language, what he is describing seems more like Velimir Khlebnikov than Mayakovsky. And yet, what should be taken away from this anecdote is that the shared predilection for rhythmic poetry further permits the mutual illumination of a poetics between the USSR and the USA, and it is the Soviet form's conceptualization that begins to resonate with Williams's evolving sense of American poetry. Describing his own technique, Mayakovsky would reject "the learning up of other people's measurements: iambus, trochee, or even this much vaunted free verse," in preference of a "rhythm accommodating itself to some concrete situation, and of use only for that concrete situation." The rejection of a "much vaunted free verse" is only conceptual, a symptom of the desire to exclude from his poetry any sort of dogmatic formalism, whereas the written outcome that is Mayakovsky's poetry was predominantly a modality of that very form. Its "concrete situation" is implied by the metaphors used to describe composition. Poetry, he says, "is a manufacture. A very difficult, very complex kind, but a manufacture," the process of which requires its own means of production: "Equipment for the plant and tools for the assembly line." Mayakovsky thus compares the freeing of rhythm to a technological breakthrough in the means of production, easing the worker's burden.[48]

In Russia, the means of production had recently been socialized, whereas in the United States they remained in the control of private interests. Perhaps this is what so famously "depends" upon the "red wheelbarrow" of poem 22—the entire relations of production and how those relations structure agrarian labor. But the North American farming class is not a working class in the Marxist sense, nor is it the kind of peasantry undergoing collectivization in the USSR, not least because these farmers mostly own their means of production.[49] Joel Nickels has accurately described Williams's sensitivity to class and ideology on this point, comparing the imagination's later manifestations to a capacity for "self-valorization," a term that refers to the freeing of labor from the capitalist means of production, whose products it would otherwise suffuse with economic value, and the redirection of it toward the positive actualization of class-consciousness and solidarity.[50] But in the United States and under capitalism, "the technology of the culture industry," which includes movie houses and baseball games, had arrived at "no more than the achievement of standardization and mass production, sacrificing whatever involved distinction between the logic of the work and that of the social system."[51] The elaboration of this point, that the class on which these poems center is profoundly alienated and that such alienation has a technological predicate, helps account for a formal peculiarity that dominates Williams's free verse. To risk putting it a little too forcefully: when Williams's prosody retains its stanzaic consistency, a manifestation of that aforementioned governance, it does so in order to better engage with the utopian "freedom," either democratic or communist, which that form might otherwise imply.

Pure Production in Sound and Syntax

The grounds for this argument become visible in a lyric described by Zukofsky as the singularly "perfect piece" of Williams's book, poem 18, an extended lyric dedicated to the poet's mentally handicapped nursemaid, Elsie.[52] This poem sustains the dialectical tension between the one and the many that we encountered in the movie house and at the baseball game by pluralizing all of its distinctive characters: "mountain-folk," "deaf-mutes," "thieves," "old names," and so on. In this case, exceptionally, the locale has been expanded out from the familiar sites of collective being to encompass much more of the United States, ranging from the mountains of "Kentucky" to "the ribbed north end of/Jersey," neither of which are metropolitan centers. The temporal coincidence of these geographically unique locations is not linked to any single event but to the division of a working week, "from Monday to Saturday," and its weekly termination in a "night" of "promiscuity between/devil-may-care men" and "young slatterns, bathed/in filth" from six days of mind-numbing labor. It is thus that the poem concretizes its abstract universal through recourse to labor. The men and women of this poem are the "pure products of America," perhaps even those who once entered "the new world naked," who now "go crazy" because of the restrictions imposed upon their imagination and the immiseration those restrictions engender. Their pathology is a symptomatic expression of the "venomous thing" from the baseball game and of the "schism" from the movie house. For Zukofsky, poem 18 is concerned with the "social determinism of American suburbs in the first thirty years of the twentieth century,"[53] but that determinism, which no amount of "promiscuity" or "adventure" will ever avert, affects the entirety of its working class. Specifically, and unlike in the USSR, where imagination had become "ebullient," here we are told that the pluralized and thus independent "imaginations" of these workers "have no/peasant traditions to give them/character." They have only movie houses and baseball games, through which they "flutter and flaunt," eventually giving vent to the repressed fervor we are seeing here. For six days a week, the imagination remains bound by the economic regulation of time and space; on the weekend it must find mindless outlet in grim libidinal expenditure: "sheer rags succumbing without/emotion/save numbed terror," a sexual reflex to a determination "which they cannot express."

This containment, regulation, or even subsumption of imagination and its otherwise revolutionary energies requires a particular technique that paradoxically combines the rhythmic freedom of free verse, its potential democratization of speech, with the economic tethering of its social content. This is one reason among many that the particular mode of free verse taken up by this poem, as well as by the previous two we discussed (which comprised solely quatrains and couplets), conforms its lines and their approximation of democratic speech to a regular stanzaic structure.

> The pure products of America
> go crazy—
> mountain folk from Kentucky
>
> or the ribbed north end of
> Jersey
> with its isolate lakes and . . .

In Thomas Whitaker's observation, the "long-short-long triplets" of this poem are "a more rigorous scheme than the later triadic line."[54] Indeed, here we have diction that is "truly democratic, truly free for all," but at the level of stanzaic and linear form, it is thoroughly "governed." As the ultimate destination for whatever energies Williams seems to have absorbed from the Russian Revolution, this is a form whose paradoxical rigor is homologous to the constraints placed upon the imagination of working-class Americans. Theirs is a state where "the aesthetic activities of political opposites are," in the words of Theodor Adorno and Max Horkheimer, "one in their enthusiastic obedience to the rhythm of the iron system."[55]

But this reading pursues an allegory without being sensitive to the deeper beauties of the thing in our hands. It neglects the utter ingenuity and aesthetic success of Williams's reframing of the abiding tension between line length and syntax, between sound and sense. In this poem, those constraints are also the path to imaginative liberty and to an irreducible "truth," expressed here by "broken / brain." This, to be sure, is the tension that is said to define all poetry, as the only guarantee of separating it from prose. In Giorgio Agamben's explanation, "the poem tenaciously lingers and sustains itself in the tension and difference between sound and sense, between the metrical series and the syntactical series."[56] The relationship between the American working class and the prosody in which that class is presented here is implied toward the poem's end, where both the class, in which the speaker now includes his own "hard pressed / house in the suburbs," and the poem are caught generating sparks of revolutionary dissonance from within the very systems that want to contain them.

> and we degraded prisoners
> destined
> to hunger until we eat filth
>
> while the imagination strains
> after deer
> going by fields of goldenrod in
>
> the stifling heat of September
> somehow
> it seems to destroy us
>
> It is only in isolate flecks that
> something
> is given off[57]

Drawn into focus here is the problem of reification within American capitalism. Elsewhere we have seen that communism has entered imagination as communal affect, but as an affective potentiality it still requires the inflammatory power of thought, which remains absent in the United States, where imagination is repeatedly foreclosed by the culture industry. How, then, does the prosody perform this? Here the short, internal lines of each unrhymed and unpunctuated triplet seem interpolated, dropped into place in compliance with the law of their circumambient form, as though to compel ("destined"), to distract ("after deer"), or to mark some vagueness about imagination's real power ("somehow," "something"). Even more so than the other poems we have looked at from *Spring and All,* these lines emphasize ideological containment as a kind of stupefaction. As such, part of all three poems' achievement is to formalize what Emerson denounced as the "jail-yard of individual relations," which for him could only be escaped, temporarily and much like the "pure products of America," by alcohol, narcotics, and "other species of animal exhilaration."[58] There is a blockage between affect and intellection, a phenomenal shadow cast by the hierarchy of unreconstructed relations of production. But, for Williams, the poem acts as a preserve for an unrealized and unrealizable imagination and the political tensions it creates. While the communist spores floating across the New Jersey skyline remain barely perceptible to that city's inhabitants, now and again they are caught by the poem, embedding in its lines so as to take shape imaginatively, in rhythm and in diction, and to do so within the structure of the unconquerably and intransigently formed stanza. The efflorescence of communism produces this stunning dissonance, but only in "isolate flecks," and so the poem ends by gazing headlong into political oblivion: "No one/to witness/and adjust, no one to drive the car."[59]

Proletarian Portraiture

The ideological containment to which Williams's poetry responds is given powerful expression elsewhere across his oeuvre, and, with remarkable consistency, it appears and reappears under the generic ensign of portraiture. As early as 1914, Williams was composing the suite of lyric poems "Pastorals and Self-Portraits," which coupled that intimate genre of mimetic depiction with the poet's cultural and aesthetic examination of the industrial modernization of New Jersey. The collection's first two poems, "Self-Portrait 1" and "Pastoral 1," enact a strange inversion of their nominated genres. The former addresses itself to the earthy substance of a tilled field and so reads more like a pastoral than a portrait. "You lie packed," it begins, "Dark: /Turned sluggishly/By plough." And, inversely again, the latter reads more like a conventional portrait than a pastoral, describing an "old man who goes about/Gathering dog lime/Walks in the gutter." From the standpoint of these generic inversions, the portrait and the pastoral may well be viewed, when undertaken by Williams at this point in his career, as the two halves of a dialectical antinomy. It should also be understood here that what is nominated as pastoral has already been stripped of its pasture, the geological site and textural substrate of that genre, which is now paved over by an anonymous street in the city. According to Raymond Williams, who theorized this dialectic as it pertained to England and English literature, "capitalism, as a mode of production, is the basic process of most of what we know as the history of country and city." Perhaps it is this, the modernizing force of capitalism, which motivated the generic inversions of these early poems: "Its abstracted economic drives, its fundamental priorities in social relations, its criteria of growth and of profit and loss, have over several centuries altered our country and created our kinds of city."[60]

This reconfiguration of the pastoral by Raymond Williams's American namesake points up its inextricable location within the historical progression of capitalism:

> The city has tits in rows.
> The country is in the main—male,
> It butts me with blunt stub-horns,
> Forces me to oppose it
> Or be trampled[61]

The gendering of these lines preempts the social logic we encountered in *Spring and All,* where the "pure products of America" both proliferate through and are simultaneously contained by their own sexual expenditure. Here the cow's udders have become the city, whereas the country, from which the cow imagery presumably originated, is associated with the "blunt stub-horns" of the bull. While these two bovine are avatars of an agrarian lifeworld, we soon learn that the purpose of either is the production of commodities, milk and meat, the extraction of which directs cows to the battery cage and condemns bulls to slaughter. "The city is full of milk / And lies still for the most part," read the subsequent lines. "These crack skulls / And spill brains / Against her stomach."[62] Rather than evoking romantic images of a "peasant tradition" as exemplified in the pastoral and portrait paintings of Jean-François Millet or Camille Pissarro, or in the pastoralism and portraiture of a poet like William Wordsworth, the subject matter of Williams's poem invokes the industrialized farm, which nevertheless abuts the city, shedding its blood upon "her stomach." In New Jersey, the subjectivity of a formerly agrarian lifeworld is relocated to the city and alienated from its tightly "packed" class. The countryside and the cityscape are brought cheek-by-jowl in their subservience to the one mode of production—namely, capitalism—figuratively evoked here by the implication of a livestock market.

The economic rationale apparent in the 1914 poems ramifies into 1935's suggestively titled "Proletarian Portrait":

A big young bareheaded woman
in an apron

Her hair slicked back standing
on the street

One stockinged foot toeing
the sidewalk

Her shoe in her hand. Looking
intently into it

She pulls out the paper insole
to find the nail

That has been hurting her[63]

These lines were initially titled "Study for a Figure representing Modern Culture," the provisional connotations of which seem equally appropriate to this portrait's internal contradictions and to its more overtly politicized inscription in the published version. Indeed, the adjective "proletarian" can refer to both a class and an individual, and here we are interested in the dynamic relationship between these two designations. The poem glimpses the worker in a moment of solitary struggle, successfully removing a nail from the inside of her shoe. While her apron and the nail suggest an immersion in particular kinds of labor, domestic or otherwise, the signifiers that would mark her class status as "proletarian" also contribute to her isolation from that class. The borderline grotesque caricature in her presentation as a "big young bareheaded woman" echoes the depiction of Elsie, who is supplied with "ungainly hips and flopping breasts/ addressed to cheap jewelry."[64] Both women are immersed in the signifiers of their class but are nonetheless made to appear sexually undesirable, which in the libidinal economy of Williams's verse is tantamount to seclusion.[65] In this poem, the imagination that otherwise coheres with the working class (in whatever debased form) has been sublimated into the struggle of an isolated individual. Here the proletarian subject looks "intently" into her shoe, thereby canceling the potentially collectivizing force that might otherwise be conveyed by that descriptor, "proletarian." Williams would later recall that Pound disliked "Proletarian Portrait," finding it ahistorical and "obvious," and that he suggested the woman "might have done as well in Russia as in the Passaic." Perhaps it was Pound's suggestion that motivated Williams to include, in a similar poem written thirteen years later, the comparison of a woman's face to that of Lenin. In that poem, the woman's legs are described as "two columns to hold up/her face, like Lenin's."[66] In such a comparison, which invokes the monumental figurehead of communism, we might find a provisional solution to the problem of genre in these early poems.

One of the lessons from "Proletarian Portrait" is that the portrait, as an artistic genre, seems poorly suited to proletarian representation. Whereas the imagination and its nativist formalization aspired, among other things, to a vision for working-class politicization in the United States, the portrait, which in a preindustrial landscape might have dynamized its depicted subjects, can now only represent the reified objects of economic subjugation. Lacking here is not the precious depths of working-class subjectivity. Rather, what the aesthetic ideology seems to be grappling with is portraiture's individualizing tendency, because the working class, as a class, cannot be represented in any individual figure. This generates some major technical difficulties for the purposes of proletarian representation. With portraiture, the aesthetic seems to conform to the reifying processes that inflict themselves upon the poem's proletarian object, individuating the represented subject from its class. There remains a tension in this, given the strong allegorical dimension of portraits in which representation might take place at the level of what cannot be concretely presented, articulating it precisely as a figure. But the poems still approach an unchecked mimesis in which the represented subjectivity is at a concrete and visual level detached from its class, thus limiting the functions of collective identity and political antagonism and perhaps even resurrecting itself as the romantic individual. The challenge for poetic imagination, then, is to make good on those tensions between what can and cannot be represented or to find a way of legitimately embracing the unresolvable ambivalence in the titular adjective "proletarian," which at once names a class and an individual.

The Portrait in Technological Modernity

Building on those preliminary thoughts about literary portraiture, I now want to think about the transformations in that genre. In particular, I want to look at how it followed the lead of imagination into engagements with the Russian Revolution and, simultaneously, helped prepare a formal strategy for *Paterson*. It was not until 1941 that Williams began to think about that poem's epic hero or central character, the formulation of which he puts as an inversion of the city's feminine gendering from 1914: "A man in himself is a city, beginning, seeking, achieving and concluding his life in ways which the various aspects of a city may embody."[67] The task here is to demonstrate how the embodying equation of "man" with "city" is the result of Williams's persistent engagement with portraiture and of communism's forceful renovation of the individual, which authorizes a formal supersession of the portrait's supposedly unique and singular subjectivity. Part of this argument is to consider how portraiture changed with the advent of photography.[68] "It is no accident," claims Walter Benjamin, "that the portrait is central to early photography. In the cult of remembrance of dead or absent loved ones, the cult value of the image finds its last refuge. In the fleeting expression of a human face, the aura beckons from early photographs for the last time."[69] When the portrait was transformed by photography, which stripped paintings of this subjective aura, the allegorical politics embodied in photomechanical technology brought the fictional medium of Williams's portrait poems into direct contact with communism, in which he would look to the USSR for a model subject.

Benjamin implies this allegorical relationship—between portraiture, photography, and communism—when he describes "the first severe crisis" faced by the "secular worship of beauty" as culminating in the "first truly revolutionary means of reproduction (namely photography, which emerged at the same time as socialism)."[70] This relationship is not just contemporaneous but also analogous: the way that photomechanical technology revolutionized portraiture produced a structural homology with the way that communism, for Marx and Engels, was to transform the reified individual. "In bourgeois society capital is independent and has individuality, while the living person is dependent and has no individuality," they write. And then, in answer to the bourgeois expositors of a rival discourse, they clarify their position: "By 'individual' you mean no other person than the bourgeois, than the middle-class owner of property. This person must, indeed, be swept out of the way, and made impossible."[71] This conception would provide an appealing alternative to the American individual with which Williams was all too familiar. Adorno offers his impression of such an American subjectivity in the dedication of a book comprising his reflections on life in the United

States. "In the individualistic society," he suggests, "the generality is realized not only through the interplay of individuals, rather the society is essentially the substance of the individuated."[72] Though Williams was highly sensitive to photography's renovation of the portrait and to the formal opportunities that renovation made available, he was just as attuned to communism's potential transformation of the subject and how it, too, galvanized poetic transformation.

The communist subjectivity that offers a serious alternative to capitalist individualism is, in its Soviet formulation, a kind of collective being, a paradoxical multiplicity of the one, the aesthetic ramifications of which Trotsky was keen to describe. In 1924, Trotsky presented his thoughts on "the dualism of every literary tendency" in relation to what he called the New Soviet Man: "On the one hand, it adds something to the technique of art, heightening (or lowering) the general level of craftsmanship; on the other hand, in its concrete historic form, it expresses definite demands which, in the final analysis, have a class character. We say class, but this also means individual, because a class speaks through an individual. It also means national, because the spirit of a nation is determined by the class which rules it and which subjects literature to itself."[73] This dual tendency may well provide a solution to the problem faced by Williams as early as 1914, that of generating a poem that simultaneously emphasizes the alienated individual as well as that individual's collective identity, bound up in both class and nation. The portrait is, to be sure, a genre that finds strong proponents in the USSR. El Lissitzky's celebrated project for a monument to Rosa Luxemburg is just such a portrait. Similarly, Mayakovsky's poetic portrait of Lenin is openly hostile to any sort of reducible individuality. "What's an individual?" it asks. "No earthly good."[74] Tempting as it is to compare Williams's poetry to these achievements in explicitly communist aesthetics, it is equally tempting to associate Williams's investment in portraiture, and especially in proletarian portraiture, with the popular photographs of working-class men, women, and children that appeared in the US press throughout the Depression. This vastly different aesthetic found its greatest exponent in Dorothea Lange, who worked as a portrait photographer until 1933, when, writes William Stott, "haunted by the distress she saw in an alley outside her studio's corner window, she 'resolved to photograph the *now,* rather than the timeless; to capture somehow the affect of the calamity which overwhelmed America.'"[75] While Lissitzky and Mayakovsky both respond to a socialized modernity, to the political imagination of a revolutionized subjectivity, the work of Lange relies on a romantically individualizing conception of the portrait. As possible solutions to the problem faced by Williams, communist portraits might be formally commendable, but they are also alien to the historical experience of regional America, and American portraits are historically apposite but formally ineffective because they revert to the individualism the form wants to overcome.

The Morning After . . .

From the late 1920s onward, a hypothetical communist subjectivity would incubate within Williams's portraiture before emerging, in the 1940s, as a fully fledged strategy for rendering everyday life in an epic poem. We encounter the inception of that subjectivity in a collection titled *The Descent of Winter,* which Williams began composing in 1927 and which was published in the 1928 edition of *The Exile,* where it featured alongside poems by Zukofsky and between Pound's now-familiar endorsements of Lenin's "new medium." The longest poem in this collection, "11/2" or "A Morning Imagination of Russia," oscillates between the gently satirical portrait of a socialist bureaucrat and the historical panorama as he either inhabits or imagines it. Inviting comparison with the visual arts, the poem begins with an insistence on the color of its depicted world.

The earth and the sky were very close
When the sun rose it rose in his heart.
It bathed the red cold world of
the dawn so that the chill was his own
The mists were sleep and sleep began
to fade from his eyes, below him in the
garden a few flowers were lying forward
on the intense green grass where
in the opalescent shadows oak leaves
were pressed hard down upon it in patches
by the night rain.[76]

The second line—"When the sun rose it rose in his heart"—inaugurates a physiognomy of the communist subject, whose catalyst is the color red, which acquires a uniquely poetic agency. The previous poem, also dated "11/2," invokes red dahlias, "mirror to the sun," held by a woman "with a red face."[77] The red of the dahlias and of the woman's face become, in this subsequent poem, "the red cold world" of the USSR. Indeed, the poem's subject is immersed in and made up of the color red—"the chill" and "the mists," which account for this world's atmosphere, are said to be "his own." For Kazimir Malevich, writing in 1918 on the aesthetic regime of socialism, red had become an intrinsically communist color. "I overheard a socialist saying he was sure that the red flag meant the worker's blood," he recalls. "I thought otherwise. If the worker's blood were blue or green the revolution would still have taken place under the red flag."[78] Williams had elsewhere situated color within the prefecture of the Russian Revolution and as a marker of difference between the USSR and the USA. "Wherein is Moscow's dignity / more than Passaic's dignity?" he asks in one poem. "A few men have added color better / to the canvas, that's all."[79] Here, however, color binds multiple meanings and tonalities within a single form—red identifies with "cold" and sits vibrantly with the "intense green" and the "opalescent shadows," which together express an affectively charged access to the sublimity of nature.

This relationship between socialist revolution and the reemergence of nature reappears throughout the poem, perhaps even threatening it with a regressive kind of romanticism. But that relationship might also be an important part of socialism, a colorful expression of its utopian promise and not just the American poet's nostalgic projection of an essentially premodern life. One of the outcomes of communism's abolition of the division of labor is opening up the possibilities of experiencing life beyond the exclusive spheres designated by capitalist production. In communism, write Marx and Engels, "society regulates the general production and thus makes it possible for me to do one thing today and another tomorrow," potentially allowing the communist subject "to hunt in the morning, fish in the afternoon, rear cattle in the evening, criticise after dinner, just as I have a mind, without ever becoming hunter, fisherman, herdsman or critic."[80] Indeed, the man is free to experience nature as an agricultural worker without necessarily being tethered to the plough and obliged to that profession with the exclusivity of economic compulsion. And so, after the morning's immersion in this environment, he leaves its natural setting and enters into a world defined by the slow advance of communist ideology through the bureaucratic machinery of socialism, from which the color dims.

That bureaucratic machinery is what we find in the first strophe's subsequent lines, against which the opening now defines itself:

> There were no cities
> between him and his desires

his hatreds and his loves were
without walls without rooms, without elevators
without files, delays of veiled murderers
muffled thieves, the tailings of
tedious, dead pavements, the walls
against desire save only for him who can pay
high, there were no cities—he was
without money—[81]

These lines can be read in several ways. First, and most obviously, they can be read as a recollection of the prerevolutionary world, with its cities and their variegated tedium. But, second, they can also be read as a reflection on the preceding lines, which now appear to have been a moment of real or imaginary reprieve from the differently tedious labor of socialism, which is required to transition from the prerevolutionary world to a communist utopia. It is this second meaning that seems to encourage the satirical overtones, which in these lines register a kind of bathos that reduces the abolition of capitalism to an ironic understatement: "he was/without money." In one of Slavoj Žižek's better analogies, the opposition between the exalted energies of revolution and the subsequent creation of a new social order is figured as the sobering experience of the morning after. "In the revolutionary explosion as an Event," he says, "another utopian dimension shines through, the dimension of universal emancipation which, precisely, is the excess betrayed by the market reality which takes over 'the day after.'"[82] The point here is that communism will mean nothing unless it is actualized in a political and economic sequence that prevents the resurgence of capitalism by imposing its new, socialist order upon the site of the event's normalization. Beyond the ecstasy of utopian fervor is another material reality that requires its own economic coordination and elaborate statecraft. In the case of Russia, communism was never just the momentary detonation of revolutionary enthusiasm that overturned aristocratic and bourgeois rule. It was also the assemblage of laws, policies, and apparatuses that were put in place to construct the socialist state, and it is within this latter situation, the unromantic morning after, that Williams's poem situates itself. As we shall see, the poem endorses both of these readings, identifying its cities with both capitalism and socialism.

The conflation of world and subject is not just the product of nostalgic romanticism, either, though it certainly bears traces of that. Within this poem, it also appears to be an outcome of that subject's reconfiguration through socialism. For Marx and Engels, "the theory of the Communists may be summed up in the single sentence: Abolition of private property."[83] And, in the absence of private property, after the removal of that which elsewhere might be nominated as "his own," what fills its place is a collective ownership of the means of production, which can only be "his own" insofar as they also belong to everybody else. As the poem's accompanying text has it in a punch line to the poem's satire, describing an economy spread dangerously thin: "There are no rich. The richness is everywhere, belongs to everyone and it is hard to get."[84] The opening strophe's second half describes the socialization of Russia as a force that legislates in favor of this collective ownership by removing cities and replacing them with soviets. "There were no cities/between him and his desires" precisely because socialism has abolished bourgeois individualism, manifest here as "the wall/against desire save only for him who can pay high," and which is later ascribed to a vision of consumer capitalism.

> Cities are full of light, fine clothes
> delicacies for the table, variety,
> novelty—fashion: all spent for this.
> Never to be like that again:
> the frame that was. It tickled his
> imagination. But passed in a rising calm.[85]

From the perspective of an abstract theory of communism, these lines would express the false freedom of a prerevolutionary individual under capitalism, according to which that freedom is only what Georg Lukács would call "the freedom of the individual isolated by the fact of property which both reifies and is itself reified."[86] The poem's adjective "full" implies the omnipresence of the "light, fine clothes" and "delicacies for the table, variety, novelty," all of which are commodities whose value is subservient to the vicissitudes of "fashion," by and from which the subject is ultimately alienated. What "tickles" the man's imagination is the eradication of capitalism—a process accounted for by the monetary term "spent"—as it takes shape in the supersession of these objects and the economic matrix that orchestrates their movements. In Brian A. Bremen's reading of these lines, he argues that the "'frame that was' is an 'ideology' whose 'grammar' determines the meaning (and price) of 'this'—a floating signifier that remains open to perpetual redefinition according to the economic 'grounding' it receives." We should add that these lines do not take place within an abstract theory or idealistic projection of communism. Rather, they attempt to provide historical insight into a Soviet man wondering at the world-historical trade-off his country has just made: selling the "cities" of glittering capital for a gamble of freedom still predicated on mud and lice and peasants. Perhaps this is why the poem reads as neither endorsement nor condemnation of the "the red cold world" and instead presents that world through a lens of ambivalent irony. The man is glad to be out of the "frame" of commodity fetishism; his imagination is "tickled," but he can see how wild the risk is. The Bolsheviks have "cut out the cancer," but "perhaps the patient will die."[87]

Given the dead metaphor of a "frame that was," which harbors fragments of the pictorial artwork's material enclosure, and given that metaphor's thematic redoubling by the fact that the poem's central subject is spatially framed by a window, there appears to be good cause for speculating on the poem's engagement with the traditional portrait. This engagement, a mutation on the genre's inborn individualism, takes place as an internal multiplication of the singular subject. It begins when the speaker notes that two peasants, "very lazy and foolish / seemed to have walked out from his own / feet,"[88] thus identifying his own limbs with the agency of two anonymous bearers of that previously mourned "peasant tradition." The multiplication is, however, a historically particular effect of the socialist experience whose previously absolutist context intrudes via analepsis.

> The very old past was refound
> redirected. It had wandered into himself
> The world was himself, these were
> his own eyes that were seeing, his own mind
> that was straining to comprehend, his own
> hands that would be touching other hands
> They were his own![89]

This individual, a sovereign defined by the proprietary "his" and "own," has been radically transformed by the socialist economy. Property is now a throwback to "the very old past," from within which he could only "strain to comprehend," and which is contrasted to the communist subjectivity from which it is recalled. Jodi Dean has explained how a communist subject embodies a unique desire antipathetic to the kind of self-possession recalled by these lines. "A constitutive component of the communist subjectification of the gap between what exists and what could be," she argues, "between working and capitalist classes, between revolutionaries faithful to October

1917 and other political subjectifications is the opposition between a collective 'we' and an individual determined in and by his singular self-possession."[90] Communism thus provides the means by which the individual can fully integrate his personal interests with those of the collective, the name for which, in this instance, is the soviet. As Bremen puts it, the "soviet" of this poem "is a participatory form of government that allows for full 'identification' in an uncertain, local, cooperative effort."[91] Note how the man's eyes, mind, and hands are all tools of labor, and note, too, the exclamatory delight at the fact that his are now "hands that would be touching other hands." This is the other side to the utopia communism projects after the abolition of the division of labor. If the first side was the freeing up of an individual's labor so that he can pursue multiple tasks over the course of each day, the second is that he will pursue those tasks communally. "And indeed," write Marx and Engels in terms that would have appealed to Williams, "this communal interest does not exist merely in the imagination, as the 'general interest,' but first of all in reality, as the mutual interdependence of the individuals among whom the labour is divided."[92]

The following lines present collectivization in its material actuality, in such a way that the soviet can now be depicted in some detail:

He decided not to shave. Like those two
that he knew now, as he had never
known them formerly. A city, fashion
had been between—

Nothing between now.

He would go to the soviet unshaven. This
was the day—and listen. Listen. That
was all he did, listen to them, weigh
for them. He was turning into
a pair of scales, the scales in the
zodiac.

But closer, he was himself
the scales. The local soviet. They could
weigh. If it was not too late. He felt
uncertain many days. But all were uncertain
together and he must weigh for them out
of himself.[93]

The first quatrain announces a positive identification with the two peasants, whom the man "had never/known" before communism because of the unassailable relations of production. The following line, "Nothing between now," signifies the removal of that rampart. The two sextets then describe a process whereby the man becomes the soviet, "turning into/a pair of scales." This "turning into" is a metaphorical expression of the man's integration into a communist ontology, wherein he is made of the same political and economic substance as everything else in his soviet. But that integration is not a reduction, the kind of flattening out of subjectivity experienced under capitalism. Instead, the man retains his subjective integrity, becoming the scales of a specifically "local soviet," the locality of which mediates between the mode of production and the irreducible self. While "all were uncertain," they were uncertain "together," and for the man that shared uncertainty forges a newfound solidarity between "them" and "himself."

Comrades Sheeler and Shakespeare

What this poem ultimately depicts is a social situation in which the individual and his historical circumstances, in the form of either class or collective, can be expressed in the same frame. The accompanying prose harmonizes this distinctly communist sociality with the challenges of proletarian portraiture. "Russia," it begins, "is every country, here he must live, this for that, loss for gain."[94] Even if (under the duress of anticommunist investigation) Williams would later describe this poem as little more than "sympathetic human feeling—non-political—roused by thoughts of Russia,"[95] its formal achievement, which reinvents the portrait's subject as an economically collectivized being, is precisely the structural effect of communism and its "local" manifestation in the "soviets." Though we should remain wary that, for Williams, communism doubles as an invitation to explore anachronistic peasant traditions—irrespective of whether that exploration takes place in a projected, utopian alternative—what remains intact is the discovery in communism of a subjectivity whose presentation maintains the tension between individual and class or, here, collective. That all of this is being thought about in terms of American portraiture is suggested by some of the poem's internal dynamics, as well as by the antecedents to which Williams compares it, which brings us back to the question of photography.

The first antecedent is Charles Sheeler, the American artist and precisionist photographer who was contracted by Henry Ford to photograph the Ford factory. "Henry Ford has asked Chas. Sheeler to go to Detroit and photograph everything," we read. "Carte blanche. Sheeler! That's rich."[96] Williams admired Sheeler's paintings, drawings, and photographs because of their exemplary fusion of concrete iconography and abstract shapes, the local setting and the universal idea, which crystallized into an aesthetic substance similar to the communist subjectivity.[97] The influence of Sheeler's aesthetic is clearly present in Williams's own portrait of Ford.

A tin bucket
full of small used parts
nuts and short bolts
slowly draining onto
the dented bottom—
forming a heavy sludge
of oil—depositing
in its turn steel grit

Hangs on an arm
that whirls it at increasing
velocity around
a central pivot—
suddenly the handle gives
way and the bucket
is propelled through
space . . .[98]

Notwithstanding the parodic overtones, everything in this portrait is connected. The tin bucket is "full" of nuts and bolts, which are "slowly draining" so as to form a sludge that is somehow "depositing" steel grit, which "hangs" on the mechanical arm that whirls "around" the machine's central pivot, until the machine unexpectedly "gives way," thus revealing the interconnectedness of large-scale industry. This structurally organic aesthetic, stretched out across one long sentence, replaces an exemplarily capitalist subjectivity with the means of production. However, we need to emphasize that, unlike the Ford factory, the Russian context does not simply delete the subject, flattening it out into whatever machinery. Rather, it preserves the relationship between that subjectivity and its economic milieu. "A city is merely a relocation of metals in a certain place," we read in Williams's gloss to the poem set in the USSR. "He feels the richness, but a distressing feeling of loss is close upon it. He knows he must coordinate the villages for effectiveness in a flood, a famine."[99] Those metals and his feelings are present together and at once, which puts him in contrast to Ford, who is presented here as all metal with no feeling.

Equating an individual with his historical situation is a social program that finds more literary precedent in a second example. "Shakespeare," we are told, "had that mean ability to fuse himself with everyone which nobodies have, to be anything at any time, fluid, a nameless fellow whom nobody noticed—much, and that is what made him the great dramatist."[100] For Williams, Shakespeare works as a literary photographer—"Because he was nobody and was fluid and accessible. He took the print and reversed the film, as it went in so it came out"—whose depicted subjects are, like those of the photographic portrait and Trotsky's New Soviet Man, dialectically connected to a greater form. As Trotsky said of Shakespeare's dramas, "the individual passion is carried to such a high degree of tension that it outgrows the individual, becomes super-personal, and is transformed into a fate of a certain kind."[101] If Shakespearean characters speak to the communist subjectivity just as much as Sheeler's photography, perhaps it is not to be wondered that Williams suggests Russia as their ideal home. "Sheeler and Shakespeare," he claims, "should be on this soviet." The text then labels this shared mode of representation, with reference to the poem's geopolitical coordinates, as "the tactical spread of realism that is the Soviets," before disengaging that "spread" from its cultural context. "Imperial Russia was romanticist, strabismic, atavistic. Style," it reads, then provides a final description of the soviet milieu into which the man has successfully integrated. "He does not blame the other countries. They fear what he sees. He sees tribes of lawyers tripping each other up entirely off the ground and falling on pillows full of softly jumbled words from goose backs."[102]

The historical passage from romance through realism requires, for Williams, a detour through the USSR that will eventually lead back to the USA. "The United States," he says, "should be, in effect, a soviet state. It is a soviet state decayed away in a misconception of richness. The states, counties, cities, are anemic soviets."[103] This metaphor returns us to the incompatibility of the USSR and the USA, of socialist and capitalist states. As the poet-doctor would have been all too aware, anemia refers to a potentially incapacitating deficiency of red blood cells, the effect of which decreases the flow of oxygen. Its meaning in this context, then, is that the localities comprised by and composing the United States are irredeemably individuated, and it is not without coincidence that their individuation results from an unhealthy lack of redness. In the USA, there is no unity of the sort that defines the USSR because of an observably supervening "misconception of richness," the name for which is capitalism. In 1942, Williams wrote to Zukofsky expressing an unequivocal admiration for the Soviet people. "I sometimes think," he writes, "that there is no longer a possibility of spontaneous and generous action left in the human soul—outside of Russia." He explains the admiration in economic terms, contrasting the USSR to England. "Perhaps the English have a plodding sort of virtue," he writes, "but the real war as ever remains to be determined between England at its worst and most successful and Russia at its best: all the overflowing wealth of spontaneous generosity, the real wealth of the plenty, of giving of plunging into virtue, the overwhelming wealth of life."[104] How, then, might the poet mobilize what he seems to be calling "realism," an aesthetic indebted to that "real wealth of the plenty," in creating a proletarian portrait for his own country?

A Portrait of Russia

Many years later, in March 1946, Williams composed the poem "Russia," which recombines his interest in photographic remediation with an antiwar response to geopolitical strife and a hope that the major allies from World War II—the USA and the USSR—would remain unopposed. "The Russian people," writes Mariani, "after all had been his greatest hope during the darkest days of the Second World War, and he had praised the courage and determination of these people, who at great personal sacrifice had first turned the German advances at Stalingrad."[105] Moreover, the USSR was still the source of a subjectivity that could be modeled in Williams's American poetry. But in the later poetry this subjectivity would become haunted by a midcentury imperialism. Unlike Pound, who finally embraced warfare as a committed fascist, Williams always considered it a threat, a phenomenon that at best alienates the individual from history and at worst allows for history to annihilate the individual. As Williams would describe the disappointment that underwrites the poem we read next: "Russia whose avowed intent has been to free the world from capitalism (for which we tentatively praised her) has turned out to be an empire seeker of the most reactionary sort."[106] Here, as with Pound, the difference between socialism and communism begins to assert itself.

If a poem about the USSR, written in 1928, invites a discourse on photography, then that invitation is returned, almost two decades later, when a photograph invites a poem about the USSR. Indeed, "Russia" begins with the description of what appears to be a photomechanical print.

> The Williams Avenue Zionist Church (colored)
> a thing to hold in the palm of your hand,
> your big hand—
> the dwarf campanile piled up, improvised
> of blue cinder-blocks, badly aligned
> (except for the inventive)
> unvarnished,
> the cross at the top slapped together
> (in this lumber shortage) of sticks from
> an old barrel top, I think
> —painted white[107]

While the first line specifies what the image depicts, the following suggests that image's medium: the representation of the church is "a thing to hold in the palm of your hand."[108] Even as the parenthetical "colored" grounds this object in technological and aesthetic history, it also signals racial segregation.

Whereas the cathedral we encountered earlier suggested ideological quiescence, this poem asks us to think about one of the deepest political fault lines in modern American history, by installing the question of race in its very first line, and again in the subsequent detail that this church is also "painted white." This will be important to us because the issue of racial segregation and its obverse galvanized thousands of Americans toward communism. As Mark Solomon has explained, "the pivotal issues then were neither tactical nor sentimental; they involved the basic structure and character of American society. Capitalism's cornerstone was seen to have been laid by slavery and fortified by racism. Therefore, the achievement of equality implied the ultimate transformation of the nation's economic and social foundations. That concept reached far beyond the racial landscape, to the recasting of the economic and psychological lives of all working people. Indeed, black striving for freedom was welded to the fortunes of the working class—creating an inseparable link between the movement of blacks of all classes to end oppression."[109] If all of this provides a broader context for thinking about the USSR, one of the church's potentially obscure details supplies that context with material specificity. To mention the "lumber shortage" is to recall lines written by Zukofsky sixteen years earlier, in which the younger poet refers to an imperialist and reactionary "embargo" set by the US Congress against the socialist state, preventing the import of lumber, pulpwood, and matches.[110] While it remains true that for Williams churches are associated with revolution and its aversion, and that racial segregation invites thinking about radical politics, to read the opening stanza of "Russia" in the context of Zukofsky's poem seals the presence of communism in what might otherwise appear to be little more than a poem written about a photograph. Though this poem, "Russia," has yet to mention the eponymous location, the communist specter is already hauntingly present.[111]

What follows the image of the church is a series of witheringly disappointed apostrophes made to "Russia, idiot of the world, blind idiot," all delivered in the first-person singular. The subjectivity of this speaker is thus framed by the growing belligerence between the USSR and the USA.

> I dream! and my dream is folly. While
> armies rush to the encounter
> I, alone, dream before the impending
> onslaught. And the power in me,
> to be crushed out: the paper, forgotten
> —not even known ever to have existed,
> proclaims the power of my dream . . .[112]

Unlike "A Morning Imagination of Russia," this poem is written in the lyric voice. The speaker is ultimately identifiable as Williams, given the poem's inclusion of multiple biographical referents ("I once met Mayakovsky," etc.) and its commencement on the outskirts of Rutherford, New Jersey. Whereas the earlier poem presented itself as a portrait, describing the man's subjectivity from a position external to his consciousness, this poem turns itself lyrically inward with a delirious excess of first-person singular pronouns, one of which is even succeeded by "alone," as though to prioritize the lyric's personal orientation. According to Hegel, one of the key differences between the epic and the lyric is the way those two genres handle the individual subject. The former, he argues, developed from the "primitive national epic and left aside both the inferior collateral types and also the poet himself," whereas the latter cherishes "the personality of the poet and the ramification of the different kinds into which lyric can expand, since it has as its principle the individualizing and particularizing of its subject-matter and its forms."[113] Between the two genres is the difference between the two social strata that Williams wants to uphold within the portrait. The lyric thus seems to be a generic model for the transposition of prephotographic portraiture into poetry, whereas the epic might be a viable destination for the representation of an entire class or nation. "Russia" consciously positions its lyric speaker, its subjectivity, as one of the "inferior collateral types," counterpoised to the imperial battle. What we might therefore expect from this poem is that its form will adhere to a similar subjectivity as was observed in the early portraits and unlike the one set in the USSR. That is to say, geopolitical belligerence diminishes the subjectively transformative energy that was present in "A Morning Imagination of Russia." With the portrait of the man from the USSR, his subjectivity was transformed into something greater than itself, but here in the USA and during wartime the portrait's subjectivity is only threatened by militarized obliteration. That difference in structure responds to the individual's correlation with its mode of production.

Williams reaches for two precedents in poetry, both of which uphold that tension between the one and the many and whose evocations help clarify the relationship between the USSR and the USA for this poem. The first appeal is to Walt Whitman.

> O Russia! Russians! come with me into
> my dream and let us be lovers,
> connoisseurs, idlers—Come with me
> in the spirit of Walt Whitman's earliest
> poem, let us loaf at our ease—a monument
> at the edge of destruction.[114]

The speaker claims to be modeled on that of "Leaves of Grass," and from this position he invites Russia and its Russians into his being. For Whitman, the individual self was always everyone all at once—a force that welcomed everything other than itself into its own being. But, given Williams's context, which postdates Whitman's romantic and democratic moment by almost a century, the invitation can only remain an ahistorical fantasy, unless it is grounded in a contemporary actuality such as that of the USSR. The poem then requests to merge the historically outmoded but regionally apposite subjectivity of Whitman with one that is geopolitically alien but historically contemporaneous. Williams makes this request with the sponsorship of Mayakovsky.

> . . . Look,
> I once met Mayakovsky. Remember

Mayakovsky? I have a little paper-bound
volume of his in my attic, inscribed by him
in his scrawling hand to our mutual
friendship. He put one foot up
on the table that night at 14th St. when
he read to us—and his voice came
like the outpourings of the Odyssey.

Russians!
let Mayakovsky be my sponsor—he
and his Willie, the Havana street-cleaner—
Mayakovsky was a good guy and killed
himself, I suppose, not to embarrass you.[115]

Of all poets writing in the English language, Whitman held pride of place with the Russian futurists. In 1914, he was described in Russia as "the first Futurist poet," and the futurists would "acknowledge only Whitman among the world's poets." Portraiture is important to this constellation of poets. For instance, Whitman's "working-class rough" portrait, which accompanied "Leaves of Grass," and which also opens the earliest Russian translation, likely inspired Mayakovsky's own self-fashioning. But after 1917 Mayakovsky embraced the difference between memories of democracy in a foreign land and the aspirations of communism in his own and turned against his American forebear. In one poem, he even populates Chicago, the perceived epicenter of global capitalism, with "all kinds of Lincolns, Whitmans, and Edisons," including an image of the famously bewhiskered poet stuffed into a "snug dinner-jacket" and "rocking like a rocking chair to an unheard-of rhythm."[116] Even if Williams still identifies with Whitman, the material conditions of "Leaves of Grass" are historically outmoded, and so Williams needs to modify his poetic analogue. However, to modify in accord with Mayakovsky is just as problematic, given that Mayakovsky's poetry responds to a socialist subjectivity, whereas Williams needs something suited for the inhospitable terrain of American capitalism. Williams has already recognized the hostile relationship between the "inferior collateral" these poets embody and the militarism of the "primitive national epic" their nations now inhabit. Whitman is "a monument / at the edge of destruction," and Mayakovsky "killed / himself, I suppose, not to embarrass you." Neither Whitman nor Mayakovsky provide a workable model for the poem's subjectivity, an impossibly non-alienated individual conceived of in the age of empire.

The poem's final three stanzas return to the United States, and to a distinctly American engagement with photographic remediation, when the speaker recalls his motivation for an apostrophe to the other two poets. We are told that what we have been reading derives from its speaker's encounter with the reproduction of Leonardo Da Vinci's "The Last Supper," found in a "poor kitchen," which brings us back to the racial and class segregation from the poem's beginning.

> And now I want to call your attention—
> that you may know what keen eyes
> I have in my dream—
> to Leonardo's Last Supper! a small print
> I saw today in a poor kitchen.
>
> Russia!
> for the first time in my life, I noticed
> this famous picture not because
> of the subject matter but because
> of the severity and simplicity
> of the background! Oh there was
> the passion of the scene, of course,
> generally. But particularly,
> ignoring the subject, I fell upon
> the perpendiculars of the paneled
> woodwork standing there, submissive,
> in exaggerated perspective.[117]

Why, then, is the speaker of this poem telling the USSR about a photograph of a painting? The painting itself provides some clues. Generically, Da Vinci is hailed as a master of portraiture. Specifically, though, "The Last Supper" represents a moment when the individual's body is shared with the multitude, when Jesus Christ divides himself up through transubstantiation to be consumed by the apostles. As Hegel comments, this painting is not interested in "ideal divinities but entirely human ideals, not simply men as they should be, but ideal men as they actually live and exist, men lacking neither particularity of character nor a connection between particularity and that universal which fills their individual lives."[118] Like the man and the soviet, the subject of this portrait is said to forge a concrete relation between the universal and the particular. The division of Christ is the collectivization of a self that retains its individual integrity. However, what the possibly photographic remediation of the painting into a "small print" achieves is the liberation of this antiquated quality, allowing for the painting's reproduced image to refocus the speaker's attention away from the aura of Christ's monumental figure. In shifting focus from "the subject matter" to "the background," the poem expresses sensitivity to the parallels between the portrait's content and the historicity of portraiture.

The stereoscopic focus that, in "A Morning Imagination of Russia," held together the individual subject and the collective soviet, transforming the former into an agent of the latter and putting the latter in service of the former, has under capitalism collapsed into an antinomy. For Williams, American poetry can have either the individual's background or it can have the individual as divorced from that context. "There you have it," begins the final stanza of "Russia": "It's that background / from which my dreams have sprung." And it is that background, comprising the "perpendiculars of the paneled / woodwork" in Da Vinci's painting and the otherwise nondescript "poor kitchen," into which that speaker begins to fade. Like the man in "A Morning Imagination of Russia," who identifies positively with the soviet, this speaker assimilates into the collective conditions of anonymous reification and imperialist threat. "Among many others, undistinguished / of no moment," the poem concludes, "I am the background / upon which you build your empire."[119] This is the paradox to which the poem builds. The speaker's individualized subjectivity, his first person singular, persists in spite of its identification with the "undistinguished" masses upon which empires construct themselves. As a mode of concrete representation this might be disingenuous in its transposition of the socialist structure into a capitalist setting. But, from a technological perspective, this is much closer to the remediating photograph, as Benjamin understood it, than it is to the original painting—as such, it marks a moment of evolutionary supersession in portraiture. For Williams, communism served as an accelerator in this aspect of modern aesthetics, supercharging the photomechanical transformation of portraiture and reconditioning along proletarian lines the ontological substance of the poetic individual.

Prehistory of an Insurgent Locale

We already know that Williams was socially and aesthetically invested in a New Jersey localism, as well as in the crafting of a nativist American poetry, and we now know that when writing about New Jersey and the USA he was often looking to the Russian Revolution and the USSR. But is there a contradiction between these local and international worldviews? While Eric White has shown that, for Williams especially, modernist localism is inextricably bound to modernism's international currents, there is still a significant tension between the ethos of American nativism and these emphatically internationalist appeals, which is felt all the more profoundly because of the major structural and, by extension, cultural differences between the USA and the USSR.[120] Williams must have been aware of the apparent tension here, given that he conjured away a version of it in the 1937 review of H. H. Lewis quoted in the introduction to this study. In the review he claims that Lewis's affection for the USSR is the "pure American revolutionary stuff" and that, rather than distract from an avowedly parochial aesthetic, it confirms the poetry's status as both regionally and culturally American.

> He speaks with fervor, a revolutionary singleness and intensity of purpose, a clearly expressed content. He knows what he wants to say; he is convinced of its importance to a fanatical degree. He has been hurt, and he yells the how, why, and wherefore. In all this he resembles the American patriot of our revolutionary tradition. There is a lock, stock, and barrel identity between Lewis today, fighting to free himself from a class enslavement which torments his body with lice and cow dung, and the persecuted colonist of early American tradition. It doesn't matter that Lewis comes out openly, passionately, for Russia. When he speaks of Russia, it is precisely then that he is most American, most solidly in the tradition, not out of it, not borrowing a "foreign" solution. It is the same cry that sent Europeans to a "foreign" America and there set them madly free.[121]

In Williams's view of Lewis, an enthusiasm for communism illuminates the American locality because it casts light on the radically democratic origins of the United States. It refers back to the kind of world inhabited by Walt Whitman and Ralph Waldo Emerson, a world that Jacques Rancière best describes in an essay on American romance. He writes that the national poet "draws his power only from his ability to nourish himself with the potential latent in collective experience, to read the hieroglyphics inscribed in the savage and multiform nature of the new continent, but also in the features and gestures of hybrid multitudes that explore and reclaim it."[122] While the object of passion is Russian, the passion itself is distinctly American. We have seen a similar illumination in Williams's verse, where visions of the socialist state resonate with an Emersonian and Whitmanesque nativism. Perhaps that is why, in an unpublished poem written by Williams in

1928 and based on prose we have already encountered, the speaker insists that the "strongest feature" of the USSR is its "local character" and that the "the first characteristic of the United States is that of so many decayed soviets." The speaker then concedes that, in America, "The general picture is that of forty eight swiftly degener-/ating soviets—the sense of local responsibility, the only—/hope in a democracy or for continual freedom, having been/milked from us almost completely."[123] Affection for the USSR appears to be analogous to affection not for the USA in the "general picture" of its historical actuality but for the America that might be or might have been. This is affection for an unrealized potential as conceived of and sustained by its "revolutionary tradition." This, to be sure, is a vision that ultimately coheres not with socialism or its extant state but, rather, with the possibility of communism as a properly transnational idea with an international program.

What, then, is the role of communism in Williams's modern epic, *Paterson,* named after that regional city in the seat of Passaic County, New Jersey? In his prefatory argument for the poem, Williams insists on the importance of Paterson as a familiar locality. He claims to know, as a poet, "that in the very lay of the syllables Paterson as Paterson would be discovered, perfect, perfect in the special sense of the poem, to have it—if it rose to flutter into life awhile—it would be as itself, locally, and so like every other place in the world."[124] The remainder of this chapter accounts for how the privileged forms we have encountered so far—imagination and its accompanying mode of verse, the collective subjectivity of the proletarian portrait—interact with the epic's local setting to produce the impression of a "decayed soviet." Jameson notes that, because *Paterson* emerged "from the immense Left force-field of the 1930s," this poem avoids Cold War ideologies, which, he says, "are contemporaneous with the setting in place of the very ideology of aesthetic modernism in the US." For exactly this reason, the poem "can plausibly continue to sustain a progressive and Left-oriented vision."[125] While the Cold War is certainly in the background to this poem—whose four principal volumes were published between 1946 and 1951—the remaining task is to demonstrate the various ways that communism irradiates the poem's ideological and aesthetic framework, shaping its political vision.[126] My sense is that communism helped expedite Williams's relatively belated migration from the lyric to the epic while maintaining the interdependence of those two genres. This migration was not a conventional case of classical poetic maturation but, rather, an effect of Williams's late turn to economic critique.

Before the Russian Revolution and its first appearance in his poetry just over half a decade later, Williams's most significant work remained a long poem, "The Wanderer: A Rococo Study," in which the speaker reflects on New Jersey as experienced by its working class. Its centerpiece passage, whose depicted event reappears several times across Williams's oeuvre, responds to the Paterson Silk-Workers Strike of 1913, a six-month industrial campaign that, according to Michael Denning, inaugurated a "connection between the arts communities and the left, between the bohemia of Greenwich Village and the movement cultures of the Debsian Socialist Party and the Wobblies."[127] The poem is reflexively aware of that relationship. Its speaker asks several strikers queued in a "bread-line" about the force that motivates their political action—"This thing heretofore unobtainable/That they seem so clever to have put on now?" —only to conclude that the workers themselves are responsible for their own breed of class-consciousness. Their "thing" remains inaccessible to the middle-class poet and unavailable to established literary forms: "Why since I have failed them can it be anything/But their own brood? Can it be anything but brutality?/On that at least they're united! That at least/Is their bean soup, their calm bread and a few luxuries!"[128] This quatrain, first published in 1914, would be rewritten and republished in 1917 and then alluded to obliquely in Book 2 of *Paterson* in 1948.

Whilst ostensibly minor, the differences between the 1914 and the 1917 versions are particularly revealing. In both, the lines conform to syntactical clauses, and each line begins on a capital letter, with the exception that, in the later version, the first sentence is not divided at all—"Why since I have failed them can it be anything but their own brood?" —which results in the first line doubling the length of the second.[129] Observing this transformation, we can suggest that the shift toward uneven lineation and the attendant change in rhythm is indicative of the relationship between the political action and the techniques Williams uses in order to faithfully inscribe that subject matter. While this particular transformation might speak to a development in the tension between sound and sense, the poet himself suggests that this relationship is meaningful on its own terms, simply as a relationship, and that it helped precipitate his epic. Williams confirms the significance of the 1914 and 1917 fragments for the radicalization not of any political commitment but, more importantly for the poet, of his evolving aesthetic. He describes "The Wanderer" as his "first 'long' poem, which in turn led to *Paterson.* It was the 'line' that was the key—a study in the line itself, which challenged me."[130]

Literature and Politics, Autonomy in Convergence

Before proceeding any further it will be worth clarifying what communism meant to Williams at this point in his career, both theoretically and in relation to his sense of poetry. In 1932, Williams seemed utterly convinced of communism's value to poetry: "Never may it be said, has there ever been great poetry that was not born out of a communist intelligence."[131] To be sure, Williams was primarily interested in how communism might advance poetry. He made this perfectly clear in a letter dated 1933, in which he accepts the editorship for the New York magazine, *Blast*.[132] In the letter he claims to "write exclusively, consciously and with a purpose to be understood by and to instruct in the object of my craft," to aid "those avowed Communists who need what I can give," and "to bring the excellences of writing to the understanding and service of men whose illumination by the principles of communism make them capable of rewarding the effort the artist would make by secrets he could not arrive at otherwise."[133] His program for the magazine, addressed to the "Red Front," is that art "must be, first, good art," that "writers (and other artists) must face their responsibilities toward the world revolution" as writers and artists above all else, without ever subordinating "training and skill to party necessity."[134] Though Williams is adamant that "there is no communistic writing," because writing must first of all be writing on its own terms, he also insists that writing has much to learn from communism, and the poems we have encountered so far are testament to this.

> There is only writing—which goes forward or back at will in order to remain in reasonable contact with [the] organization of its materials, [or to respond] to a continually revalued estimate of the nature of its materials. Now it must go back according to the new stress which Communism places on words and their uses. Communism has cut away whole bales of misconception in form—art then quite naturally retreats, to organize its position. It must retreat. It isn't flattered to do so. It doesn't set out to serve the proletariat. It remains art, but it retreats. Takes its place not where it will but where it can. Absorbs some of the warmth, perhaps, in doing so. Retains its integrity. And for *this* must be valued. By its integrity.[135]

This, for Williams, is a fruitful alternative to the subordination of art by politics, a different way of engaging with what he describes as communism's "revision of the code," which presents to the artist "an opportunity to regain an understanding."[136] Irrespective of whether an artist endorses or rejects a political belief, that artist should place his or her political disposition in the service of art. "But," he cautions, "the artist makes a mistake if he believes that there is no way to serve the new mode implied in a present-day Communism—which is intellectually inescapable—save by jettisoning his personal integrity as an artist." To engage with communism as a writer with integrity, then, means responding to communism via the "organization of its materials"—that is, with literary technique. Appreciating this will be all the more important here because, unlike the verse we have encountered so far, the poem we are now interested in here contains relatively fewer direct references to communist phenomena and fewer still to the socialist state.

Despite the apparent absence of the Russian Revolution and its ebullient imagination, the literary strategies we have seen evolve in relation to that event remain active in *Paterson.* Indeed, many are modified so as to better serve the epic. These strategies are mentioned in the italicized, prefatory note to Book 1, which seems to strategize Williams's intention for the pages to follow. Pitched somewhere between verse and prose, the note is reminiscent of Williams's riposte to Eliot. Here the poem announces itself as the manifestation of a "local pride" and as a distinctly working-class "reply to Greek and Latin with bare hands." The subjectivity of the proletarian portrait, which evolved by envisioning the bureaucrat from the USSR and later by contrasting the USSR and the USA, is figured here mathematically, "by multiplication and a reduction to one." The result is a singular individual who is simultaneously the sum of his or her multitudinous class. What the note seems undecided on, however, is the circumambient frame in which these forms will be presented and drawn together: "hard put to it; an identification and a plan for action to supplant a plan for action."[137] In the pages that follow, we look at the importation of these strategies from the shorter poems, and how they change for the epic while continuing to bear traces of communism, before finally posing the question of the epic as its own genre somewhat more insistently. The point of that question is to determine what exactly makes *Paterson* an epic and to explore the extent to which communism persists into this late-career shift of genre.

New Ideas, Old Forms

Perhaps the most conspicuous of the literary practices to have migrated from Williams's shorter poems and into the modern epic is the subjectivity that was exemplified in the proletarian portrait and developed in relation to the USSR. In the preface to Book 1 we read of "the city/the man, an identity," about which the poem insists "it can't be/otherwise—an/interpenetration, both ways." From the outset, the poem insists upon that concrete relationship between the individual and his urban form, a fusing together of the singular character and the multiplicity of its social relations. This subjectivity is the focus of Book 1, in which the city of Paterson is described as one of two sleeping giants. If one giant is the city, the other is a mountain, which is variously likened to a female counterpart. "And there, against him, stretches the low mountain," we are told. "The Park's her head, carved, above the Falls, by the quiet/river."[138] The biblical metaphor of two sleeping giants enacts the epic inversion of that familiar collective subjectivity. Though figural gigantism is, of course, a prominent trope in Soviet propaganda—which frequently depicts revolutionaries as giants, with numerous images making Lenin truly colossal—that is not what we are seeing here. For Williams, if the giants bear any relation to communism, they are more likely to do so as an expression of the subjectivity we encountered in the two poems set in or in relation to the USSR. In the shorter poetry, the formal challenge for the individual or lyric speaker was reconciliation with the panorama of his or her milieu. Here that panorama is the poem's epic subjectivity, as in Whitman, but without a stable voice attempting to hold that panorama within the speaker's consciousness. Instead of relegating an individual to either the foreground or background of the historical frame, that individual is conceived of in wholly new proportions.

In these lines from the opening strophe of Book 1, the poem's epic subjectivity is rendered as the organic whole of the localized mode of production:

> Immortal he neither moves nor rouses and is seldom
> seen, though he breathes and the subtleties of his
> machinations
> drawing their substance from the noise of the pouring
> river
> animate a thousand automatons. Who because they
> neither know their sources nor the sills of their
> disappointments walk outside their bodies aimlessly
> for the most part,
> locked and forgot in their desires—unroused.[139]

Despite the abundance of personifying pronouns, we should be wary of referring to this as "subjectivity" in any conventional sense of the term, owing to its realization as a machinelike factory of slumbering elements. But, as we shall see, this gigantic embodiment achieves something on the order of Whitman's speaker, incorporating anything and everything into its own sentient form. The first sentence begins in the epic register, with the adjective "immortal," whose object rapidly identifies as a kind of mechanized hydropower: a "river" that powers "machinations" and "automatons." In that way, these lines preempt a description of the river as "half steaming purple from the factory vents,"[140] connecting this natural feature of the poem's landscape with the local industry. The second sentence describes those "automatons," equipping them with a collective consciousness that remains unaware of the immense thing that conjoins and sustains them. The "bodies" here are unknowingly disappointed, aimless "for the most part," and alienated from their own "desires." Like the gigantic thing of the first sentence, which "neither moves nor rouses," here its working parts remain "unroused." But note the dynamic relationship between the pronouns in these two sentences, with the third-person singular "he" and "his" laying claim to the "machinations" of the "automatons," which then become the "who" and "they" of the second sentence. Note, too, that both sentences are predominantly iambic, transferring rhythmic energy from one to the next, so that the consciousness of the second sentence is formally akin to the machinery of the first sentence. Though Williams offers no totalizing noun to encapsulate this entire process, its expressive connectivity—as engineered between the river, the machines that syphon its power, the social relations it sustains, an emoting consciousness, and an everyday routine—recommends that what we are encountering here is a localized manifestation of the mode of production.

James E. B. Breslin takes these lines as evidence that "Williams could have written a polished, elegant poem about Paterson, but only by maintaining the kind of distance from his subject that this panoramic view of the city requires."[141] The poem's middle-class narrator, a physician modeled on Williams and named after the city itself, Paterson, is similar to the Soviet bureaucrat in that he claims a privileged access to the mode of production he inhabits. "Who are these people," asks Dr. Paterson, "(how complex/the mathematic) among whom I see myself/in the regularly ordered plateglass of/his thoughts." But, unlike the Soviet man, there is an almost forcible schism between Dr. Paterson and the epic's population of frequently named minor characters: a class division, perhaps, in which Dr. Paterson can observe but never experience the lives of those around him, which together evince a political history for Paterson. These minor characters range up and down the class spectrum, from David Hower, "a poor shoemaker with a large family, out of work and money," through a shop owner, Lambert, who "was the first/to oppose the unions" and who comes to embody a petit-bourgeois sense of proprietary entitlement: "This is MY shop. I reserve the right (and he did)/to walk down the row (between his looms) and/fire any son-of-a-bitch I choose without excuse/or reason more than I don't like his face."[142] The parenthetical interjections made in the narrator's voice foreground that these lines comprise reported speech, that everything outside of parentheses is spoken by Lambert in his own voice, and they simultaneously characterize Lambert's speech as historical fact. These are different from Pound's pronominally identifying interjections into the world of Sigismondo Malatesta, because they emphasize that, while the narrator might not be able to identify with the working class, he is also unable or perhaps even unwilling to identify with the capitalists. Whereas Pound's interjections often embedded the poet within the contexts he described, Williams's interjections imply critical distance.

Elsewhere, we are given a close-up of the kind of face that might have earned a firing in Lambert's shop, that of a migrant workman who enters New Jersey by way of Soviet cinema. In Book 2, a family of Italian immigrants in the park, drinking, dancing, and speaking in demotic—"Come on! Wassa ma'? You got/broken leg?"—invite the following comparison:

Remember

The peon in the lost
Eisenstein film drinking

from a wine-skin with the abandon
of a horse drinking

so that it slopped down his chin?
down his neck, dribbling

over his shirt-front and down
onto his pants—laughing, toothless?

Heavenly man![143]

In David Kadlec's reading of these lines, the inclusion of this single "verse-clip" from Sergei Eisenstein's incomplete Mexican fantasia "serves to mock America's insatiable taste for sexual suppression. More than that, it challenges the very methods of assemblage that undergird both Williams's and Eisenstein's varieties of modernism."[144] Rather than viewing this as social criticism or as an aesthetic challenge, we might read it as another expression of proletarian portraiture. As a self-contained proletarian portrait, this image might be the next logical step in the technological evolution of that genre, which elsewhere draws inspiration from photography. "The cinema," wrote André Bazin, "can actually multiply the static interpretations of photography by those that derive from the juxtaposition of shots."[145] These couplets loosely emulate the visual syntax of cinematic montage, with its cuts and zooms and tilts: each couplet conjoins two separate frames into an animated whole, and all four couplets together animate a single filmic sequence. By depicting this man as a sequence from "the lost Eisenstein film," the poem does not, as Kadlec suggests, tame the dialectical force of montage. Instead, it suggests that this man is just several frames in a greater panorama of images, to be threaded together into the continuum of a totalized whole. What makes this man so "heavenly" might therefore be the same social and aesthetic sensibility that distinguished the individual faces at the baseball game: his face registers a flash of singular beauty not separate from but within the crowd. Ironically, however, this face emerges from a strong peasant tradition —and, knowing that, the film's status as fantasy pushes back against the speaker's reverie, returning his gaze to real inhabitants of the park.

What Williams previously called "imagination" returns here as well, and it once again figures a division between collective affect and a noticeably absent intellection. We have seen this absence already, in the "thousand automotons" that "neither know their sources nor the sills of their disappointments" and who "walk outside their bodies aimlessly," as well as in the Eisensteinian caricature, whose slop reads as hyperbole on what Williams once described as the dampening "selfspittle" that prevents any kind of revolutionary ignition. This becomes clear in Book 2 of the epic, which reveals that, in Paterson at least, imagination has been conscripted once again for ideological manipulation.

—and the imagination soars, as a
voice beckons, a thundrous voice, endless
—as sleep: the voice that has ineluctably called them—
                                        that unmoving roar!
                churches and factories
                                        (at a price)
                together, summoned them from the pit . . [146]

As in the shorter poems, the imagination registers as collective affect, here finding comparison in "a thundrous voice" that reverberates up through the mode of production, sounding out through its churches and factories. The second description of the voice, "that unmoving roar," owes its oxymoronic realization to the fact that the energy and intensity of the "roar" sustain an "unmoving" stasis. Of course, this voice is one we have heard Williams attempt to modulate throughout his career by utilizing idiomatic language and a restricted free verse that, together, are capable of stirring the imagination. Here, however, the soaring imagination is "beckoned" by the voice of capital, summoning forth workers from the Miltonic "pit," drawing them into the containment of its "churches and factories." As with "Russia," the juxtaposition of religion and labor is important, for it is the church that helps sustain the relations of production, perpetuating this "endless" recruitment into capital. This part of Book 2 contains an epiphany made to similar effect, realized in the shadow of "a massive church," "that those poor souls had nothing else in the world, save that church, between them and the eternal stony, ungrateful and uncompromising dirt they lived by . . . An orchestral dullness overlays their world."[147]

The division between affect and intellect is presented as an outcome of the relations of production more clearly than it was in the shorter poems. In Book 1, "the decay of the middle class," which opens a feudal-sounding "moat between the high and the low," is blamed for the restriction of knowledge and for the perpetuation of social "stasis."[148] Later, in Book 2, the "frank vulgarity" of a sunbathing couple focalizes a diagnosis of that stasis and its attendant stupefaction.

> Minds beaten thin
> by waste—among
>
> the working classes SOME sort
> of breakdown
> has occurred. Semi-roused
>
> they lie upon their blanket
> face to face,
> mottled by the shadows of the leaves
>
> upon them, unannoyed,
> at least here unchallenged.
> Not undignified . .[149]

Here we have a version of the variable foot, which again uses hard enjambment to play off the tension between sound and sense, and which is again used to allegorize the situation of the working-class imagination as only "semi-roused." The ostensibly condescending emphasis of that capitalized word, "SOME," encodes a social disconnection between the middle-class speaker and the working-class man and woman he voyeuristically observes. But that word is not just condescending. It also prevaricates. The emphasis of an approximate determiner reflects the speaker's uncertainty about the "breakdown" to which he bears witness. That uncertainty repeats in the equivocal language he uses to describe the couple, in his claim that they are "unannoyed," "unchallenged," and in the double negative of his compliment, that these two are "not undignified." The extremely awkward phrasing of that final tercet, with the repetition of "un-" in three past participles, recalls a quotation from John Addington Symonds about Greek poetry from the end of Book 1, which describes "the harmony which subsists between crabbed verses and the distorted subjects with which they dealt—the vices and perversions of humanity—as well as their agreement with the snarling spirit of the satirist." While these lines are not satirical—at least not in a way that snarls at their objects of description—they are certainly dealing with "distorted subjects," and the form seems to reflect this in its own ungainliness. "Deformed verse," we were told in that quotation, "was suited to deformed morality."[150]

Hometown Communism: A Mirror to this Modernity

What we have seen of *Paterson* so far takes up the ideas developed earlier in Williams's career and in relation to communism, modifying them for the new generic frame of the modern epic. The subject of the proletarian portrait has returned in the metaphor of the giant, in the speaker's synonymy with his location, and in the panorama of characters that emblematize their class. Imagination is, once again, conspicuous in its suppression, and once again the choice of language and the structure of verse reflect this. Here, more so than in the earlier poems, the formal strategies are overtly engaged with their mode of production and the economic construction of their local setting. While these strategies now serve in a depiction of the USA, we no longer encounter the detailed, referential engagements with the USSR that we were seeing in the other poems, or at least we are not seeing them in the same way. In the closest thing to the socialist state we have encountered so far, even Eisenstein finds himself on the other side of the planet. The most obvious driving force behind this transformation is revealed by the epic's one and only direct reference to the USSR, in an unfinished line for the incomplete draft of Book 6, written in the late 1950s and early 1960s, which refers to "the murders of a Staline."[151] There are several competing explanations for why direct references such as this are excluded from the rest of the text, but above all is the fact that those murders —in the trials and the famines and the gulag—can only have curtailed whatever sympathies might have remained for the socialist state. If, in the earlier poetry, Williams was openly and actively invested in the USSR, then its relative absence from his late-career epic is likely to be, at least in part, an attempt to distance himself from what that state had become under Stalin. Another similarly contextual reason for the exclusion of Soviet particulars is that, by the end of the 1940s, the USA and the USSR were entering into armed conflict that militated against Williams's investment in the USSR as a source for utopian imaginings. A short poem, published in 1949, marks a final disarticulation of the USSR from its communist aspirations.

> Russia! Russia! you might say
>   and furrow the brow
> but I say: There are flowers upon
>   the R. R. embankment
> woven by growing in and out among
>   the rusted guard cables
> lying there in the grass, flowers
>   daisy shaped, pink
> and white in this September glare.
>   Count upon it there
> Will be soon a further revolution.[152]

When the double exclamation of the proper name "Russia" is accompanied by the confusion or disappointment or exasperation suggested by an interlocutor's furrowed brow, the speaker seems to insist on the USSR's latent potential, but only in relation to another political paradigm. While these lines depict the deterioration of communist utopianism in Russia, as implied by the metonymy of "rusted guard cables," this deterioration is referred back to the socialist state's inception, as though to recall the utopian premise on which it was founded. The conventional shorthand for railroad, in "the R. R. embankment," encodes a reference to the Russian Revolution, and, as though to memorialize the geographical site of that event, flowers interweave through the guard cables. The emphasis on flowers and grass in these lines knowingly recalls the aesthetic predilections of Whitman, whose democratic context was for Williams defined by a similar kind of utopianism. In earlier versions of these lines, the final word, "revolution," was written as "dispensation," chiming with Eliot's "Journey of the Magi." Had the earlier version remained, it would have produced an entirely different poem, one whose theological undertone might even prophesy a shift from socialism into an altogether different mode of production. Ending the poem with "revolution" hearkens back to the utopian potential seized in 1917, and, by associating that potential with Whitman, the poem relates the communist utopia of the Russian Revolution to that of American democracy. For Williams, by this point in history neither the communist nor the democratic projects had come to their utopian fruition, but his poetry remained interested in that "further revolution," irrespective of how unlikely it must have seemed.

By this stage in Williams's career, the Russian source of communist desire had become unnecessary—for here and now the poem finds utopianism in the living men and women of its eponymous location. Persisting from the earlier engagements with socialism both in and out of the USSR is an almost romantic vision of communism as a force that remains irreducible to statist realpolitik and that takes shape as a larger sense of humanity's capacity to organize production and decision making along collectivist lines. If there are direct references to communism, they no longer point to the socialist state in Russia but instead to the political history and everyday realities of Paterson. There are three references of this nature, which we can summarize briefly as they acquire definitive meaning only when taken together. One block of prose from Book 2 narrates the propaganda emanating out of an industrial battle, concluding with a rhetorical question that positively contrasts a travesty of communism to a corrupted parliamentary democracy: "I refuse to get excited over the cry, Communist! they use to blind us. It's terrifying to think how easily we can be destroyed, a few votes. Even though Communism is a threat, are Communists any *worse* than the guilty bastards trying to undermine us?" In Book 3, we encounter an autobiographical fragment lamenting the apparent decline of Paterson's radicalism: "Rose and I didn't know each other when we both went to the Paterson strike around the first war and worked in the Pagent. She went regularly to feed Jack Reed in jail and I listened to Big Bill Haywood, Gurley Flynn and the rest of the big hearts and helping hands in Union Hall. And look at the damned thing now."[153] And, within the satirical exchanges from Book 4, we listen to a short piece of doggerel read by one of the poem's minor characters—the middle-aged and wealthy Corydon—written to her youthful employee and nurse, Phyllis.

You dreamy
        Communist
Where are you
        Going?

To the world's end
        Via?
        Oh oh oh oh

That will
        really
be the end .
        you

dreamy Communist
        won't it?
Together
        together[154]

Included here is another jab at Eliot. That the opportunistic socialite, Corydon, is echoing the apocalyptic sentiment of *The Waste Land* and reproducing its adaptation of idiomatic song ("Oh oh oh oh" sonically replicates Eliot's "O o o o") would be, in Williams's view, equally damning for both poets. Indeed, Phyllis triangulates the desire of two competitive suitors, the unsuccessful Corydon and the poet's own surrogate, Dr. Paterson, with whom she has an affair. It is as though, in a strangely elaborate allegory or even a crude wish fulfillment, she embodies the native spirit that Williams once tried to preserve against the corrupting cosmopolitanism of Eliot. More interesting, however, is the bathos that comes with transitioning from political to sexual desire, when social dreaming devolves into "dreaminess" and when the solidarity conveyed by "together" morphs into amatory coupling.

It might be easy to dismiss these citations—as a rhetorical counterpoint for parliamentary politics, as a charming anecdote about youthful rebellion, and as mocked-up poetry purpose built for seduction—but nevertheless there is consistency between them. As a material referent, communism is no longer a geopolitical or economic force but something minimal: a social alternative, animated by personal want or even by the inarticulate longing for a different mode of government, for generosity in organized labor, and for sexual desire that transcends the relations of production. Communism here is less world historical and more a circumstantial feature of the city and its inhabitants—an irreducible part of their local character, which yearns for things to be otherwise. Political desire still resonates with communism, but it is a communism decoupled from the geopolitical sequence that began in 1917.

All of which is perfectly consonant with the poem's genre. In 1932, Williams announced what he was hoping to write in the future. "The epic if you please is what we're after," he claims, "but not the lyric-epic sing-song. It must be a concise sharpshooting epic style. Machine gun style. Facts, facts, facts, tearing into us to blast away our stinking flesh of news."[155] Though there are certainly pages of facts, which bear more resemblance to Williams's prose excerpts than to Pound's lineation of documents into verse, that is not what defines the poem's purchase on totality. As a whole, this poem reads much more like what Williams disparaged as "the lyric-epic," a genre that seems, in this instance, to have emerged from the multiple tropes and devices that evolved in Williams's lyric poetry. In order to understand why this genre is in fact epic, as opposed to just an overlong lyric, and why this iteration of the genre might want to exclude references to the USSR, it is worth recalling Lukács's account of "minor epic forms," in which he argues that the narrator, poet, or speaker in that genre will

> adopt the cool and superior demeanor of the chronicler who observes the strange workings of coincidence as it plays with the destinies of men, meaningless and destructive to them, revealing and instructive to us; or he may see a small corner of the world as an ordered flower-garden in the midst of the boundless, chaotic waste-lands of life, and, moved by his vision, elevate it to the status of the sole reality; or he may be moved and impressed by the strange, profound experiences of an individual and pour them into the mold of an objectivized destiny; but whatever he does, it is his own subjectivity that singles out a fragment from the immeasurable infinity of the events of life, endows it with independent life and allows the whole from which this fragment has been taken to enter the work only as the thoughts and feelings of his hero, only as an involuntary continuation of a fragmentary causal series, only as the mirroring of a reality having its own separate existence.[156]

This is how the eponymous speaker of Williams's epic, Dr. Paterson, appears throughout the poem: as a calm observer, witnessing the interplay between the localized mode of production and the men, women, and children who inhabit it. In this view of the regional city, there is little room for the development of an international perspective, which would encroach upon the local more than it would enhance an experience or depiction of it. That this poem has absorbed forms developed not only in relation to the USSR but also under the sign of the lyric is important to its specific version of the epic. In minor epics, argues Lukács, "a fragment of life is transplanted by the writer into a surrounding world that emphasises it and lifts it out of the totality of life; and this selection, this delimitation, puts the stamp of its origin in the subject's will and knowledge upon the work itself: it is, more or less, lyrical in nature." However, and this is what differentiates the new genre from the kind of poem we encountered with "Russia," that lyricism is itself made epic. "It is not," says Lukács, "the swallowing of a solitary 'I' in the object-free contemplation of its own self, nor is it the dissolving of the object into sensations and moods; it is born out of form, it creates form, and it sustains everything that has been given form in such a work."[157]

But in what ways does Williams's sense of the lyric formalize an epic totality, imposing a unifying technical procedure on the panorama of heteronymous images and dialogistic voices present here? And what, similarly, makes this transformation in communism, from statist to local, anything more than pure romanticism? "How," asked the speaker of the 1914 poem that inspired this one, "shall I be a mirror to this modernity?"[158] The answer to these questions brings our study of Williams to a close by demonstrating how the poem's epic totality, like the forms and tropes and themes it includes, shares a history with communism at the level of political economy.

Economics, Finally

In "The Poem as a Field of Action," a talk given in 1948, Williams summarizes the spirit of his age. "Briefly then," he insists, "money talks, and the poet, the modern poet has admitted a new subject matter to his dreams—that is, the serious poet has admitted the whole armamentarium of the industrial age to his poems."[159] Despite this insistence, it can be argued fairly that, unlike Pound and Zukofsky, Williams's investments in communism have been at something of a remove from that idea's requisite grounding in political economy. And yet it is precisely this belated turn to political economy that secures the totality of Williams's modern epic, drawing together its multiple lyric forms into a coherent whole. The economic diagnoses that synthesize the poem's multiple working parts into an unstable totality are what bear the traces of communism most visibly, even while the socialist state almost entirely escapes the poem's sphere of reference. In chapter 2, on Pound, we encountered the suggestion that, in communist thought, capitalist industry is a privileged site for revolutionary sociality, and we encounter it again at length in chapter 4, on Zukofsky. The idea is that, from the standpoint of communism, capitalism forges revolutionary combinations antagonistic to the bourgeois, capitalist class, even if those combinations rarely become revolutionary because ideology frequently forestalls that potential. In this sense, ideology functions similarly to the way in which Williams seeks to account for the dissociation of imagination, which, we recall, separates collective affect from critical intellection. But, while Pound and Zukofsky were both readers of Marx, Williams was not. "I have not read Das Kapital," Williams wrote to Pound in 1946, "nor any of the landmarks of present day thought—except in the form of excerpts."[160] Of course, an anthological communism built of snippets will bear some resemblance to the modern epic—and, in the case of Williams's major poetic interlocutors, Pound and Zukofsky, their epics anthologized numerous excerpts from "Das Kapital" that might now find resonance with the economic thought in *Paterson*. To make this argument for the determining presence of communism's economic analyses, we need to account for Williams's economic views before returning to the poem.

In a speech delivered at Harvard in 1951, Williams mounted a critique of capitalism that was, in its emphasis on Social Credit, clearly influenced by Pound's infatuation with C. H. Douglas and Silvio Gesell. Having entered into what Williams calls the "Power Age," in which industrial technology ought to ease the burden of human labor, he argues that the United States needs to reassess its forces of production. "This is an age in which the productive capacity of one man has been increased, by machines, forty times over that of the past," he says, "but during which, purchasing power, as represented by wages or their equivalent, though it should have been expanded forty times to meet this contingency, has remained relatively stationary." While he insists that Social Credit "must bridge this gap," and that this theory displaces the ideology of "defunct capitalism," much of what follows in the speech is subtended by thoughts of socialist revolution. "Let me acknowledge, and it is an important point," he says, "that the original conception of a revolutionary America, in the minds of such agitators as Samuel Adams Freneau and some others, was not very different from the objective of those advocating a classless soviet today!" For Williams, the means by which a classless society can be achieved in the United States is a return to rugged individualism, a nativist version of Pound's factive personality, which here finds its exemplars in "Lenin, Mussolini—and my grandmother." This bathetic construction is clearly satirical, and yet there remains some truth in one its nominations. While Mussolini receives no further discussion, and Williams's grandmother is a figure for localism as well as a means of parody, Lenin was defined, says Williams in a somewhat counterfactual register, by a "dynamic determination, at all costs, to achieve that personal liberty of belief upon which society must always fall back for its regeneration." What makes this impression counterfactual is the way it covers over the socially collective aspirations of communism, even in its most demiurgic embodiment.[161]

That Williams effectively Americanized Lenin, turning him into a rugged individual or an expression of democratic voluntarism, is not just a willful distortion. It also results from a recognition that the kind of revolution engineered by Lenin would have appealed to an American sensibility in the model that Williams seeks to advocate.

> A labor revolution by a society seeking to be in fact classless is both great and traditionally American in its appeal. Its strength lies today in a continued need for the bare necessities of life by tens of millions of the inhabitants of this wealthy nation as well as the emotional appeal of brute action to all degrees of intelligence which might be involved. To violently affect, by brave stroke, the ejection of an inhuman and anti-social domination by those who have an effective control over the means of our common livelihood for their private gain—would appeal to the American character if once put into motion.[162]

This stance does not make Williams an advocate of communism. To be sure, Williams disapproves of what he calls the "narrowing of the attack to a fanatical and static fixation on a class war," because, in his view, it desires "to suppress all liberty of thought so characteristically American, once power should be assumed."[163] Instead of "class war," Williams advocates the idea of Social Credit, which might offer a remedy to economic ills without the need for dismantling capitalism.

But here and in the poetry, Williams's ideal form of Social Credit seems conspicuously divorced from that idea's historical and economic content. This is, as Jameson avers, what separates Williams from Pound on the question of economics. "Perhaps," says Jameson, "it is this very indeterminability of Williams's economic thoughts as opposed to Pound's only too clear ones that marks a formal advantage," allowing for the totalizing force of political economy without succumbing to overt propaganda.[164] While such a loose mode of economic thinking is open to all manner of ideological currents, including but definitely not limited to those of communism, it is also difficult to pin down any one of its conceptions to a specific ideology, communist or otherwise. This is what we encounter in Book 4's lengthy explorations of Social Credit, which develop a series of positivistic equations analogizing economic reform with the abstract and politically neutral universalisms of nuclear physics. While a page from a Cold War-era article on economics appears to be reproduced in full, claiming that to defeat the USSR "we must reform our finance system," all contextualizing and politically charged details have been excised from it, including the original subheading: "Our Treasury Officials Support A Legally Protected, Dishonest Plan Which Will Accomplish Lenin's Wish to Bankrupt America. There's Still Time to Wreck Lenin's Wish."[165] That is to say, the socialist state and the afterlife of its creator have been actively suppressed from the page, even in quotation. Rather than indicating some muffled sympathy for the USSR, this tactical omission invites speculation on the extent to which the poetry allows for that resonance between the revolutionary traditions of the USA and the USSR, those moments of volition that Williams sensed were distinctly American and simultaneously a defining feature of Lenin and the USSR: a collective enthusiasm for a class war that the poem does not openly or even consciously endorse but which nevertheless infiltrates its sense of economic totality.

Revolutionary Imagination, Part 2: A Great Beast

In Book 1 we are introduced to a malevolent energy that is identified with the history of Paterson:

A history that has, by its den in the
rocks, bole and fangs, its own crane-brake
whence, half hid, canes and stripes
blending, it grins (beauty defied)
not for the sake of the encyclopedia.

Were we near enough its stinking breath
would fell us. The temple upon
the rock is its brother, whose majesty
lies in jungles—made to spring,
at the rifle-shot of learning: to kill

and grind those bones:[166]

This sounds a lot like the revolutionary "thing" we glimpsed at a baseball game many years earlier, which "smiles grimly" from within the multitude. This time, however, it embodies the force and movement of history itself and not just history's agents. That is what gives the prosopopeia its frisson, the forced congruence between the epic's elusive object, "history," and the vitality with which that amorphous object is figured. Williams is drawing on a zoomorphic imagination here to depict the abstract forces of history as a wild animal, a creature that defies the idealism of beauty as well as the categories of the encyclopedia—a moving figure we cannot properly envisage with the description provided. All of which is, of course, congruent with Benjamin's theses on history, with their figuration of the political impulse, both Left and Right, as having "a nose for the topical, no matter where it stirs in the thickets of long ago," always anticipating "the tiger's leap" into the reactionary past or the revolutionary future.[167] Indeed, for Williams, history is what "lies in jungles," ready to attack "at the rifle-shot of learning." This metaphor, likening education to ballistics, creates a scenario hypothetically analogous to that of political activation, in which an exploited class turns against its exploiters, and, as Marx put it, we see "the expropriation of a few usurpers by the mass of the people."[168] Here the wild animal of history responds aggressively to the acquisition of knowledge, with which it becomes the positively murderous, bone-grinding biomass of the revolutionary proletariat.

We soon learn that this creature is indeed the industrial workforce, conceived of not by Marx but, rather, by Alexander Hamilton, the Federalist politician who in the late eighteenth century sought to industrialize the growing township of Paterson.[169] With his first appearance in the poem, he takes inventory of Paterson's population, enumerating its division precisely as though for the above-mentioned encyclopedia: "From the ten houses Hamilton saw when he looked (at the falls!) and kept his counsel, by the middle of the century—the mills had drawn a heterogeneous population. There were in 1870, native born 20,711, which would of course include children of foreign parents; foreign 12,868 of whom 137 were French, 1,420 German, 3,343 English—(Mr. Lambert who later built the Castle among them), 5,124 Irish, 879 Scotch, 1,360 Hollanders and 170 Swiss—." What reads like politically abstract, encyclopedic enumeration is the material of an economic vision, which will integrate a "heterogeneous population" into the mechanisms of capital before transforming that population into the working-class masses among whom Dr. Paterson walks in the park. "Even during the Revolution Hamilton had been impressed by the site of the Great

Falls of the Passaic," we are told. "His fertile imagination envisioned a great manufacturing center, a great Federal City, to supply the needs of the country. Here was water-power to turn the mill wheels and the navigable river to carry manufactured goods to the market centers: a national manufactury."[170] Central to Hamilton's thought was an understanding that "the rich seek social stability to preserve their advantages, but the poor work for social change that would bring them a larger share of the world's rewards."[171] On that score, Hamilton was deathly afraid of the poor, whom he famously likened to "a great beast," coining the Benjaminian metaphor that Williams repeats and that likely informed his animate figure of history.

In its first iteration in the poem, the metaphor of "a great beast" refers to a rioting crowd from 1880, "numbered some ten thousand," which destroys the property of a homicidal landowner, William Dalzell. From this first mention we know that the "great beast" is capable of tremendous collective violence—or, more specifically, a kind of insurrectionary justice. "Immediately after the shot," we are told, "the quiet group of singers was turned into an infuriated mob who would take Dalzell into their own hands. The mob then proceeded to burn the barn into which Dalzell had retreated from the angry group."[172] The second and third iterations of the "great beast" bookend the poem's lengthy account of a Sunday spent in the park, when Dr. Paterson strolls among the working class enjoying its designated respite from exploitation. "Their Sunday relaxation," writes James E. Miller Jr., "suggests the nature of the other days of their lives—days in the factories and business of Paterson earning the money for survival."[173] Indeed, we see those other days written legibly onto their bodies, which Williams engages along gender lines, voyeuristically aestheticizing the feminine: "the ugly legs of the young girls, / pistons too powerful for delicacy! / the men's arms, red, used to heat and cold, / to toss quartered beeves."[174] Though this image arguably recalls the cinema of another Soviet director, Dziga Vertov, who frequently engineered visual links between mechanical parts and human limbs, where communism sediments here is in the revolutionary undercurrent that subtends description. These arms and legs might be ugly and indelicate but, because of their use in physical labor, they are also powerful. As a result of those six days of labor, the girls now have the impossible strength of large-scale industry, their limbs having become mechanical "pistons," and the men's arms have likewise taken on the same "red" color of the massive chunks of animal flesh, the "quartered beeves," that they toss. As working organs of the great beast, these bodies and the subjects to whom they belong are collectively powerful. All that lacks is the "the rifle-shot of learning," the catalytic force of imagination that would transform these young girls and these working men into a revolutionary army.

Even though *Paterson* is punctuated by riots, mob violence, and what might be thought of as the upsurge of revolutionary energy or as the expression of an incipient class war, this modern epic has indeed moved away from any more detailed engagement with the socialist state as we saw it in the earlier poems. In a letter from 1947, written just after he had completed Book 2, Williams confirms that in *Paterson* "the social unrest that occasions all strikes is strong," but in the same letter he concedes that he has consciously omitted communist language and implies that the object of revolutionary praxis is alive and well but speaking sub rosa: "In Part of Book II, soon to appear (this fall, I think), there will be much more in the same manner, that is, much more relating to the economic distress occasioned by human greed and blindness—aided, as always, by the church, all churches in the broadest sense of that designation—but still, there will be little treating directly of the rise of labor as a named force. I am not a Marxian."[175] Williams might not identify with Marx, but despite shifting a field of reference from the USSR back to the USA, the poetry has nevertheless retained the forms and structures that took shape in relation to communism. And, when the "great beast" leaves the park, "before the plunging night," the absence of this discourse is noted, elevating communism to the level of supplement precisely in its verbal preterition: "Missing was the thing Jim had found in Marx and Veblen and Adam Smith and Darwin—the dignified sound of a great, calm bell tolling the morning of a new age."[176] What follows immediately after this sentence is the poem's anguished attempt to rethink the formal strategies with which "to unslave the mind," and it does so in language that echoes Marx in his hortatory, rhetorical mode—the mode of commonly anthologized excerpts of his writing, those Williams is most likely to have been read. Here is an example of that language, which we can easily imagine would have appealed to Williams: "Along with the constantly diminishing number of the magnates of capital, who usurp and monopolize all advantages of this process of transformation, grows the mass of misery, oppression, slavery, degradation, exploitation; but with this too grows the revolt of the working class, a class always increasing in numbers, and disciplined, united, organized by the very mechanism of the process of capitalist production itself."[177] While this rhetoric is eminently quotable and quite clearly bears a propagandistic overtone, it nevertheless derives from and appears within Marx's critique of political economy, the totalizing ambitions of which have been approximated in Williams's handling of the epic. In a remarkably similar register to Marx, Williams proceeds to claim a desire to "accomplish the inevitable," addressing that task to none other than the beneficiaries of communism: the "poor, the indivisible, thrashing, breeding," the working men and women tossed upon their "debased city."[178] Even if Williams fully believed democracy to be the political paradigm in which a nativist vision might be worked out, in this moment of self-definition, and perhaps even unconsciously, the poem reaches for the communism that its hierarchy of reference tries to deemphasize.

4 Louis Zukofsky

Cosmic Communism, Cybernetic Socialism

Tell Me, Mother Russia

Vladimir Lenin never completed his theoretical masterpiece, *The State and Revolution.* Written in hiding and only published after the Bolsheviks seized power, this book was intended to arm socialists with the conceptual means to act effectively in revolutionary situations. Its content was assembled in response to one specific imperative: "explaining to the masses what they will have to do to emancipate themselves from the yoke of capitalism in the very near future."[1] The published explanation contains Lenin's theories on statecraft, a detailed conceptualization of the dictatorship of the proletariat, multiple critiques of social democracy, and historical sketches of the French Revolution and the Paris Commune, as well as responses to the thinking of Karl Marx, Friedrich Engels, Georgi Plekhanov, and Karl Kautsky. What remained incomplete was an account of the book's own revolutionary situation, the political and economic circumstances of nineteenth- and twentieth-century Russia. It remained incomplete precisely because that situation erupted into full-scale revolution, drawing Lenin away from his writing and into the lived actuality of politics. As the postscript to the book's first edition explains,

> This pamphlet was written in August and September 1917. I had already drawn up the plan for the next, the seventh chapter, "The Experience of the Russian Revolutions of 1905 and 1917." But except for the title, however, I was unable to write a single line of the chapter; I was "interrupted" by the political crisis—the eve of the October Revolution of 1917. Such an "interruption" can only be welcomed; but the writing of the second part of this pamphlet ("The Experience of the Russian Revolutions of 1905 and 1917") will probably have to be put off for a

> long time. It is more pleasant and useful to go through the "experience of the revolution" than to write about it.[2]

For Louis Zukofsky, this final axiom would be reframed one decade later as a measure for poetic value: "a 'poet,'" he wrote in 1927, "who is not conscious of Lenin's statement that it is better to have lived thru a revolution than to write about it is not worth his salt."[3] Endorsement of this sanction may well sound peculiar given that, from the perspective of the balance of political forces in the United States, the barest possibility of Zukofsky, who was anything but an activist, living through revolution seemed altogether unlikely. This disjuncture has not passed unnoticed. In Mark Scroggins's assessment, "Zukofsky's career as a fellow traveler, and the degree to which his very serious leftist commitments influenced the theories of poetics he propounded in the early thirties, represent an early and important instance of an American poet trying to come to grips with the tension between the political and literary spheres."[4] As we shall see, the assimilation of Lenin's postscript into Zukofsky's modern epic is a specific manifestation of that tension.

The problem of authorial experience in times of political upheaval is a staple of bourgeois aesthetics, reaching something like its apogee with the Lake Poets and their felt distance from French Revolution, but for Zukofsky the problem is more about the substance of history than it is about literary authority, and in his case it is also peculiar to the utopian aspirations of communism. Zukofsky's poetry of the late 1920s and the 1930s struggled to see any way of realizing Soviet-style socialism in the United States, even while the Popular Front kept the idea of communism alive as a real social force. In contrast to Ezra Pound and William Carlos Williams, who both drew aesthetic energies and formal inspiration from the Russian Revolution before witnessing the collapse of its legacy into Stalinism, Zukofsky was forced from the start into a different kind of distillation. He was obliged to extract lessons from socialism's utopian potential, its communist immanence, while knowing perfectly well there was no possibility of correlation between the USSR and the most advanced industrial economy on earth, that of the United States. While neither Pound nor Williams believed Soviet-style communism to be a solution to economic problems in the United States, their engagements with communism began in much closer historical proximity to the Russian Revolution, and so they encountered communism at its most internationally promising moment. Zukofsky, a significantly younger writer, viewed communism as a desirable alternative to capitalism, but his was a communism postdating the first waves of revolutionary internationalism that had captured the attention and imagination of his poetic forebears. Part of the difference between Zukofsky and the other two poets, then, derives from the belatedness of his arrival to modernism; he started writing poems several years after the energies of 1917 had already settled into the machinations of a distant, socialist state.[5] But the distillation is felt all the more poignantly in Zukofsky's verse than in the verse of Pound and Williams precisely because, unlike the other two poets, he identified positively as a communist.

There are a number of reasons that help us account for Zukofsky's profound and positive investment in communism. Some of them are biographical. Having been raised by Russian peasants turned working-class Americans who only immigrated to Manhattan in the 1890s, Zukofsky must have embraced the Russian Revolution at a more affecting, personal level than did those multigenerational US natives who preceded him in modernism. Written in 1926 and published in 1928, Zukofsky's first significant work, "Poem beginning 'The,'" includes an early indication of communism's affective gravity and how it would influence Zukofsky's handling of the modern epic. Here communism intercedes through the maternal lineage:

195 Speaking about epics, mother,—
196 Down here among the gastanks, ruts,
cemetery-tenements—
197 It is your Russia that is free.
198 And I here, can I say only—
199 "So that an egoist can never embrace
a party
200 Or take up with a party?
201 Oh, yes, only he cannot let himself
202 Be embraced or taken up by the party."
203 It is your Russia that is free, mother.
204 Tell me, mother.[6]

The "epic" takes hold between two politically antithetical space-times distilled into one setting by the silent figure of the speaker's mother. The "gastanks, ruts," and "cemetery-tenements" of Manhattan amalgamate into a vision of capitalist poverty to be contrasted with her "Russia," that place of familial origins, which is now "free." The words between quotation marks are adapted from Max Stirner, and, within this context, their original advocacy of an individualist anarchism reads as refusal to align with the specific "party" that had lately liberated Russia and which the poem's Eliotic reference list will punctually confirm is "The Bolsheviki."[7] As might be suggested by this quotation, the means by which Zukofsky will construct his own epic is going to be a version of Pound's method, "including history" through the combination of multiple textual documents. Zukofsky identified this technique as fundamental to poetic modernism. "The immediacy of Pound's epic matter," he writes, and that matter's transcription as verse, are "as much a fact as those facts which historians have labeled and dissociated."[8] Under Zukofsky's hand, the methodological combination of historical sources into relationships denied by historicist dissociation is used willfully to develop associative resonances between modernist writing in the United States and the history and ideas of communism, especially as they pertain to Russia. The internalization of Lenin's statement, about writing and the experience of revolution, injects that technique with what this chapter describes as its utopian impulse, a desire to "live through" the kind of revolution to which the poem's documents attest. That impulse further illuminates the Russian freedom Zukofsky was asking his mother about from an experientially insurmountable distance.

The argument for this chapter is that Zukofsky's poetry was committed to the specifically utopian dimensions of communism, which guided him to make use of forms that might lay claim to an unknown and unknowable future. His aesthetic armature, argues Norman Finkelstein, operates through an array of "utopian tropes for a poetry capable of reconciling the immediate particulars of the world as given with 'the will to change' or historical process."[9] While it will be shown that the particularity of these forms is largely motivated by the perceived utopianism in Russian socialism, those forms only engage the socialist state on their own terms, approaching it as an object lesson in the aspiration toward utopia but not as the completed attainment. That difference, once again between socialism and communism, is crucial for Zukofsky. It underpins the aesthetic ideology of his poetry, which consistently distinguishes between the historical actualities of capitalism and socialism, and the unrealized potential for communism. "Every concept he deploys," claims Luke Carson, "is split into its ideological presentation and its utopian promise."[10] Indeed, Zukofsky's utopianism is especially potent because it is forced into being from the realm of inescapable subsumption—from what Finkelstein describes as "an America in which capitalism has left no sphere of human activity free of its homogenizing ideologies of imperialism and consumerism."[11] Here we are interested in how some of

Zukofsky's aesthetic achievements result from the poetry's identification with a communism that, from the historical and social situation in which he was writing, seemed structurally impossible. For that reason, we situate Zukofsky's utopianism within his observation of the USSR through a gathering of tropes that might cohere as science fiction, a genre which, in Fredric Jameson's words, is concerned with "affirming as it does that even our wildest imaginings are all collages of experience, constructs made up of bits and pieces of the here and now."[12] Two distinct layers of the poetry's utopianism are treated here. While the chapter's first half is interested in what might function as an affective catalyst for social transformation, mobilizing a deeply felt and profoundly animate desire for the inauguration of a new social reality, its second half accounts for the poetry's utopian program, the systematic means by which utopia can be forecast from "the here and now." The chapter thus modulates between two kinds of science fiction in correspondence to that distinction: first, utopia as the destination of an extraterrestrial voyage and, second, utopia as the concrete result of earthbound cybernetics.

Interstellar Futures

In Lenin's first appearance in *"A"*, from its sixth part, he voices the now-familiar axiom about experience and revolution. What then follows is a good indication of how the poem will rise to the challenge set by its inclusion of these words:

> "It is more pleasant and more useful,"
> Said Vladimir Ilytch,
> "To live thru the experience
> Of a revolution
> Than to write about it."
>
> The women held the world cornice,
> The Red Army was buttressed by women.
>
> The star, Venus, bathed
> In the sunsets
> of elegant, imperial islands—
> Mr.—'we own your, this government
> benefits by our protection. . .'—
> And in Haiti
> Mars

Bloody
Tinkered with the other
Stars.[13]

The lines after Lenin's pronouncement invest in an aesthetic form through which poetic consciousness apprehends its revolutionary referent, while nonetheless conceding experiential distance from it. There is an argument to be made that Zukofsky is witnessing 1917 through Sergei Eisenstein's monumental restaging of the October Revolution, in which the women on the roof of the Winter Palace attain a similar architectural magnitude as this. But what these lines have that Eisenstein's film does not is a properly cosmic sensibility. The architectural metaphors ("cornice" and "buttress") used to describe the strength of the socialist women are also applied to the "world," announcing that their revolution conceived of itself as inaugurating political reconstruction on a planetary scale. This is how Lenin described the significance of women to communism and the significance of communism to women: "Many of them work day and night in the Party or among the masses of the proletariat, the peasants, the Red Army. That is of very great value to us. It is also important for women all over the world."[14] Or, consider the heroic words of Alexandra Kollontai, Lenin's mainline to Russia before the Revolution: "Without the participation of women, the October Revolution could not have brought the Red Flag to victory. Glory to the working women who marched under that Red Banner during the October Revolution. Glory to the October Revolution that liberated women!"[15] In Zukofsky's unrhymed couplet, revolution is elevated to a worldwide undertaking that begins and ends with women; indeed, their participation offers a more concrete, historical reason why Zukofsky related Russia's freedom to his mother and not his father.

The following lines transport those women and their political program from the terrestrial world to an extraterrestrial constellation. "The star, Venus," is a mythological and astrological symbol of the feminine, and, simultaneously, it serves as an astronomical and interstellar metaphor. After the sun and moon, Venus is the brightest celestial object, and it frequently appears during twilight as the evening or morning star, scintillating not when the sun has already set on those "elegant, imperial islands" but in moments of transition between day and night. Yet, while Venus is rising in the East, Mars remains visible in the West. Contemporaneous with the Russian Revolution was the American marines' occupation of Haiti, where they engaged the national rebels in bloody conflict, ultimately reestablishing imperial rule on that island.[16] Here, the Red Army's women are collectively portrayed in the figure of "Venus," the American marines are "Mars / Bloody," and their contested territories are "the other Stars." The cumulative effect of these figures is the reimagining of political history—specifically, of socialist revolution in Russia and of capitalist counterrevolution in Haiti—with reference to astrological and astronomical events. Historical particulars and phenomenal contingencies are supplanted by a vision of celestial boundlessness. Following hard on the quoted injunction from Lenin, these lines project revolution into a cosmic realm that, while distant from earthbound experience, has always been used to orient or guide human activity, through navigation, mythmaking, and so on. This kind of thinking, for Georg Lukács, is emblematic of both epic literary production and utopian joy. "Happy," he reflects, "are those ages when the starry sky is the map of all possible paths—ages whose paths are illuminated by the light of the stars."[17] Zukofsky's comparison of socialism and the cosmos is, in that sense, a generic expression of the modern epic's commitment to an exclusively utopian modality of communism.

The first time Zukofsky wrote about Lenin was in 1925, one year after his death and four years before the first part of *"A"* was published. Composed as an elegy, "Constellation: In Memory of V. I. Ulianov" is one of the earliest instances in which Zukofsky's verse articulates political commitment through astronomical operations, but it is not the first. It recaptures and amplifies the effect of "Sun, you great Sun, our Comrade," a line from "Poem beginning 'The,'" which, according to the reference list, is the poem's second reference to "The Bolsheviki."[18] The elegy opens with one long sentence, broken up into semiautonomous units and sequenced into a whole by punctuation marks that conjoin semicolons and dashes.

Immemorial,
And after us
Immemorial,
O white
O orbit-trembling,
Star, thru all the leaves
Of elm;—
Lighted-one, beyond the trunk tip
Of the elm
High, proportionately vast,

Of mist and form;—
Star, of all live processes
Continual it seems to us,
Like elm leaves,
Lighted in your glow;—
We thrive in strange hegira
Here below,
Yet sometimes in our flight alone
We speak to you,
When nothing that was ours seems spent
And life consuming us seems permanent,
And flight of stirring beating up the night
And down and up; we do not sink with every wave.[19]

Scroggins is surely correct to identify this as "one of Zukofsky's less compelling early voices."[20] Indeed, these lines are formally regressive in their undeniable pastiche of a distinctly Tennysonian lyricism, which also entailed achingly sentimental expressions of grief, a pronounced affection for assonance, and an emphasis on arboreal perception. "The moan of doves," writes Tennyson, "in immemorial elms."[21] However, Zukofsky's cosmic imagery prefigures the aesthetic we have already encountered in the maturing verse of *"A"*, and for that reason we might want to speculate on how it breaks from the sentimental nostalgia of Victorian poetics to approach something more decisively modern. Analogous to the women's Red Army and its portrayal as Venus, Lenin is figured as an orbiting "star," set in the heavens to guide a migratory "us," an indeterminate yet pronominally collective subjectivity occupied in "strange hegira." Coupled with the fact that the star is white as opposed to red, all of this imagery makes it seem we are gazing upon an actual star and not just a political or poetic symbol. The shift to a cosmic frame of reference here more than canonizes Lenin as a communist saint. It also reframes global history: like looking through the wrong end of the telescope, it asks us to consider as shibboleths all our frozen conceptions of what is materially possible. As Ruth Jennison proposes, for Zukofsky the Russian Revolution established "a differently centered globe in which core nations might be viewed in parallax from the position of counterhegemonic peripheral regions," thus illuminating "an American political life whose claims to the unmediated liberal principles of evenly developing equalities and freedoms were experiencing a Depression-era crisis of legitimacy."[22]

This star, despite its actuality, is nevertheless portrayed as an indeterminate image. The adjectives "high" and "vast" imply that its luminosity is observed only from a distance and from below. The nouns "mist" and "form" are almost oxymoronic, insofar as "form" denotes visible appearance, whereas "mist" confounds vision and occludes visibility. Though we are certainly looking at a star, we nonetheless struggle to see it with any objective clarity.

The indeterminate descriptors that attend Lenin's star acquire definite political meaning when compared to the collective subjectivity in the subsequent lines:

Travels our consciousness
Deep in its egress.
Eclipsed the earth, for earth is power
And we of earth.
Eclipsed our death, for death is power
And we of death.
Single we are, tho others still may be with us
And we for others.[23]

These short, two-line, end-stopped sentences are formally distinct from the sprawling twenty-three-line sentence preceding them. Simultaneously "immemorial" and "after us," Lenin's star is not bound by the "consciousness" within which the speaker claims to be "alone." The difference in syntactic length and the shift to regulated punctuation reflect this opposition between the celestial and the earthbound by shifting to a substantially more regulated prosody for the latter, similar to what we encountered with Williams's restrained free verse. Assuming "our consciousness" is grammatically the object in all four sentences, the description of its starlit "egress" might not be as earthbound as the earlier "here below" implied. When the speaker's consciousness is given to "eclipse" the limits of both "earth" and "death," it does so in ascent to a structurally communist subjectivity: "Single we are . . . And we for others" is both conceptually and rhetorically reminiscent of "from each according to his ability, to each according to his need," an axiomatic definition of communism we encounter elsewhere in Zukofsky's verse. It would seem that the poem's "flight" wants to be taken literally. The experiential passage to revolutionary consciousness is, for this poem, the experience of leaving earth and approaching a new cosmic entity.

This interpretation accords with Williams's reaction to these lines. "You are wrestling with the antagonist under newer rules," he wrote to the younger poet: "But I can't see 'all live processes' 'orbit-trembling' 'our consciousness' 'the sources of being'—What the hell? I'm not finding fault I'm just trying to nail what troubles me."[24] Of course, Williams "can't see" the poem's radiant objects, precisely because its interplanetary destination is not a place but a series of negative echolocations. "It may be," Williams signs off, "that I am to [*sic*] literal in my search for objective clarities of image." But this poem does not just neglect objective clarity. It seems aggressively opposed, in its deepest structural impulses, to anything of the sort. Even though, in this instance, the form is unable to fully extract itself from the tradition of elegiac verse, it nonetheless initiates Zukofsky's mission to generate what he called "the revolutionary word," a formal answer to the problem of political inexperience when looking to the distant USSR, as well as a means of capturing communism's utopian impulse.[25] There are two dimensions of this aesthetic that require individual interpretation so as to fully apprehend its historical location and political coordination. The first dimension is the irreducible negativity, the fact that this poem's forms are resistant to the ontologically positive content of historical particulars. The second dimension is the projection of the resulting negativity away from earth and onto the stars.

The Promise and the Problem of Utopia

To write about revolution without having lived through it is to be confronted with a unique kind of abstraction: "for the more surely a given Utopia asserts its radical difference from what currently is, to that very degree it becomes, not merely unrealizable but, what is worse, unimaginable."[26] Belonging to Jameson, this formulation provides a deft theorization of what Williams characterized as Zukofsky's "wrestling with the antagonist under newer rules." From the standpoint of capitalism, and when lacking any sort of meaningful revolutionary praxis, utopia does not mean bourgeois fulfillment or any sort of luxurious idyll. Rather, utopia in this sense means determinate negation without knowable criteria: it is what comes after the alleviation of exploitation and suffering—an antipode approached only by way of abolition. This is what Marx and Engels mean when they define communism as the movement that "abolishes the present state of things," a notion that is readily legible in the poetry. In Zukofsky's elegy, for instance, the titular nomination of Lenin invites poetic form to respond to a projected version of utopia from the site of "what currently is" or "the present state of things." The poem's structural negation of recognizable content, as well as Williams's inability to "see" and appreciate its images, together stand revealed as an expression of the same historical reality. This technical decision to obscure is thus indicative of a conscious inability to imagine utopia. "Art," writes Theodor Adorno in a formulation even more stringent than that of Jameson, "is no more able than theory to concretize Utopia, not even negatively. A cryptogram of the new is the image of collapse; only by virtue of the absolute negativity of collapse does art enunciate the unspeakable: Utopia."[27] Even if Zukofsky believes that utopia has begun localizing itself on Russian soil, there remains a sense that any attempt to define utopia from within the United States will only impose upon it forms created by and for the social world of capitalism.

Lenin was all too aware of utopia's challenge to consciousness, that it resists positive content. For instance, in a late interview, Lenin responded to positive descriptions of his political persona by denying a comparison between his legendary capacities for speaking publically and the prose of Leo Tolstoy. "Like him," the interviewer suggests, "you have the broad, unified, firm line, the sense of inexorable truth."[28] Lenin's response to this compliment is redacted into verse, in the eighth part of *"A."*

I thought of workers and peasants;
It's good nobody hears
Your national, psychological hypothesis
Or someone might say
"The old man is flattered by country."[29]

The first line refers to the fact that, when Lenin initially "became a speaker," he drew courage by thinking generically "of workers and peasants" rather than of his immediate audience. This tactic suggests Lenin's disarticulation from the psychical energies of his local situation in order to engage something bigger, more abstract, even planetary. For Lenin, communist rhetoric is not just about the immediate situation of its delivery but also about workers and peasants everywhere, addressed as an international commonality. Communism, from this perspective, cannot be limited to one country; to believe that it could be nationalized, as Stalin did, is to abandon truly utopian desire and embrace parochial flattery. Lenin's reaction against psychoanalysis is also recorded here. As he wrote to Maxim Gorky in 1908 and in a letter which also appears in *"A"*, "Our empirio-critics, empirio-monists, and empirio-symbolists are floundering in a bog," insofar as they have been willing to (in Zukofsky's version) "drink the stinking source of some French 'positivists.'"[30] Empiricism is similarly reductive, imposing unwonted constraints upon revolutionary aspiration, and for that reason the "psychological" is just as untenable as the "national." The lesson here is that the principal subject of the Russian Revolution actively resisted established hermeneutics, the theories of which flourish, says Lenin, "in the dirty soil of society."[31] That communist utopianism presents a challenge to positive representation and that the revolution's chief architect and living embodiment held to the same thought helps to explain the abstraction of Zukofsky's verse. And yet, there has to be a way to focus historical particulars, be they geopolitical or psychological, through a lens crafted by this utopian imagination, and of using that lens to project the bare lineaments of a new world. That is to say, desire needs an object, even if inaccessible. This new world, the object of utopian desire, is what we discover in the generic organization of Lenin's elegy and of his first appearance in *"A"*, both of which conceive of revolution in relation to extraterrestrial and otherworldly phenomena.

Utopian Stargazing

"Felt deeply," Zukofsky would exclaim in one of his privileged form's most dazzling affirmations, "poems like all things have the possibilities of elements whose isotopes are yet to be found. Light has travelled and so looked forward. How do we know?" he asks. "We look at the stars and because the light from them has travelled we see them shining tonight into tomorrow."[32] And yet, star imagery is itself highly traditional, with celestial and intergalactic visualization proliferating in verse by Sir Philip Sidney, William Shakespeare, John Milton, William Blake, William Wordsworth, Percy Bysshe Shelley, and John Keats, not to mention the preponderance of stars in T. S. Eliot's late turn to a vast, interstellar darkness. Nevertheless, for all of these poets, stars also encoded a distinct sense of longing: they appear in poems either as impossible objects of desire ("Astrophil and Stella," "To the Evening Star," "Bright Star") or as navigation points from which to draw guidance (Sonnet 116, "Throw of the Dice," "The Hollow Men"). To repurpose literary stargazing in order to write a political and historical poem is to therefore formalize a utopian longing, the desire for another world, by gesturing at objects that are irreconcilable with earthbound experience but might nonetheless direct the trajectories of earth's inhabitants. Perhaps that is why this mode of figuration has such a rich history within communist thought. For Louis Auguste Blanqui, writing in the final days of the Paris Commune and immediately before the Communards' liquidation, the stars provided an analogue for earthbound politics and the apparent foreclosure of utopian possibility.

He believed that "the entire life of our planet, from birth until death, is being minutely detailed day by day on myriads of brother-stars."[33] Walter Benjamin developed his understanding of the constellation from Blanqui, among others, using it to account for the relationship between disparate historical events and, in particular, between multiple revolutions. In Benjamin's view, Blanqui's eventual resignation to the revolution's defeat—written from a cell in the Fort de Taureau—is the moment at which he is finally "brought to his knees with such force that the throne begins to totter," precisely because that society's attack on any utopian thought appeared then and there to circumscribe all history and to deny all possible histories opposed to that of capitalist modernity. And this, for Benjamin, is why Charles Baudelaire excluded stars from his poetry; the utopian otherness expressed in the firmament is literally and figuratively invisible from the city. "In any case," he argues, "the artificial lighting does away with all transition to night. The same state of affairs is responsible for the fact that the stars disappear from the sky over the metropolis."[34]

Similar imagery is taken up in political discourse from the USSR. It was in the period immediately before the Russian Revolution that utopian science fiction began to merge with political reality. Osip Mandelstam viewed the newly founded socialist state as a properly astronomical event, doing so from a poem written in and about Petrograd just months after the Russian Revolution.

> A wandering fire at a terrible height—
> can it be a star shining like that?
> Transparent star, wandering fire,
> your brother, Petropolis, is dying.
>
> The dreams of earth blaze at a terrible height,
> a green star is burning.
> O if you are a star, this brother of water and sky,
> your brother, Petropolis, is dying.[35]

To imagine revolution as igniting the firmament only makes good on what politics had already taken from literature. Lenin named his pamphlet of 1902 after Nikolai Chernyshevky's utopian novel of 1863, *What Is to Be Done?*, the narrative of which provided an early conceptualization of political commitment for Russia's socialist underground. One of Lenin's political adversaries, Alexander Bogdanov, famously composed the novel *Red Star,* which tells the story of a scientist-revolutionary who travels to Mars so as to experience the Martian version of socialism. The thematic of intergalactic socialism was carried into the visual arts, usually motivated by the Soviet cosmologist, Konstantin Tsiolkovsky. Lenin himself explained a utopian ambition to H. G. Wells in 1920: "Human ideas—he told Wells—are based on the scale of the planet we live in. They are based on the assumption that the technical potentialities, as they develop, will never overstep the 'earthly limit.'" According to Lenin, interplanetary discovery would provide the solution to material scarcity, one of the core premises for capitalism (and precisely the kind of thing Lenin was raging against with his attack on empiricism). "If we succeed in making contact with other planets, all our philosophical, social and moral ideas will have to be revised," he claimed, "and in this event these potentialities will become limitless and will put an end to violence as a necessary means of progress."[36] The combination of these poetic and political traditions is what takes place in Zukofsky's elegy to Lenin: a collectivized subjectivity "oversteps" its "earthly limit," and by doing so it transcends the material bounds of a philosophical, social, and moral earth-being.

Zukofsky was not alone in this endeavor, as other modernist poets were similarly utilizing star imagery to think about revolutionary history. Joseph MacLeod's *Ecliptic,* published in 1930, is a useful point of contrast for Zukofsky's interstellar aesthetic. This densely symbolic sequence of poems uses the zodiac to determine its perspective on the first decades of the twentieth century, including several opaque intimations of historical totality. Here, for instance, are the opening lines of Gemini, which figure historical transformation under the sign of that constellation and its mythic cognate, the twinned Dioscuri:

Flow full, Eurôtas river, we hymn Castor dead.
Flow from your fond Borêan watershed
Alone to wide ship-bare Laconian bight.
You almost are Arcadian, sprang to light
A few miles from that Paradisal border,
Mapped out for all eternity, by order
Of a moment: yes eternally removed
From such a country as you might have grooved
Luxuriantly. But languish not to alter,
Where to fantasticise would be to falter,
To falter weakly, unachieving change.

Flow full through the commercial countries strange
And hostile, which your tributaries shred;
Flow full, Eurôtas river, we hymn Castor dead.[37]

While Zukofsky certainly knew of this poem, and while its sense of hard-won "change" outflowing from an unnamed paradise into "the commercial countries" would have appealed, its symbolic structure is something he consciously set out to avoid. In a letter to Pound—who served as an advocate for MacLeod—Zukofsky claimed to appreciate the versification but to have been less convinced by the interpolation within the zodiac.[38] Unlike MacLeod, Zukofsky addresses history not only by way of astral symbolism but also with a sense of interplanetary wonderment, in which the stars are real stars just as much as they are symbols or structures. Much closer to Zukofsky, then, this wonderment is what we also encounter in the fourth and final section of "Jerusalem the Golden," by Charles Reznikoff, which Zukofsky published through the Objectivist Press in 1934. The poem's third section depicts a pantheistic god as an otherworldly and abstract entity: "He is the stars, / multitudinous as the drops of rain."[39] Then the following section repurposes that imagery to introduce a rhapsodic prophecy of the communist utopia, whose subtitle indicates its dedication to Marx.

We shall arise while the stars are still shining,
while the street-lights burn brightly in the dawn,
to begin the work we delight in,
and no one shall tell us, Go,
you must go now
to the shop or office you work in
to waste your life for your living.
There shall be no more war, no more hatred;
none of us shall die of sickness;
there shall be bread and no one hunger for bread—
and fruit better than any a wild tree grew.
Wheels of steel and pistons of steel
shall fetch us water and hew us wood;
we shall call nothing mine—nothing for ourselves only.
Proclaim to the seed of man
throughout the length and breadth of the continents,
From each according to his strength,
to each according to his need.[40]

These lines produce their paradisiacal forecast in the model of Gonzalo's utopian speech: work is delightful, machines oblige humans, there is no private property, and the relations of production culminate in Marx's axiomatic and aphoristic definition of communist sociality. The presentation of that sociality is, strictly speaking, utopian. Note the abundance of negative propositions: "no one shall tell us," "no more war, no more hatred," "none of us shall die of sickness," "no one hunger." While the poem is deeply invested in the negation of capitalism, its positive content is only conceived of within a properly utopian state, as the antipodean other to the way things are. The first line's modal verb, "shall," is wagered on the temporal conjunction "while," whose repetition implies the necessary simultaneity of two clauses: "the stars are still shining" and "the street-lights burn brightly in the dawn." In order for the poem's collective subjectivity, its "we," to "arise" and inhabit the new world of communism, the stars and the streetlights must be visible together and at once. This is (to recall Benjamin's reading of Baudelaire, for whom "the big city knows no true evening twilight") a material impossibility and the reason why metropolitan poetry is denied access to a certain type of utopian presentation, because it cannot perceive beyond the experiential space of capitalism and that mode of production's illuminating technologies. In this poem, grammar equates communism with the stars' impossible luminescence, and the form seems to know as much, given how a desire to dim the lights of capitalism is felt just as powerfully as a will to affirm Marx's words.

Adams and Adams: American Antecedents

Arranging these different versions of utopian stargazing into a functioning optic, through which the world might be thought anew, the most important of Zukofsky's intertextual fields for this aesthetic are the writings of Henry and John Quincy Adams. It is widely known that Zukofsky composed his graduate thesis on Henry Adams and that Adams's grandfather, John Quincy, served as the first US ambassador to Russia. "The man who taught me most about history," Zukofsky once claimed, "was Henry Adams."[41] Here I want to argue that Henry and John Quincy Adams served as a screen through which the USA could appreciate the USSR, a uniquely American optic for telescoping the socialist navigation points that, without this mediation, might have been imperceptible through the glare of capitalism's reactive ideology. The younger Adams's hermeneutic lends itself to the presentation of utopia as we have encountered it so far, as an alien phenomenon potentially taking root on a new planet. His writing frequently engaged in acts of historical estrangement, transforming realities into forms that begin to seem otherworldly. In Jennison's summary of what Zukofsky learned from Adams, "facts must be falsified—made strange, in the Brechtian sense—in order that their structuring conditions—or truths—can be made visible. In other words, facts can no longer signify belligerently; they must assume a difficult concord with the more capacious 'honesties' of larger historical context."[42] This presentational strategy, a different version of the documentary method that we saw Pound develop through reading and rewriting Malatesta, allows for the inclusion of an absolutist prehistory to Russia's revolutionary present, where that "larger historical context" is shown to cast off the unsuspected sparks of revolutionary ignition.

The pertinent encounters with Henry and John Quincy Adams begin with a reference to the senior's famous description of stargazing as an almost miraculous encounter with the "light-houses of the skies."[43] Here the phrase is used to introduce the diplomat's account of an observatory in Cincinnati, which he visited in 1843:

> "Light-houses of the skies," John Quincy Adams . .
> something
> Of awful enjoyment . . observing the rising and
> setting of the sun . . that
> Perpetual revolution of the Great and Little Bear
> round the pole;
> Orion from . . horizontal . . to . . perpendicular . .
> Of sorrow in reflecting how little we can ever know
> of it . . of
> Almost desponding hope that we may know more
> of it . .
>
> As cold as Nova Zembla.
> In the morning awakened by the hail—the
> Train frozen to the rails
> Could not be broken free for an hour.
> I felt as if I were incrusted in a bed of snow.[44]

These lines are thick with allusion. For John Quincy Adams, celestial observation meant the experience of sublime divinity. "To me," he writes in the text from which this material derives, "the observation of the sun, moon, and stars has been for a great portion of my life a pleasure of gratified curiosity, of ever returning wonder, and of reverence for the Creator and mover of these unnumbered worlds."[45] Sublime experience is nominated by "awful enjoyment," which in the context of modernist verse cannot help but allude to W. B. Yeats's "terrible beauty," a phrase coined in response to another political insurrection.[46] And, while this episode might also be a variation of Mallarmé's celebrated constellation, whose stars comprise Ursa Major and Ursa Minor, which Zukofsky rename "the Great and Little Bear," its reappearance in these lines observes that constellation before a distinctly revolutionary horizon.[47] Carson has argued this point convincingly. "The citations," he says, "are made to echo with the citations concerning the revolution of the great Russian bear, and therefore also the place of 'awful enjoyment' in historical revolutions."[48] The bear is, of course, the national symbol of Russian federation, but, more importantly, the stars' motility in "perpetual revolution" echoes the communist formulation of "permanent revolution," a concept popularized by Leon Trotsky, who used it for the title of a book published in 1929. According to Trotsky's version of the theory, the logic of "permanent revolution" explained how socialism could take place in anachronistic societies, like Russia, that had not already achieved the preconditions of advanced capitalism. Trotsky's theory argues, first, that the bourgeoisie in underdeveloped capitalist countries is incapable of developing the productive forces that ought to generate an industrial proletariat and, second, that the proletariat in those countries must therefore seize social, economic, and political power, leading an alliance with the peasantry. "Russian Marxism," he writes, "can justly be proud of having alone explained the direction of this development and foretold its general forms."[49] From the standpoint of the United States, as with the view from Cincinnati upward and upon the stars, this kind of revolution remains distant to the point of being experientially unknowable, the internalized affect of which ramifies "sorrow" through an "almost desponding hope" to know more about an undefined "it." All of this makes for a misprision of John Quincy Adams that needs him in order to perceive the Russian Revolution from American soil and simultaneously allows for the Russian Revolution to inhabit a distinctly American text. As with the elegy to Lenin, this parallax shift from the unknowable thing to the subjectivities that witness its ascent effectively deforms the poem's syntax. The movement of the stars, from "horizontal" to "perpendicular," animates a long, paratactic sentence, whose elliptic punctuation and syntactical elisions imply perpetual movement. America, from which all of this is observed, is "frozen" and "incrusted" by a stasis that locks prosody into truncated, end-stopped sentences, the final two of which exist on two single lines, as though the poem itself is frozen to the rails.

A continued detour through Russia's revolutionary prehistory consolidates the poem's investment in permanent revolution before returning us to an interplanetary utopianism. An account of Russian absolutism, sourced from Henry Adams, begins when the poem announces an arrival into the twentieth century and goes on to emphasize the uniqueness of Russia in relation to its surrounding continent, as well as the singularity of its regional anachronisms.

> 1901. Henry Adams.
> Active, vibrating, mostly unconscious, and quickly
> Reacting on force . .
> (Brooks: men work unconsciously . .
>   perform an act, before they can explain why;
>   often centuries before)
> Russia . . nothing in common . . with . .
> Any . . world . . history knew;
> She had been the oldest source
> Of civilization in Europe, and
> Had kept none for herself . .
> Luminous . . salt of radium . .
> But with . . negative luminosity
> As though she were a substance whose
>   energies had been sucked out—
> . . Inert residuum—with movement of pure inertia.
> —herders deserted by their leaders and herds.—
> —wandering waves stopped in their wanderings—
> —waiting for their winds or warriors to
>   return and lead them westward;[50]

Even before 1917, Russia presents itself as a different "world" to anything known in "history," a bizarre entity whose people are energized by inexplicable and invisible forces. Russia, we are told, "had been the oldest source/ Of civilization in Europe," whose bourgeoisie had been depleted by its own imperialism. Russian culture, then, comes to resemble "a substance whose/ energies had been sucked out." What remains of this hollowed state is the divided labor of two distinct work forces: the proletarian "men" who are said to "work unconsciously" and the peasant "herders deserted by their leaders and herds." In the absence of a living bourgeois culture, the proletariat and the peasantry are conjoined by their shared investment in an unknown future. While laboring "unconsciously," the members of the proletariat nonetheless "act, before they can explain why," disposing themselves "often centuries before" they are due. Analogously, the peasants have "stopped in their wanderings" and await "winds or warriors to return and lead them westward" to the industrial homes of the proletariat. That these movements and their future reckoning are defined by inevitability, "movements of pure inertia," further suggests that these lines are associated with permanent revolution. Connecting this association with Russia's figuration elsewhere as "luminous," as giving off "negative luminosity," refers us back to the radiance of the stars. Though "negative luminosity" echoes Keats's "negative capability," the phrase is technical and describes how the stars that are closest to earth appear brightest because their apparent magnitude has not dissipated as widely: a star with "negative luminosity" is closer to earth and therefore appears brighter than a star with positive luminosity. Simultaneously, and in the nontechnical, Keatsian sense, the phrase is almost oxymoronic and lays claim to the practical truth of this kind of utopianism—that it can only be conceived from the realm of what already exists.

Unlike the train that had "frozen to the rails" somewhere near Cincinnati, here in Russia another locomotive draws across the steppe, passing through St. Petersburg (soon to become Petrograd, and in Mandelstam's poem Petropolis) before arriving at a moment of unrealized actualization and proleptic becoming.

From the first glimpse one caught
From the sleeping-car window,
In the early morning, of the
Polish Jew at the accidental railway station, in
All his . . horror,
To the last . .
Of the Russian peasant
Lighting his candle and
Kissing his ikon before
The railway Virgin in
The station at St. Petersburg . .

Dreary forests of Russia . .
Stockholm . . thru a New England landscape and
                                        bright autumn . .

Discovered Norway
Triangulated . . vast surfaces of history . .
All his life against the beer-swilling
Saxon boors whom Freeman loved . . peering
At the flying tourist . . the lights of an electro-magnetic
civilization . .
The infinite seemed to have become loquacious:
An installation of electric lighting and telephones . .
Beyond the level of the magnetic pole . .
Look back across the gulf to Russia . .
The glacial ice-cap still pressed down . .
Dusky and oily sea . .
Ice-cap of Russian inertia . .

Nothing to say.
For him, all opinion founded on fact must be error,
Because the facts can never be complete,
And their relations must be always infinite.
Very likely, Russia, would instantly become—[51]

Perhaps this is what we had been observing from the "light-houses of the sky," the newly lit "lights of an electro-magnetic/civilization." In terms of narrative, these lines describe the exit from a Russia whose candlelit idolatry and superstitious "dreariness" are now being illuminated by the "installation of electric lighting and telephones." Indeed, the train's journey bears a striking resemblance to the electrified map in the Red Army Club at the Kremlin, as Benjamin described it approximately one decade prior to Zukofsky's rewrite from Adams: "Beside it is a handle. When the handle is turned, the following is seen: one after the other, at all the places through which Lenin passed in the course of his life, little electric lights flash."[52] As we shall soon see, technology played the integral role in Zukofsky's engagement with communism. For the time being, however, we need only confirm that electricity was not only materially but also ideologically significant to the Russian Revolution. This is made apparent nowhere more powerfully than in Lenin's frequently derided equation: "Communism is Soviet power plus the electrification of the whole country."[53] The electrical illumination of Russia, "the lights of an electro-magnetic civilization," further clarifies the previous episode's "luminosity" by combining its image with the astral metaphor, "light-houses of the skies," and contributes to the vision of postrevolutionary Russia as modernizing in coherence with the stars' navigation points. The electrification of Russia thus opens up lines to a hitherto unforeseen hereafter. "The infinite," we are told, "seemed to have become loquacious," as though it speaks through all of Russia by way of the electrical grid, preparing that nation-state to make its leap into the future from the anachronistically importunate or economically underdeveloped past. The repeated emphasis on "inertia" similarly recalls the outcome of permanent revolution, the combination of workers and peasants into soviets now working together under the glowing radiance of an electrical sun. And the utopian futurity and "infinite" relations of that revolution are given powerful invocation in the final line's curtailment with the grammatically unclaimed object of "become," for it is never revealed what exactly Russia is becoming. That line comprises the unfinished beginning of Henry Adams's original sentence, which if completed would direct this episode toward one final, unrealized astral metaphor: "Very likely Russia would instantly become the most brilliant constellation of human progress through all the ordered stages of good."[54] But the brilliance must remain, for Zukofsky, properly inconceivable. The constellation abides beyond the horizon of historical prediction: it is made properly utopian in its abstention from prerevolutionary representation. While the stars might guide socialism, the socialists are yet to reach them. Communism, which animates this expedition, is still to be seen.

Alien Space Encompassing

That all of this material predates 1917 does not obviate against its relevance to the perceived utopianism of Russia. While it provides an American optic through which communism is conceived of under the guise of permanent revolution, the Adamses' shared predilection for stargazing has at least one correlative in postrevolutionary Russia. Appearing before any of the Adams material is an episode in which high-altitude balloons arise into Soviet airspace: "Nineteen kilometers in the stratosphere, / Further than Podolsk is from Moscow, / Three kilometers above the record / they made in Europe."[55] This episode motions toward a state-sponsored reclamation and aesthetic recuperation of Lenin's star from 1924. The orbital sphere is, in this instance, a stratospheric balloon, elevated over "the Central Asian Desert" in the name of Soviet innovation. Again, an inclusive multitude, the "dense mass of people," collectively gazes heavenward. The balloon's skyward trajectory replaces the elegiac rhetoric of the earlier poem with the language of science, figured in the episode's superabundance of numbers:

"Three kilometers," "echoed by millions," "22 automobiles," "eighty-six days, 5, 721 miles." These are the same Russians we passed by on the train in 1901, now galvanized toward Soviet futurity by technological acceleration. The horizontal progression of the train has become the vertical ascent of the balloon, with it rising higher "than Podolsk is from Moscow." That both "the balloon" and "the automobiles" are "each part soviet make" suggests a collective pride very different from the chauvinistic labor we encountered with Pound in Canto 22. The repetition of "our" ("'It is ours.' Our balloon. Our automobiles. Our trucks.") reinvests pride not only in the technological objects but also in the collective that produced and owns those objects. "We have caught up with them, passed them this time," claims one voice, perhaps grounding collective affect in permanent revolution, whereby the most backward of European states has broken free of its absolutist containment and appears to have surpassed the rest of that continent. "Blazoned with red flags," the poem celebrates the scene with a delightfully lyrical image: "Party-colored flowers."

Several lines later, we glimpse an image of earth seen from the balloon, as though looking down from a nearby planet, from which Soviet scientists gaze further still into the future.

> In the stratosphere the color of the sky
> Would be a deep soft violet he said.
> And he was right. With a chromatic scale of colors
> we saw the sky,
> We did not, as we had expected, see
> The curvature of the earth.
> Our instruments may yet record it,
> The naked eye could not.
>
> Possibly we'll bear witness
> To long distance flights at terrific speeds
> In altitudes where resistance of air-pressure's
> Reduced to a minimum:
> But come back to the Soviet after ten years
> To see what we shall have done.[56]

Of all the available gestures to be made within finite experience, perhaps this comes closest to the realization of utopian consciousness. Humans use technology to extend life beyond the confines of the planet but are not yet capable of venturing outside its atmospheric boundaries—to a terrestrial space so different from our own that terra firma's very "curvature" is expected to appear in full relief. But, at this moment, irreducibly within the historical situation of the USSR, only "instruments may yet record it," whereas "the naked eye cannot." The epistemological impasse is an objective correlative to the presently impossible; that vision from above, mediated by way of the machine, is the situational antithesis to an event that cannot yet be written. Though it might be a given in modernity that machines do our sensing for us, with each poet possessing what Eliot would describe as "a mechanism of sensibility which could devour any kind of experience,"[57] here that mediation is repurposed to sense a reality that can neither be devoured nor experienced. As with the train journey in 1901, which projected a future that it refused to predict ("Very likely, Russia, would instantly become—"), the second strophe articulates technology back within the conditional and the subjunctive, within the realm of possibility, before directing it on a line of flight toward a future, dictated by the imperative and declarative, indexed to the productive capacities of the first two Five-Year Plans. Socialism attempted to sustain the utopia longed for in these lines and the scientific project to which they bear witness. Come 1957, Zukofsky would remark that "Krushchev / won't debate / satellites."[58]

Interplanetary and extraterrestrial utopianism as conditioned by futuristic machinery connects these episodes to numerous instances in which Zukofsky's poetry approaches communism through its purchase on technology. Before accounting for the conditioning web of explicitly communist ideology through which Zukofsky inscribes technology in verse, however, these tropes—the astral, the technological, and permanent revolution—can be seen to have reached their utopian summit with the poem's one depiction of Lenin. Though his disembodied words and thoughts appear all throughout *"A"*, the closest we come to an encounter with the man himself is the following, which augments those elegiac lines from 1924, pitching their lyric vision into a properly epic register:

> He (Lenin) came to this earth, to drive
>   out Kuchak, Tajiks!
> Kuchak (Adam).
>
> He slays the dragon, with golden arms
> Born of the moon and the stars,

When the world was made he helped, too
Comrades of Uzbekistan

The strength of one man can be reckoned
        1/20 of a horsepower—
Think, then, 10 turbines are 900,000 horsepower.
The gas flame of the automatic welder
        burns thru steel
And is not put out by water[59]

The first two strophes redact their material from a *New York Times* article written in 1935, one decade after Lenin's death. The article recounts the mythic story told by the Tajik people in Afghanistan, who believed that Lenin avenged their wrongs by driving out their Kuchak adversaries. The article also claims that in "other myths of Eastern peoples of the Soviet Union Lenin is depicted as a knight slaying foul monsters, like St. George and the dragon; as a hero with golden arms, born of the moon and stars, and even as a participant in the creation of the world."[60] The second strophe's almost balladic half-meter, multiple assonances, and imperfect rhymes combine to create a peculiar musicality, giving this version of the Lenin myth a jaunty and fairytale quality. The form and its content are both juxtaposed to the following six lines, wherein musicality is occluded by a numerical fraction difficult to recite aloud, by a multiplication, and by what reads like a technical manual: a machine-age auxesis. What we encounter between them is the generic schism between fantasy and science fiction, two genres with which the modern epic reaches toward the utopian object it cannot experience historically. Fantasy, in Jameson's conception, "breathes a purer and more conventional medieval atmosphere, and dreams this non-historical vision along certain sharply articulated lines, from religion to village life, from superstition and legends all the way to the great struggles between the nobility and the peasantry." Generically encoded in the prosody, then, are those images from Henry Adams, depicting Russia's belatedly medieval absolutism, and whose embodiment of permanent revolution is, in these lines, reimagined as heroic quest. Typical of the genre, all of this is centered on the paradigmatically fantastical figure of the dragon. "Meanwhile," adds Jameson, "in fantasy itself the dragon can be seen as the equivalent of the spaceship or of teleportation in SF. Yet as a living being the dragon is also able to incarnate sheer otherness, so that its symbolic capacities well exceed those of inanimate machinery." But here the dragon faces off against a technologically superior extraterrestrial—an impossible, world-building, utopian figure, miraculously "born of the moon and the stars"—and is expeditiously supplanted by a machine whose strength is calculated at 900,000 times that of twenty men and whose "gas flame" "burns thru steel/And is not put out by water." And so Jameson continues, having returned from fantasy to science fiction, "these are machines that have already become Others, and have been promoted into something like a new and distinct, alternate, species to the human." What the poem knows is that the real magic behind the fantasy, a mythic story in which Lenin appears from the heavens and slays the dragon of monopoly capitalism, is that of inanimate machinery made into a living being by socialist collectivism. If communism's utopian impulse is of the stars that are, in this singular instance, brought down to earth by a mechanized Lenin, then its program will reanimate the machine—and for that reanimation, which we are about to encounter, the poetry requires a whole new branch of science fiction.[61]

From Satellites to Cybernetics

The opening to the eighth part of *"A"* temporarily regrounds the poem on terra firma with a rhapsodic hymn to labor.

And of labor:
Light lights in air,
                    on streets, on earth, in earth—
Obvious as that horses eat oats—
                    Labor as creator,
                                        Labor as creature,
To right praise.[62]

The socialist "lights" in the sky have been cast down to "earth," and because of that the poem requires another, different branch of utopian presentation to operate simultaneously with its interstellar aesthetic. Specifically, it requires a means of apprehending the utopian energies that inhered within the United States during the 1920s and 1930s, from where Zukofsky was reading the socialist star system. Attending that transition from the extraterrestrial to the earthbound is a subgeneric modulation in the poem's science fiction. We just encountered this other branch of science fiction in the depiction of Lenin as a dragon-slaying machine-god from another planet and in that depiction's promotion of a biological form's integration with industrial machinery. The aesthetic we are interested in for the remainder of this chapter concerns itself with that integration of technology with organic life, as it pertains to Zukofsky's immediate historical context. In short, my argument for what remains is that Zukofsky's poetry internalized a specifically communist interpretation of what might be called cybernetics and that this internalization helped direct him toward the closed-form prosody that would eventually be included within the epic.

My interpretation of cybernetics here takes less from Norbert Weiner's theory of complex systems and feedback loops than it does from that theory's uptake into Donna Haraway's account of the cyborg, a figure she defines as "a hybrid of machine and organism, a creature of social reality as well as a creature of fiction," or better yet what N. Katherine Hayles describes as follows, amalgamating the theories of Weiner and Haraway:

> Central to the construction of the cyborg are informational pathways connecting the organic body to its prosthetic extensions. This presumes a conception of information as a (disembodied) entity that can flow between carbon-based organic components and silicon-based electronic components to make protein and silicon operate as a single system. When information loses its body, equating humans and computers is especially easy, for the materiality in which the thinking mind is instantiated appears incidental to its essential nature. Moreover, the idea of the feedback loop implies that the boundaries of the autonomous subject are up for grabs, since feedback loops can flow not only *within* the subject but also *between* the subject and the environment.[63]

Here I want to insist upon such theory's origins in socialist thought, and specifically on the role of labor as primary mediation between the organic and the cybernetic, between the carbon and the silicon, between the body and the machine. In short, within the context of industrial capitalism, the "creature" and "creator" named labor only exists in the interplay between humans and their complex apparatuses, or as what Marx would call the "forces of production." Here I show that while Zukofsky was looking to the USSR as a utopian navigation point in modernity's night sky, he was simultaneously sensing that his own geopolitical situation, the USA during the 1920s and 1930s, contained unrealized utopian potential and that such potential was born from industrial capitalism's forces of production.

There are some obvious contextual reasons for Zukofsky's depiction of Lenin as an unambiguously cybernetic entity. For instance, even after Lenin's death, his body remained a biomechanical marvel. "Why is it that Lenin lies intact in Moscow?" asks a fictional comrade in a novel from 1930. "He is waiting for science—he wants to be resurrected."[64] Zukofsky was conscious of that technological preservation, and he even alludes to it in a short poem from 1931.[65] But the relationship between communism and biomechanical technology expresses itself more diffusely throughout the socialist state. For instance, Trotsky's New Soviet Man prophesied a utopian moment when the organically human subject was "to extend the wires of his will into hidden recesses, and thereby to raise himself to a new plane, to create a higher social biologic type, or, if you please, a superman."[66] In cinema, Dziga Vertov championed a race of Kinoks, the cybernetic integration of men with movie cameras, of eyes with lenses, limbs with tripods, and so on. In literature, Mayakovsky recognized that a "futurism of naked technology with the superficial impressionism of smoke and wires" also "has the enormous task of revolutionizing the paralyzed, obese, and ancient psyche."[67] And, in the visual arts, constructivists such as Alexander Rodchenko reimagined the biomechanical subject using photomontage and monochrome to promote the visual and technological horizons of a postbourgeois life. "All new approaches to art," said Rodchenko, "arise from technology and engineering and move toward organization and construction."[68] If, as Jameson avers, cybernetic technology as defined by capital "tends to transform the organic into a machine far more than it organicizes machinery," thus shaping a situation in which "cybernetic technology becomes if anything even more 'unnatural' than the older heavy-industrial kind,"[69] within a socialist context we might find cause to expect the reverse. As we shall see, Zukofsky's poetry approaches cybernetics just us frequently from the opposite direction, equipping "heavy-industrial" technology with distinctly organic features. This specifically communist sense of techno-utopianism would contour Zukofsky's reading of Marx and the application of Marxism to the large-scale industry of his own historical situation.

The Mother of Antagonism

Zukofsky's engagement with technology is informed by Marx's argument for it as the privileged medium of epistemological access to modes of production. "Technology," summarizes the poet, "throws light upon mental conceptions." This line derives from a footnote to *Capital,* in which Marx argues that technology "discloses man's mode of dealing with Nature, the process of production by which he sustains his life, and thereby also lays bare the mode of formation of his social relations, and of the mental conceptions that flow from them." What differentiates technology from the other phenomena adjoined to the mode of production is that technology is resolutely inorganic; it is neither person nor nature but an inanimate thing. Our "dealing with Nature," "social relations," and "mental conceptions" are all phenomenally bound to carbon-based organisms; technology, by contrast, is lifeless. Or, rather, technology is lifeless until it enters into production's ecological matrix and is met by human labor. "In so far then as labour is such specific productive activity," writes Marx, "in so far as it is spinning, weaving, or forging, it raises, by mere contact, the means of production from the dead, makes them living factors of the labour-process, and combines with them to form the new products." Technology is dead until the mode of production integrates it with human bodies, at which point industrial machines acquire tremendous productive power and are born anew.[70]

This shorthand rendition of Marx's interpretation of technology is ultimately diagnostic: a politico-economic description of technologies and their application within the social context of capitalism. But Marx's aspiration for unlocking the epistemological secrets to the mode of production was that, when equipped with this knowledge, the working class might also change it, replacing capitalism with communism. Zukofsky knew this theory, and we can see a redoubled emphasis on the political side of Marx in the fact that he reads Marx through Lenin and the Russian Revolution and in relation to his own American context. See, for example, this theoretical gesture toward a legal framework in which people can be unequal without being exploited on that basis, the content of which is taken from Lenin's gloss on Marx:

> Friends too tired to see differences,
> This, Marx dissociated:
> "*Equal* right . . presupposes inequality,
> Different people are *not* equal one to another."
> But to make the exploitation by one man of many
> impossible!
> When the opposition between brain and manual work
> will have disappeared,
> When labor will have ceased to be a mere means of
> supporting life,[71]

These lines combine Marx's theory and Lenin's commentary into a theoretical imagining of the transition from capitalism to socialism and then from socialism to communism. Zukofsky's lines begin with Marx's critique of bourgeois right under capitalism, the legal basis for which consolidates a reality wherein "every right" presupposes economic inequality because, with "an equal share in the social consumption fund, one will in fact receive more than another, one will be richer than another, and so on."[72] Such a reality, which is manifestly that of the Depression-era United States, is one in which "different people" are "equalized" as values within an exploitative economic order. And indeed, because this inequality also applies to entire branches of industry, its Depression-era manifestation affected individuals employed across a range of different professions and in different geographical locations: "The development of US domestic policy was itself highly uneven. This was true not only regionally, and especially as regards the South, but also sectorally: some industries, such as agriculture and textiles, remained notoriously vulnerable to any downturn in prices."[73] Nevertheless, by attributing an inability "to see differences" to the gently humanizing and socially differentiating noun, "friends," the opening two lines push back against the American caricature of Marx as the proponent of leveling and an undesirable type of economic equalization as cultural homogeneity. Zukofsky's second sentence belongs to Lenin and develops a political corrective to capitalism in the guise of what the original text refers to as the "first phase of communist society."[74] During this "phase," which we know as socialism, "differences, and unjust difference, in wealth will still exist," but it will nonetheless succeed in negating bourgeois right; it will, as Zukofsky puts it, "make the exploitation by one man of many impossible!"[75] While Lenin's text was written immediately before the 1917 revolution, we might read the exclamation mark, which is Zukofsky's addition, as an enthusiastic affirmation of a socialism to which the original text had no historical access. One of the things we might therefore learn from these lines is that Zukofsky read Marx through the kaleidoscopic overlap of at least two different perspectives. On the one hand, he reads Marx through the context of capitalism in his own country, and on the other, he reads Marx through Lenin, through the Russian Revolution, and through the socialist state. According to Lenin's reading of Marx, the historical sequence from capitalism to socialism and from socialism to communism would be predicated on technology—and especially what will evolve into the American technology we encounter later in this chapter, in Henry Ford's automotive factory.

Technology enjoys revolutionary theorization in the two occasions when Marx finds it essential to quote from *The Communist Manifesto* on the pages of *Capital,* thus allowing the resolutely utopian but also practical dimension of his thought to shine through his critique of an otherwise unassailable economic system. The first of these two quotations accounts for the coming of the machine age and with it the bourgeoisie's blasting asunder all residually feudal and absolutist fetters. The bourgeois revolution, we are told, is patently technological because it is based in a systematically motivated lust for industrial innovation. "The bourgeoisie," says Marx, "cannot exist without continually revolutionising the instruments of production, and thereby the relations of production and all the social relations."[76] For Marx, history thus entered capitalist modernity by way of technology, namely, "the instruments of production," and by doing so it produced a social fabric no longer bound by religious superstition but instead divided into classes, wherein each human relates to the next only in accord with their position within the relations of production. It is precisely in those constantly evolving technologies and the social relations they consolidate that we find potential for overturning capital. Such is the lesson of the book's second quotation from the *Manifesto*: "The advance of industry, whose involuntary promoter is the bourgeoisie, replaces the isolation of the labourers, due to competition, by their revolutionary combination, due to association. The development of Modern Industry, therefore, cuts from under its feet the very foundation on which the bourgeoisie produces and appropriates products. What the bourgeoisie, therefore, produces, above all, are its own grave-diggers."[77] Here, then, is one of capitalism's fundamental contradictions—and one that we have already encountered with Williams. Technology's acquisition of organic structures in the passage from manufacture to large-scale industry, the way it revolutionizes a social world by integrating the bearers of labor power into its own form, also generates an association between individual members that make up the vast armies of men and women brought together by industrial production. That association is what hypothetically encourages collectivization, and, united by modern industry, the collective is said to form the engine room of socialism if not communism: the proletariat. Lenin sensed this to be the case for Russia as early as 1913. "The role," he wrote, "of a truly advanced class, a class really able to rouse the masses to revolution, really capable of saving Russia from decay, is played by the industrial proletariat."[78]

In Zukofsky's epic, the gothic metaphor of capitalism's graveyard finds its way into his treatment of a workers' chorus.

> Light lights in air blossoms red
> Like nothing on earth

Now the chains
Drag graves to lie in
This is May
The poor's armies veining the earth![79]

In these lines, the shackles of capitalist exploitation, "the chains," have not simply been cast aside under the "blossoms red" of socialism. Instead, they are expropriated and put to work once more, now dragging the "graves to lie in," as the "poor's armies" consign their bourgeois predecessors to "the earth." The poetry complements these allusions to a mass grave for the bourgeoisie with its characterization of technology as simultaneously pertinent to the beginning of a new economic life cycle. Zukofsky quotes one of Marx's 1868 letters to the German gynecologist Louis Kugelmann, in which Marx refers to his published descriptions of large-scale industry as a material precondition for communism: "Not only as the mother of antagonism, but as the/producer/Of the material and spiritual conditions for resolving/that antagonism."[80] Returning us to the maternal aspect of Zukofsky's verse—his interest in the Russian Revolution was first mediated by his mother, and the verse presented that revolution as an essentially feminine event—these lines condense one of Marx's favored expressions, in which capitalism is said to quite literally give birth to its communist antithesis: "the productive forces developing in the womb of bourgeois society create the material conditions for the solution of that antagonism."[81] Technology's mechanical structure is thus recast in the quintessentially organic metaphor, "the mother of antagonism," whose recipient, a gynecologist, may well read it more literally than Marx probably intended. Here, between metaphors of death and life, I want to underline that to depict the technologically enabled transition between modes of production using figures of human scale is to begin supplying that technology with organic features.

Later, and in a similar mode of epistolary clarification, the idea of a technological "association" is reiterated, using the jargon proper to historical materialism but with Zukofsky's subtle modifications of the original text.

"What I did" said Marx, "was to prove"
One) that the existence and war of the classes
Springs from the means of production
Further) that class war brings on of itself
The dictatorship of the proletariat
Last) (and without repetition)

This dictatorship dies, is the end
of the classes.[82]

These lines derive from another of Lenin's glosses on a letter from Marx, reading it within the context of the Russian Revolution and using it to develop that Leninist conception of the "dictatorship of the proletariat" into a workable political strategy. There is an argument to be made that Zukofsky replacing Marx's sequential numbers with the syntactic gradation of a noun, adverb, and another noun ("one," "further," and "last") reshapes technical description as something more narrative and perhaps even more human than mechanical. If, however, that would overstate what is only suggested at the level of descriptive content, the organic quality of these lines is far more apparent in their figuration. While they describe a process in which "class war" or "war of the classes" emerges from "the means of production," they do so using that now-familiar rhetoric of organic life cycles. "Springs," the term used for this emergence, applies to both machines and bodies, but when it is coupled with the terminal verb "dies," the industrial process described here acquires a distinct biological quality. And so that life cycle clarifies itself: the socialist vanguard "springs" to life from "the means of production," and in the abolition of classes, the final shift from socialism to communism, that vanguard also "dies."

Working Like a Horse

If the organic quality of these redactions from Marx remains so subtle as to be easily overlooked, we see its heightening in the dramatic presentation of Marx himself, who is depicted as a flesh-and-blood writer using lines appropriated from a letter to Engels sent in 1865. "I am now working like a horse," he writes, laboring with such intensity that he now suffers carbuncular symptoms. Marx also claims to be "doing some differential calculus" but only in order to procrastinate and avoid writing his critique of capitalism. For him, all literature has become labor—the "literary-historical" consistently "drives" him back to the "work" of his "writing"—and mathematics thus serves as a leisurely escape.[83] Perhaps this is why the aesthetic dimension to this episode bears witness to the organic underpinnings of Marx's labor. As Mark Scroggins observes, the equine simile recalls Zukofsky's own depiction of the modern artist from his essay on Charlie Chaplin. "There exists probably in the labors of any valid artist," writes Zukofsky, "the sadness of the horse plodding with blinkers and his direction is for all we don't know filled with the difficulty of keeping a pace."[84] By turning Marx into a full-blooded literary character, a physicality on the order of Chaplin, Zukofsky supplies the economist's intellectual labor with its biologically human contingency, a body suffering from "carbuncles." These do not yet damage his all-important "brain pan," and their "local" as opposed to cerebral manifestation recalls the division of physical and mental labor under capitalism. In this way, the depiction of Marx performs what the poem elsewhere describes as "our most valuable capital," namely, "labor's arterial blood."[85] And yet, while this organic detail might recall the bodily substance of human labor—the "expenditure of human brains, nerves, and muscles"—what we are yet to see is how that substance integrates with industrial technology, from which Marx as an intellectual laborer remained physically disconnected.[86]

We can see a version of industrial labor in Zukofsky's exemplary depiction of a cornmill.

> The clock and the corn-mill
> (The water-mill, that is,)
> The clock, the idea of applying automatic device
> (Moved by springs) to production.
> The mill the essential organism of a machine:
> The mechanical driving power; the transmitting
>   mechanism ; the working machine,
> Which deals with the material. Each
> With an existence independent of the others.
> The mathematicians, so far as they occupied themselves
> With practical mechanics and its theoretical side,
> Started from the simple corn-grinding water-mill.
> The actual work . . beating, crushing, grinding,
>   pulverisation . .
> Was performed from the first without human labor
> Even tho the moving force was human or animal.
> This kind of machinery is therefore very ancient,
> At least in its origins, and
> Actual mechanical propulsion was
>   formerly applied to it.
> The German asses . . great at these small things . .
> Calling the use of animal power machinery . .
> Deciding a plough is a machine . .

While the spinning-jenny, in so far as it is
worked by hand, is not.[87]

The textual origin for this material is another of Marx's letters to Engels, from 1863, in which he describes the difference between tool and machine as relative to the historical progression from manufacture to large-scale industry. Marx's letter refers to a "re-reading" of his own book's "technical-historical extracts," which clearly informs this description of the machine in large-scale industry.[88] "Here we have," Marx argues in one of those extracts, "in place of the isolated machine, a mechanical monster whose body fills whole factories, and whose demonic power, at first hidden by the slow and measured motions of its gigantic members, finally bursts forth in the fast and feverish whirl of its countless working organs."[89] Marx's principal metaphor for technology is the organ, the dual character of which is defined at once by autonomy and contingency: though an organ's function is unique, every organ functions in relation to other organs; their interaction constitutes a larger organism. In these lines the mechanical organism is characterized as an entity whose individual parts are defined by what Zukofsky also calls "an existence independent of the others." The syntax with which Zukofsky forms Marx into verse reflects as much. The opening eight lines include no fewer than ten definite articles, the effect of which produces a dense cluster of semiautonomous noun phrases, each naming a separate working organ of the machine but articulating those organs together as a system of machinery. This repetition of definite articles does not establish a paratactic list of independent, sequential objects. Rather, it overlays and imbricates noun phrases as though arranging them into an organism. These lines also contain a technical description of machinery's acquisition of its "organic" qualities, by assimilating "the moving force" previously undertaken by either "human" or "animal" labor. To be sure, the machine performs the "actual work" of "pulverization" only because it has conjoined with or completely subsumed animal and human labor. When the final lines criticize the false distinction according to which formerly animal labor is deemed mechanical ("a plow") while formerly human labor ("the spinning-jenny") is not, Marx's history of the machine as combinatorial organism and Zukofsky's translation of that history into his epic have already debunked this distinction: under capitalism humans and machines have been integrated as one. This integration is what, for Marx and Lenin, cultivates an association between human laborers and precedes both socialism and communism.

Meanwhile, in Siberia

But if socialism is supposed to derive from the forces of production that have been made antagonistic to the bourgeoisie in their maturation through large-scale industry, then we need to acknowledge that the Russian Revolution took place where the means of production were yet to mature. This technological disjunction between the USA and the USSR becomes apparent in an episode whose adjacencies were mentioned briefly during the chapter on Williams, with the church whose cross was "slapped together" out of scraps during a "lumber shortage."

> 12 years after Ilytch's statement
> When the collectivists
> Raised the great metallurgical plants
> In Siberia,
> For a people's idea,
> As well as their practice;
> Tariffs;
> The U. S. A. embargo
> On pulp-wood from Russia,
> Tho the U. S. A. needed the pulp-wood.
> If there must be nations, why not
> Make it clear they're for business?[90]

The first long sentence is broken up by the single word "tariffs," whose position between semicolons elevates it to the status of a rhetorical lever between two syntactically adjacent yet both grammatically and geopolitically contained locations. The USSR has reconfigured its subjects' relationship with the means of production by building cooperation into a socialist collectivism, whose workers now raise "the great metallurgical plants" in accord with a "people's idea." In the United States, by way of contrast, politically motivated embargos block the importation of timber from Russia, even though the country "needed the pulp wood." The two halves of this sentence appear to reverse the assumed distributions within a situation of uneven and combined developments, here rendering Siberia and Russia industrially active as opposed to America, which appears industrially backward. The point, however, is that it has taken twelve years for the USSR to make good on large-scale industry, whereas the USA—which has had that kind of industry for years—only ever uses it for the sake of "business." For Lenin, the socialist state is that "which, while safeguarding the common ownership of the means of production, would safeguard equality in labor and in the distribution of products."[91] And, as Joseph Stalin later recognized, technical ingenuity born in the United States played an integral role in Lenin's design for the New Economic Policy and then in the Five-Year Plans. "The combination of the Russian revolutionary sweep with American efficiency is," he claimed, "the essence of Leninism."[92] Each state is economically dissimilar from the other because of the radical difference not only in the means of production but also in the public access granted to them by each government. In the USSR, the metallurgical plant belongs to the state and its people, whereas in the USA, people will suffer because of their elected leaders' political divisiveness.

Despite the construction of these metallurgical plants, Siberia's Kulaks ("landlords, rich men, bloodsuckers," according to Lenin's infamous Hanging Order[93]) continue to inhabit a presocialist ideology whose fetish for exchange value is echoed in the bourgeois rationalism of Henry Ford.

> "We've got to find new uses for wheat," said Henry;
> The time was when its shipment would
> Have done good to Ivan
>   still waiting for his own tractor—
> Kulak unable to see that there was any
> Good in anything without any money.[94]

In modern Russia the tractor has often served as an interface between communism and the peasantry. As Lenin dreamed in 1919, "If we could give 100,000 first class tractors tomorrow, provide them with gasoline, with mechanics (you all know quite well this is a fantasy), the middle peasant would say, 'I am for communism.'"[95] In other words, communism was slow to take hold because its means of production were yet to advance to a point equal to or beyond that of capitalism, whereas in Ford's America industry generated agricultural overproduction. Jennison provides a satisfyingly damning account: "Henry Ford's desire to find new nonfood commercial uses for wheat," she argues, "reads as obscene in the global context of both Depression-era food insecurity within the United States and a technologically underdeveloped Russia, where metallurgical plants were not yet forging tractors for cultivation."[96] For a poem dedicated to grasping the role of technology in transitioning to a postcapitalist utopia, American industry should present itself as the site of revolutionary potential. Yet its capacity for realizing that potential is ultimately blocked by ideology. The bearers of labor power remain oblivious to their revolutionary potential and in some cases retain an allegiance to capital, as does the stupefied Nevadan (an obvious and inverted echo of Pound's Canto 16) encountered later in the epic landscape: "Dem Rooshans ain't rational, why! / De damn fools would pard'n 'nfanticide / An' make 't—phwhat nerve!—international— / Bolshewiki; wher' do they git that stuff—"[97] However, as several drafted lines that were edited from the published poem suggest, while some might claim to have destroyed the influence of Marxism on the American working class, Marxism lives on elsewhere as both an economic critique and an electrifying political force. According to those lines, that proof is indeed historical socialism, realized in the form of a state.[98] While there is an obvious material divide between the USSR and the USA, for what remains of this chapter, we look at how the theoretical lessons from Marx and Lenin translate into Zukofsky's American context and how they inform a type of poetry designed as anathema to what appears as an ideological blockage in the forces of production.

Henry Ford's Industrial Bucolic

Before Zukofsky employed Marx and Lenin to theorize the revolutionary potential of technology under capitalism, he had already used Ford to demonstrate that potential as inherent to the geopolitical culture within which his poetry is produced. Adapting material from a 1930 interview, Zukofsky quotes Ford on working conditions in the United States and specifically in the Ford factory. "Many people are too busy to be unemployed," Ford says, before the poem levels its satirical barb against him in a parenthetical apposition: "Especially those who have their own factories / to take care of."[99] Ford's advocacy of productive busyness and his criticism of a perceived inability for disenfranchised labor to transform itself into productive capital are only the effect of his positive relationship with the means of production—he is one of "those who have their own factories." With that additional detail, his charge against the unemployed reads like his obscene attempt to find profits in wheat during Depression-era scarcity, redoubling the force of satire. Ford then dismisses the threat of communism in the United States on the basis that, in his factories, potential communists are "treated so well there was no danger of our having any trouble with them."[100] That is to say, the relative benefits enjoyed by Ford workers foreclose against the revolutionary and communist aspirations industrial technology is supposed to foment. This is the internal dynamic of capitalist class power in the United

States, whose "key industrial innovations together reorganized mass production in such a way as to mark a high-wage proletariat compatible with and actually functional to industrial capitalism."[101] Instead of showing class antagonism, the engagement with Ford presents industry as the source of ideological circumscription, the likes of which we have already seen Williams grappling with in multiple poems.

"Industry itself," Ford continues, "is a part of culture."[102] While this line resembles Zukofksy's redaction from Marx, that technology "throws light upon mental conceptions," such negotiation with a relationship in which the economic base articulates its cultural superstructure by way of industry or technology is central to literary modernism more generally. "Around 1900," reads Benjamin's canonical account of this relationship, "technical reproduction had reached a standard that not only permitted it to reproduce all transmitted works of art and thus to cause the most profound change in their impact upon the public; it also had captured a place of its own among the artistic processes."[103] Zoning in on that cultural and aesthetic placement, Zukofsky continues his ventriloquism of Ford in order to more accurately present a description of poetry in relation to industry.

> "*That's* poetry," he was told.
> "It's fiction, too, isn't it," said Henry,
> "I read poetry, and I enjoy it
> If it says anything,
> But so often it doesn't say anything."[104]

These five lines of Ford's interview material respond to a question about his favorite work of fiction, which he answers, "Maud Muller," a sentimentally bucolic poem by John Greenleaf Whittier, published in 1856. Ironically, the captain of large-scale industry's ideal work of fiction is a romantic lyric about preindustrial and agrarian labor, the narrative content of which hinges on the reification of sociality into two asymptotic classes. While Zukofsky excises this answer, despite its obvious potential for sharpening an already pronounced satire, the excision means that Ford, whose political tactics have more or less proved effective against communism, seems to be articulating something true, which derives not from his sentimental taste in literature but from his managerial strategies. Because of Zukofsky's tactical revisions, Ford appears to be arguing that poetry fails to say anything about the fact that technology is indeed a part of culture. What follows immediately after these words is a performative account of poetic language succumbing to the "culture" of industrialization that insinuates itself into every aspect of modern life.

The demonstration rewrites material from Zukofsky's essay on Pound. In particular, it reworks a description of the radical juxtapositions achieved in Pound's transhistorical compressions.

> The common air includes
> Events listening to their own tremors,
> Beings and no more than breath
>   between them,
> Histories, differences, walls,
> And the words which bind them no more than
> 'So that,' 'and'—
> The thought in the melody moves—
> A line, flash of photoplay.[105]

"Postulate beings and there is breathing between them and yet maybe no closer relation than the common air which irresistibly includes them," the source essay reads. "Movements of bodies, peoples through history, differences between their ideas, their connections, are often thus no closer knit, no further away than 'So that' and an 'and' which binds them."[106] Here, however, that compaction is achieved by way of industrialization, so that whatever "thought" resides "in the melody" of each poetic "line" submits to an industrialized aesthetic of "photoplay." This strophe both theorizes and formalizes what Marx, Lenin, and Ford have had to say about technology. The "beings" of industrial capitalism are organized together into an association, presented in union by the "breath between them" and the "words that bind them." Power thus becomes poetry in the same movement that commonality mutates into communalism. However, while this culture's economic base has aggregated its subjects into an army of potential revolutionaries, the same superstructural articulation prevents the realization of that potential. This is capitalism's self-perpetuation of its own technological determinism, in which words really do "bind" a subjectivity that behaves exactly as though its consciousness is always already determined by the economy and stamped out by its technological regime. For Zukofsky, the goal of a poetry that takes so much from Marx and Lenin but also from Ford is to sink an ideological depth charge into these forces of production, so their emancipatory potential can be awakened as revolutionary vanguard. Such is the meaning of an unpublished essay, "Matter That Thinks: Or Notions towards Action," in which Zukofsky uses Lenin and Engels to argue that literary preeminence in the United States is reactively backward. Against this situation, Zukofsky recommends purchasing the *Manifesto* and following Lenin's advice: "Movement, in its turn, is to be considered not only from the point of view of the past, but also from the point of view of the future."[107]

Insect Prosody: Form as Exoskeleton

The design for this poetry first made itself known in 1934, immediately before the poet embarked upon the immense eighth part of his epic. It took shape between the poem "Mantis" and its accompanying "Interpretation," which were published together in that year's October issue of *Poetry.* "Mantis" describes an encounter with Depression-era poverty using an image of the titular insect cast adrift in the Manhattan subway. Of course, other modernist insects have been similarly associated with thought—in Yeats's well-known simile, the mind's silent dexterity resembles "a long-legged fly upon the steam"; and, in Cummings' "r-p-o-p-h-e-s-s-a-g-r," spatial arrangement allows for the reader to recreate, in mind, the cognitive effect of a grasshopper leaping. But what makes "Mantis" unique is that it casts itself within the closed form of a sestina, which functions as a kind of insectoid exoskeleton for the poem's fleshy content. As a closed form, the sestina necessitates the arrangement of discrete lexical units into cohesive patterns based on common sounds. It comprises six stanzas of six lines and an envoi of three lines, all of which are decasyllabic, and it repeats the same six end words in each stanza but in different orders, with the envoi grouping all six words within its three lines. There are arguments to be made elsewhere about the historical particularities of this form and about the ideological hopes or fantasies it has acquired, not least of all within Pound's emphasis on Occitan-Provençal and the troubadours in his history of the lyric. As Pound would have it, the sestina is "a form like a thin sheet of flame, folding and infolding on itself."[108] Here, however, I want to echo David Caplan's reading of Elizabeth Bishop's "A Miracle for Breakfast," according to which "the sestina's demands are so harshly arbitrary that they ask to be used metaphorically," in that for Bishop the sestina's structure comes to echo the brutal schedule faced by workers during the Depression. "Shivering outside, the poor pray for a miracle to break the day's grim routine," he insists. "But just as society offers further humiliations, the sestina insists that the poem follow its harsh demands."[109] If, for Bishop, the form's metaphorical value resides in the way it "organizes its implicit recognition of contemporary culture's particular contours," for Zukofsky it would view those contours from the standpoint of socialism: its routine is one not just of exploitation and immiseration but also of collectivism.

This complex form, a mechanical imposition on the untamed stuff of language, writes itself deep into the mind's organic substance. Zukofsky describes the poem's cerebral multiplicity as "The actual twisting/Of many and diverse thoughts," and, in response to the rhetorical question "What form should that take?" he answers,

> The sestina, then, the repeated end words
> Of the lines' winding around themselves,
> Since continuous in the Head, whatever has been read,
> whatever is heard,
> whatever is seen
> Perhaps goes back cropping up again with
> Inevitable recurrence again in the blood . . .[110]

Of course, all of this natural imagery comes from the form's history. Since its twelfth-century invention, by Arnaut Daniel, this most complicated of verse forms has been said to be exemplary in its approximation of human thought. According to the Comte de Gramont, who in this definition looks skyward, the sestina should serve as "a reverie in which the same ideas, the same objects, occur to the mind in a succession of different aspects, which nonetheless resemble one another, fluid and changing shape like the clouds in the sky."[111] But what burnished figurations such as these neglect is the absolutely mechanical quality of writing into such an intensely complicated yet arbitrary structure, as though to insert the stuff of nature into a machine, as well as the irreducible fact that because the sestina is so eminently recognizable it invariably emphasizes the poem's construction. Unlike Pound, author of "Sestina: Altaforte" and "Sestina for Isolt," Zukofsky exploits both of these features, and he does so in such a way that collocates the closed form with what we have been calling cybernetic technology.

In Michael Davidson's reading of "Mantis," Zukofsky is using the sestina to construct a critical immanence to the culture of which it is a part. "Rather than being *about* commodities or labor per se, the poem uses its own status as an aesthetic object as a lens for viewing social alienation." That view—of commodity capitalism from the standpoint of the commodity—is, for Zukofsky, singularly equal to representing "the most pertinent subject of our day." It grants a unique perspective on those marginalized by that system. "The poor," he writes—with shades of the poem by Carl Sandburg we encountered in the introduction—are the future site of a revolutionary event. Within this poem, they have been animated from within and against the structures of capitalism: "But the mantis *can start*/ History etc./The mantis situation remains its situation,/Enough worth if the emotions can equate it." This political animation, the revolutionary mantis's leap of history, is conditioned by and contingent upon the closed form, whose aesthetic novelty and formal complexity sustains "the original shock" of an encounter with poverty precisely so "that the invoked collective/Does not subdue the senses' awareness." Instead of giving way to any sort of ideological torpidity, the closed form manifests as an impassioned call to arms. Its late acceleration, when the six end words of the first six stanzas are recycled in only three lines, suggests historical urgency. It demands revolution. "Unprompted, real, as propaganda."[112]

Though "Mantis" includes a direct reference to communism when its speaker addresses the eponymous insect as "you whom old Europe's poor/call spectre," and though its closing envoi resembles the socialist anthem, with its references to an uprising by "armies of the poor" which will "build the new world in your eyes," what we are most interested in here is how the poem also retains an emphasis on the biomechanical integration and industrial association we have seen theorized throughout Zukofsky's epic. The poem employs some clearly cybernetic imagery in the final stanza. "Android," the speaker describes the mantis, "loving beggar, dive to the poor," then infuses it with distinctly mechanical animation: "Graze like machined wheels."[113] This imagery derives from an essay by Roger Caillois, for whom that insect is used to allegorize the process of reification. "The assimilation of the mantis to an automaton," he says, comparing its "anthropomorphism" to that of "a female android," results from "the conception of an artificial, mechanical, inanimate, and unconscious machine-woman incommensurable with man and other living creatures."[114] If the figure of the mantis can be a cybernetic organism, half organic and half machine, the poem itself might be a kind of mantis, because it enacts a comparable admixture at the levels of form and content.

Mantis! praying mantis! since your wings' leaves
And your terrified eyes, pins, bright, black and poor

Beg—"look, take it up" (thoughts' torsion)! "save it!"
I who can't bear to look, cannot touch,—You—
You can—but no one sees you steadying lost
In the cars' drafts on the lit subway stone.[115]

The convergence of multiple "thoughts," woven together by the repeating single-syllable words that are destined to recur, makes good on a dialectic unmatched by the adjacencies found in the early parts of *"A"*. Its mode of delivery integrates the organic process of thinking into the highly structured and inorganic design of the sestina, which acts here as a kind of mechanizing automaton set to accelerate. When that thinking turns on the question of "the poor," the men and women who for Marx and Lenin will comprise the revolutionary association born of industry, the poem is using its form to enact a similar process as prosody. It is thus that the cybernetic quality of the closed form finds resonance with the poem's communist content and with the communist theories of technology we have seen developed on the pages of Zukofsky's epic. What all of this wants to make clear is that, for Zukofsky, the closed form might serve as the poetic object with which to proclaim and embody utopian potential from within capitalism, not only because of its capacity for enacting thought but also because it enacts as form what industry does with its workers, forcibly arranging organic subjects into a mechanical association.

If the closed form of "Mantis" provides a means of staging the revolutionary potential of industrial technology as literature, then that solution owes itself to the seventh part of the epic, written several years earlier in 1930. It uses seven Petrarchan sonnets to animate a scene of street labor, from which seven impoverished workers ride off to "a meal" and to revolution on horses that are also representative of the sonnet itself.[116] But these sonnets only prepare for the political formalism that takes shape after the technically clarifying "Mantis" and its "Interpretation," and emerges fully fledged in the eighth and ninth parts of the epic. To be sure, it is not until the poem's eighth and ninth parts and their turn toward accentual-syllabic verse that the closed form's revolutionary capacity is truly felt. As Scroggins describes it, with reference to part eight, the poem's "easy, often long-lined free verse" is repeatedly interrupted by "a far tighter and more rigorously determined form,"[117] as though the avatars of history and the content of the epic have themselves collectivized into industrial associations—revolutionary cells made up of tightly bunched lines that find strength in combination.

Dickinson's Pod, Marx's Manifesto

That political formalism is what we see in this mutation of Spenserian prosody, one of several nine-line stanzas made up of alternating hendecasyllables or alexandrines. Here, in the final stanza of the first interrupting cluster of closed forms from part eight, the poem seems to reflect upon the fixity of its own construction within a specific geopolitical context.

> Proletarians massed on each nation's curtain
> Of fire, fighting to stop the haggling of nations,
> The void fills, the music of old glass is playing new
> Announcements of economies, As one object
> Speeding in the light in a calculus of speed,
> Revolution is the pod systems rattle from,
> Yet no frame breaks being elastic, the column
> Of the wake continues into the wave, Disdain
> To shunt aims, To each his needs, the Manifesto.[118]

At the level of description this one long sentence refers to a revolution whose actors have amassed against economic imperialism, expressed here in the "curtain of fire" that attends each nation's "haggling." While that depiction of imperialism should recall the adjacency of the USA and the USSR, the stanza's two allusions, woven together by the closed form, instantiate both a revolutionary impulse and its technological program as they direct the poetry toward communism. The first allusion is to a lyric by Emily Dickinson, in which she reflects on the American and French Revolutions by way of botanical metaphor.

> Revolution is the Pod
> Systems rattle from
> When the Winds of Will are stirred
> Excellent is Bloom
>
> But except its Russet Base
> Every Summer be
> The Entomber of itself,
> So of Liberty—
>
> Left inactive on the Stalk
> All its Purple fled

Revolution shakes it for
Test if it be dead.[119]

For both Dickinson and Zukofsky, the revolution is stalled—"no frame breaks being elastic"—and, consequently, their poetry's shared situation is one of political stasis. But the almost cryonic metaphor of "pod systems" situates that revolution as a future event, which anticipates natural blossoming from its "Russet Base," the fittingly red substance in which it thrives. Zukofsky's second allusion, in the final line, announces an economy through words taken from Marx's *Critique of the Gotha Program* and its translation from Blanqui, which Zukofsky incorrectly ascribes to "the Manifesto."[120] "To each his needs" is, of course, a gnomic condensation of Marx's definition of the communist utopia on the other side of socialism.

> In a higher phase of communist society, after the enslaving subordination of the individual to the division of labor, and therewith also the antithesis between mental and physical labor, has vanished; after labor has become not only a means of life but life's prime want; after the productive forces have also increased with the all-around development of the individual, and all the springs of co-operative wealth flow more abundantly—only then can the narrow horizon of bourgeois right be crossed in its entirety and society inscribe on its banners: From each according to his ability, to each according to his needs![121]

In any other context the coupling of Dickinson and Marx would appear eccentric, yet here they combine to produce a self-allegorical figure for the revolutionary poem. The lines' central metaphor, in which the proletariat is encountered as "one object" moving "in a calculus of speed," has two destinations, both of which galvanize the earlier appearance of Marx's apparently escapist mathematical labors, combining them with a revolutionary aesthetic. It metaphorizes the laboring body under capitalism, in which industrial "calculus" forces the association of multiple workers into "one object," and, simultaneously, it metaphorizes the poem's form, which facilitates the combination of these independent contingencies, Dickinson's revolutionary desire and Marx's revolutionary program, into a unified whole. The aforementioned "pod systems" that Zukofsky takes from Dickinson contain the revolution prophesied by Marx, and both are enclosed by the prosody. Indeed, the arrangement of Zukofsky's enjambed parataxis as spread across lines unobstructed by punctuation synthesizes the syntax from which it quotes. Dickinson's fragments are compressed together, while Marx's prose is stripped of its logical connectives and critical exegesis; hypallage thus conglomerates with prosody to conceive of and to enact as poetic form the possibility of communist revolution from within the industrial space of capitalism. And yet, despite their aesthetic ingenuity, these lines from Zukofsky do not appear as interested in the material exigencies or political programs of Marx and Lenin, or the industrial logic of Ford, as the free verse they interrupt. Their lyrical beauty seems to occlude the language with which Zukofsky conceives of such a program.

Impulse to Action

Perhaps even more so than this Spenserian prosody with its adaptations from Dickinson and Marx, the Villon ballades that close part 8 revert to an almost romantic endorsement of communism as detached from the socialist preconditions that Zukofsky has only just been stipulating in the long stretches of free verse.[122] But these lines seem to know as much, that theirs is ultimately an idealism, commencing as they do with a "pretty May note" and concluding with a repetition of that blazoned hymn to labor with which part 8 commenced.[123] Immediately thereafter, the ninth part of *"A"* and its adaptation of the canzone instantiate the matured expression of the communist poetry to which Zukofsky has been building with these experiments in closed form. Considered by Dante as the most musical of all verse forms, the canzone is made up of five stanzas of fourteen hendecasyllables articulated by fourteen terminal and twelve internal rhyme sounds. Potentially intensifying the synthesis of organic thought and mechanical form, in the canzone 52 out of every 154 syllables are deployed by its structuration.[124] After centuries in obscurity, the canzone reemerged in modernism by way of Pound's translation of the medieval Italian poet, Guido Cavalcante. In his work on the canzone, Pound emphasized the virtue of that form's capacity for transposing the intellect into song. That Pound championed the canzone over "the stock and trade sonnet," suggesting that the sonnet "occurred automatically when some chap got stuck in the effort to make a canzone," would undoubtedly have been significant for Zukofsky, given that the seventh part of *"A"* was written as a series of sonnets. But more relevant to the relationship between the canzone and communism is the peculiar analogy Pound uses to describe its historicity. While the sonnet is figured in the language of finance capital, condemned here as "stock and trade," for Pound the canzone once expressed a "tone of thought" as threatening as "a conversation about Tom Paine, Marx, Lenin and Bucharin" in "a Methodist bankers' board meeting." By the twentieth century, however, because of the canzone's supposedly lyrical stability, it was "no longer considered dangerous."[125]

All of this should be familiar to scholars of Zukofsky. To summarize the closest reading to that which is pursued here, Julian Murphet cites much of the same material on closed forms to argue that Zukofsky's prosody is a means by which the poem metabolizes and reacts against its own status as commodity. Though Murphet also reads this kind of verse as a formal expression of communist utopianism, I argue that Zukofsky's deployment of the canzone, like his use of the sestina and some of the closed forms in part 8, constructs a homology between poetic technique and industrial technology under capitalism, especially as it might be redeployed in the name of communism. From this perspective the closed form might be seen, in the age of free verse, as a piece of superannuated technology left behind by the main currents of aesthetic development. As Zukofsky claimed in 1968, "the so-called 'modern' will say you cannot write a sestina anymore, that Dante did it and it's dead and gone. But every time I read Dante, it's not dead. The poet is dead, but if the work is good, it's contemporary."[126] The closed form in Zukofsky's handling is thus exemplary of what Adorno describes when reminding us that the term "technique" is "a borrowing from antiquity, which ranked the arts among artisanal activities," and that "all artistic procedures that form the material and allow themselves to be guided by it coalesce under the technological aspect," while maintaining a minimal distance from the capitalist industry into which it refuses assimilation.[127] While such distance from industry must either be an anachronism or an aristocratic if not bourgeois luxury, it is precisely for this reason that the sestina, ballade, canzone, and the sonnet come to bear an allegorical relationship to the anachronistic conditions of the Russian Revolution. Here it is necessary to remind ourselves once more of the technological distinction between the USSR and the USA at the onset of the twentieth century—the Russian Revolution took place where the means of production were yet to mature. Socialism, as institutionalized by the USSR, is not what Marx prophesied; it is what Lenin created. That is to say, Lenin's version of socialism, through which Zukofsky has been reading Marx, was an adaptive forcing of the revolutionary event out of the very primitiveness of the means of production. This is why Lenin and Stalin were both so thoroughly obsessed with the expansion of the small but organized and active industrial proletariat, which in 1917 served as the energetic nucleus of the Russian Revolution—and that might be the historical content formalized into the epic by Zukofsky's deployment of closed forms.

Throughout the landscape of Zukofsky's epic, we encounter instances of industrial technology met by poetic technique, transforming the subjects of capital into densely related and politically animate collectives. We encounter it most powerfully of all in the canzone from the first half of the epic's ninth part, the first strophe of which reads,

An impulse to action sings of a semblance
Of things related as equated values,
The measure all use is time congealed labor
In which abstraction things keep no resemblance
To goods created; integrated all hues
Hide their natural use to one or one's neighbor.
So that were the things words they could say: Light is
Like night is like us when we meet our mentors
Use hardly enters into their exchanges,
Bought to be sold things, our value arranges;
We flee people who made us as a right is
Whose sight is quick to choose us as frequenters,
But see our centers do not show the changes
Of human labor our value estranges.[128]

The textual source for these lines is *Capital* and that book's legendary act of theoretical ventriloquism in which Marx imagines the commodities speaking between themselves. Here the commodities announce their own fetish character, revealing that their embodied value is only manifested through "congealed labor," the productive reality of which is obfuscated through the process of exchange. According to the shift in pronominal register from "their" and "they" to "us" and "our," the strophe can be split into equal halves of seven lines, which delineate between two separate voices. The first is that of the poem's speaker, introducing the "goods" or "things" before speculating on what "they could say" if they were "words." The second voice belongs to those commodities as imagined by that speaker, whose descriptive labor renders that projection itself a commodity made of words, thereby negating the subjunctive "were" by replacing a dramatization of commodity speech with an actually speaking commodity. It is thus that the poem not only dramatizes but also accepts its own submission to a "culture" of industrialization that unknowingly prepares for communism. But the speech is not attributed to just the commodities. In the first instance, it is said to emanate from "an impulse to action," which cannot refer to the speaking commodity but only alludes to those it encounters: a sociality of anonymous and alienated embodiments of living labor power, grouped together as "one or one's neighbor" and as the "people who made us," the name for whose collective being is industrial proletariat. The poem later emphasizes that sociality's classed and technological predication, contending that these commodities are forged by the laboring "poor" and through "pawl," "ratchet," and "machine's terror," the affective gravity of which has been noted. "They continue," says Jennison, "to force the wheel of industry forward, trapped anew in grooves with each forward tick of the ratchet," in lines whose "language, like the industrialist's machines, scores the repetitions of the working day."[129] We are in the factory, the site of labor's exploitation but also the site of its combination and association; simultaneously, we are (much like Marx but unlike Lenin) at the writer's desk, immediately involved in the labor of poetry, crafting a form whose anachronism might serve as an ideological double to the machines with which these workers produce their miraculously speaking commodities. As such, the objects of industrial and poetic labor merge into one, a microcosmic reflection of the forces of production, the realization of which leaps the division between intellectual and manual labor, yielding a monadic entity that contains the very association from which communism might be built. After this, the first half of the epic's ninth part, Zukofsky would turn away from communism before composing the poem's second half, which borrows from Spinoza instead of Marx. But here, prosody serves as a stepladder on which labor might extend itself from within the blackened matrices of capital to glimpse the glowing stars of socialism and the communist utopia toward which they direct.

Epilogue

The Heat of the Setting Sun

Our story began in 1917, with the dawning of a red sun over Moscow. We witnessed the Russian Revolution and its creation of the socialist state, viewing those events from the perspective of its own personalities and from that of poets in the United States. Since then we have seen major power shifts in the USSR—from Vladimir Lenin to Joseph Stalin, with Leon Trotsky recording the changes from near and afar—and we have also seen this socialist sequence illuminate the relations of production on the other side of the globe, where capitalism retained its dispensation. This book has aimed to demonstrate some of the ways that modernism engaged with communism as amplified by the Russian Revolution and the USSR. Its thesis—that modernist literature found a complicated political analogue in communism—was introduced as a theoretical relationship, motivated by the modern epic's totalizing impulse and by an anti-capitalist alliance between avant-gardes and vanguards. That theoretical relationship was drawn into actuality by a series of mediations, comprising the obstinacy of labor, the socialist state, and an investment in technological immanence, which together seal the relationship between modernism and communism as historical fact. This thesis has been pursued across three very different though consistently modern epics, in which communism entered and transformed the poetry and poetics of Ezra Pound, William Carlos Williams, and Louis Zukofsky.

The writers of our chosen epics moved to remodel the genre's presentational strategies in an attempt to apprehend a world that had been split in two by adversarial modes of production. All three evolved poetic form in such ways as to capture the world-historical antagonism between capitalism and communism. And, of course, these two forces were not only modes of production. For our poets, the antagonism shaded into geopolitical ideologies, broader views on reality and ways of living daily life, and above all the dreams of an uncertain future. The modern epic did not simply welcome or denounce communism. Instead, it attempted to map the historical totality of which communism had become a significant part, thus synthesizing a vast array of historical impressions into its ever-evolving form. Moreover, it did so via poetic reconfigurations of productive and reproductive technology, the utopian potential for which remained and remains unrealized under capitalism. Indeed, whether determinately or not, communism reverberated through the aesthetic machinery specific to the modern epic: in each chapter we have seen the various ways that it seized upon or was seized by modernist poetry. Communism thus engineered a literary recalibration in admixture with several other forces. The most prominent of these forces has been capitalism, which conditioned the lived reality of the poets we have encountered and which not only rivaled communism but also provided the grounds of possibility on which a future communism might have taken place, even while it actively foreclosed that potential.

The study concludes at a moment in history, not long after World War II, when the USSR had become a very different entity from the one that Lenin and Trotsky intended or Karl Marx and Friedrich Engels might have imagined. In the introduction, I mentioned that this historical moment would be the endpoint to a particular narrative in the relationship between communism and modernism, one that is bound up in the historical process of socialism. As Eric Hobsbawm once recalled, Stalin's mode of authoritarianism "would have outraged Lenin and the Old Bolsheviks, not to mention Marx."[1] What the USSR mutated into under Stalin's reign curtailed much of the already conflicted enthusiasm that multiple poets harbored for the socialist state and, too, for that state's communist aspirations. This is true of our three case studies. Pound's engagement with the USSR had become predominantly satirical, and this satire was directed at Stalinism. Williams refrained from referencing the USSR directly in his modern epic, save for a belated mention of Stalinist atrocities. And, after modeling a canzone on Marx's theory of the commodity in the ninth part of his epic, Zukofsky would also disarticulate his poetry from the politics it had been invested in up until that point, so as to retrain his literary focus on Spinozan philosophy and domestic life. Of course, to say that this moment is an endpoint for communism as a whole would be overplaying the significance of Stalin and his state apparatus. The idea of communism was still alive and well in the USSR, in the Popular Front, and in various other manifestations across numerous global territories. But for these profoundly influential modernists, whose interest in communism was so fundamentally bound up in the USSR, Stalin made socialism untenable, and an untenable socialism meant an increasingly unlikely communism. What appears to be a shared sentiment here is exemplified by British poet Basil Bunting in a 1936 letter to Pound: "I'd rather have a revolution, blood and skulls, but since Stalin has reduced himself to a larger Hitler and pretty good imitation of someone else, I doubt whether I could work with communists except for exceedingly strictly limited objects and there's no other revolutionary party in sight."[2]

And yet, other revolutionary parties soon reared into view, leaping into history in a way that was capable of restarting this dialectic of communism and avant-garde poetry all over again. Even though the political sequence inaugurated in 1917 had been compromised beyond ideological recuperation, China was soon to present itself as a principal location for the next communist event of a comparable magnitude. Leszek Kołakowski outlines the historical coordinates. "Some characteristic features of Chinese as opposed to Russian Communism were already visible in the late 1920s," he writes. "It was only after the Chinese Communists' victory in 1949, however, that their ideology, including in particular Mao's utopian vision, began to take on a definite form."[3] This transposition of political energy and utopian enthusiasm inaugurates the second stage of what Slavoj Žižek describes as the "displacement" internal to historical communism, the dynamic of which is "concentrated in two great passages (or, rather, violent cuts): the passage from Marx to Lenin, as well as the passage from Lenin to Mao."[4] Like the Russian Revolution, the advent of Chinese communism would be geographically and culturally specific, and its arrival at state socialism can be traced back to regional origins, in the Jinggang Mountains, where Mao Zedong first rallied an army of socialist guerrillas in the late 1920s. Radically dissimilar to Russia's prerevolutionary situation, which was an absolutist world defined by economic power's concentration in the nation's capital, these variegated provinces served as a germinal site for the Red Army that would seize Beijing twenty years later, thereby completing the discontinuous passage between Lenin's Russia and Mao's China.

The impact of communism's geopolitical displacement from Russia to China is visible in avant-garde poetry from the postwar period. Zukofsky, for instance, seems to have sensed it from as early as 1930: "The roving Red bands of South China," he writes. "The poor would give to the poor, / when incited."[5] But it is Charles Olson's "The Kingfishers," first published in 1949, that provides the first notable instance of American poetry viewing Russia and China as bound together by political succession.

I thought of the E on the stone, and of what Mao said
la lumiere"
          but the kingfisher
de l'aurore"
          but the kingfisher flew west
est devant nous!
          he got the color of his breast
          from the heat of the setting sun![6]

These lines capture the transnational conveyance of communism. The words from Mao, quoted in the French through which Olson first encountered them, adapt an epic method from Pound to represent a new dawn in the Far East—another red sun. Flying in the opposite direction and on indented lines, the poem's eponymous kingfisher travels west, toward the USSR and into what the poem elsewhere describes as an "apparent darkness (the whiteness which covers all)."[7] Perry Anderson's historical interpretation of these lines is illuminating. "Contemporary revolution," writes Anderson, "came from the East, but America was subjoined to Asia: the colours of dawn in China and of the flight into the West reflected the light of a single orbit."[8] For Olson, the sun was setting on the USSR just as it was rising over China. The poem bears witness to that realization.

Olson may have been the first poet to incorporate this historical transition, but he was not the last. Communism's political succession from Russia to China makes its impression elsewhere in postwar poetry, most notably in Allen Ginsberg's "Kaddish," a poem written for his dead mother. While the poem recalls Naomi Ginsberg's commitment to communism and her affection for the Russian Revolution, the geopolitical succession appears early on, materializing on the remote horizon of an apocalyptic daydream.

Dreaming back thru life, Your time—and mine accelerated toward Apocalypse,
The final moment—the flowing burning in the Day—and what comes after,
looking back on the mind itself that saw an American city
a flash away, and the great dream of Me or China, or you and a phantom Russia,
or a crumpled bed that never existed—
like a poem in the dark—escaped back to Oblivion—[9]

There are shades of Zukofsky's "The" in these lines, written in 1956, in the maternal connection to Russia, but this time the distance between poet and revolution is even more pronounced. Here communism occupies a seemingly impossible time and place—an unimaginable future projected from a now-distant past as dreamt about in the poem's present. It is a backward glance at looking forward. Here and now, either speaker, "Me" or a new socialist state, "China," will sustain "the great dream" once embodied in what has become "a phantom Russia." But it will be a dream and nothing more. For the American poet, communism, whether in China or in Russia, remains as good as fantasy—it is tied to a domestic image "that never existed," in a purely hypothetical space-time somewhere between "Apocalypse" and "Oblivion." Of course, Mao's China would appear elsewhere in Ginsberg's poetry, and in greater detail, but here that most venerated of all the postwar poets announces sensitivity not only to the shift from Russia to China but also to just how distant that sequence was from the "mind itself that saw an American city." Or so Robert Duncan would muse several years later, thinking similarly about the intractable division between the United States and Mao's China, rendered apparent "in the phantasm of a blinding fear of communism, of the primal peoples of the world, and of the depths of Asia. And from China," he insists, triangulating those three forces, "in the inspired poetry of Mao Tse-tung, there were signs of the ancient empire of the Mongols reawakening."[10]

Emerging from a comparably guerrilla context but approximately one decade after Mao entered Beijing, the Cuban Revolution as engineered by Fidel Castro and Che Guevara also found its way into American poetry and poetics. While Amiri Baraka, in "Cuba Libre," and Lawrence Ferlinghetti, in "Poet's Notes on Cuba," occupy themselves with this socialist state, it is once again Ginsberg who provides the most recognizable answer, in his letter-manifesto of 1961, "Prose Contribution to Cuban Revolution," in which he links a perceived problem with political transformation to the socialist projects of "Russia, China, Cuba." Here the poet asks just what the Cuban revolution can achieve, not for class and government and economy, but for being itself.

> What to do about Cuba? Can the world Reality (as we know it through consciousness controlled by the Cortex part of the brain) be improved? Or, with expanded population & increasing need for social organization and control & centralization & standardization & socialization & removal of hidden power controllers (capital-

> ism), will we in the long run doom man to life within a fixed and universal monopoly on reality (on materialist level) by a unison of cortex-controlled consciousness that will regulate our Being's evolution? Will it not direct that evolution toward stasis of preservation of its own reality, its idea of reality, its own identity, its Logos?[11]

It's hard to know how seriously we can take any of this. While the hippie psychologism is clearly fogged by narcotic haze—and indeed, the letter's second half (written the morning after) makes a plea for legalization—these sentences nevertheless acknowledge that Cuba, as a revolutionary socialist state, has the potential to implement such changes to consciousness. That this is framed as a choice between two alternatives preserves the possibility of the improvement of reality by way of the cortex. As with Russia, Cuba opens up a potential reality alternative to the one prescribed under capitalism. In his more sober amendments, Ginsberg seems to rewrite his proposition as something more teleological, as though to imply that statewide material transformation might yet serve as the pretext for a new psychic life. "Now," he continues, "the Cuban Revolutionary government as far as I can tell is basically occupied by immediate practical problems & proud of that, heroic resistances, drama, uplift, reading & teaching language, and totally unoccupied as yet with psychic exploration in terms which I described above."[12] Here we can speculate on that phrase, "as yet," and all the futurity it implies. Though less interested in the world-historically transformative political projects that appealed to the modernists, Ginsberg sensed that, in Cuba, the utopian stirrings of a wholly new reality might nevertheless be upon us.

While these two contexts, China and Cuba, serve as potential points of departure into an ongoing story about the importance of communism to avant-garde poetry in the United States, "The Kingfishers" by Olson and both "Kaddish" and the "Prose Contribution" by Ginsberg denote the endpoint of the present story, precisely because they mark a significant endpoint for literary modernism and the onset of a new postmodern poetics. "It was here," recalls Anderson, thinking about Olson, "that the elements for an affirmative conception of the postmodern were first assembled."[13] That Olson and Ginsberg were instrumental in poetry's shift from modernism into postmodernism renders the periodization of avant-garde poetry coterminous with the displacement of communism from Russia to China and to Cuba. The USSR's political vitality departed for China, where it had already found living embodiment as the People's Republic, and to Cuba, where it was carried forward into the future by guerrilla combatants. American poetry from the second half of the twentieth century would attend to this fact, registering it as seminal to the transition out of modernism and into postmodernism. Olson's and Ginsberg's poems are the first of many to preserve the political legacy from modernism—a recalcitrant, ambivalent, and aesthetically fertile commitment to the spirit of communism—but in new forms and new verses, from the standpoint of which the actualization of that revolutionary sequence, in Russia in 1917, would feel so far away and long ago as to be nothing less than miraculous.

Notes

Chapter 1. Introduction

1. Leon Trotsky, *The First Five Years of the Communist International* (New York: Monad, 1972), 49.

2. Karl Marx and Friedrich Engels, "The German Ideology," in *The Marx-Engels Reader,* 2nd ed., ed. Robert C. Tucker (New York: Norton, 1978), 162.

3. Marx and Engels, "Manifesto of the Communist Party," in *The Marx-Engels Reader,* 491.

4. Trotsky, *The First Five Years,* 49.

5. Walter Benjamin, *The Work of Art in the Age of Its Technological Reproducibility and Other Writings on Media,* ed. Michael W. Jennings, Brigid Doherty, and Thomas Y. Levin (Cambridge, MA: Harvard University Press, 2008), 81.

6. Jacques Rancière, *Dissensus: On Politics and Aesthetics,* trans. Steven Corcoran (London: Continuum, 2010), 152.

7. Ezra Pound, *Literary Essays of Ezra Pound,* ed. T. S. Eliot (New York: New Directions, 1954), 58.

8. Alain Badiou, *The Age of the Poets,* ed. and trans. Bruno Bosteels (London: Verso, 2014), 93, 95.

9. Franco Moretti, *Modern Epic: The World System from Goethe to García Márquez* (London: Verso, 1996), 50.

10. James Joyce, *Ulysses* (London: Penguin, 1992), 610.

11. Joshua Clover, "Georgic for the World-System," *Lana Turner Journal* 5 (2012), www.lanaturnerjournal.com.

12. Joyce, *Ulysses,* 602.

13. See Paul Thomas, "Critical Reception: Marx Then and Now," in *The Cambridge Companion to Marx,* ed. Terrell Carver (Cambridge: Cambridge University Press, 1991), 45.

14. C. D. Blanton, *Epic Negation: The Dialectical Poetics of Late Modernism* (Oxford: Oxford University Press, 2014), 136.

15. Ibid., 9.

16. T. S. Eliot, *The Complete Poems and Plays* (London: Faber and Faber, 2004), 72, 79. A thorough reading of these lines would follow Michael North's interpretation, according to which the Russian Revolution triangulated Eliot's royalist tendencies with his romantic anti-capitalism, thus producing an irreconcilable paradox, with the world-historical embodiment of anti-capitalism annihilating its nation's absolutist aristocracy. See Michael North, "Eliot, Lukács, and the Politics of Modernism," in *T. S. Eliot: The Modernist in History,* ed. Ron Bush (Cambridge: Cambridge University Press, 1991), 169–90.

17. Eliot, *Complete Poems and Plays,* 79.

18. Eliot, "A Commentary," *Criterion* 6.2 (August 1927): 98.

19. Jenny Goodman, "'Presumption' and 'Unlearning': Reading Muriel Rukeyser's 'The Book of the Dead' as a Woman's American Epic," *Tulsa Studies in Women's Literature* 25.2 (Fall 2006): 268.

20. Muriel Rukeyser, *The Collected Poems of Muriel Rukeyser,* ed. Janet E. Kaufman, Anne F. Herzog, and Jan Heller Levi (Pittsburgh: University of Pittsburgh Press, 2005), 29.

21. Peter Bürger, *Theory of the Avant-Garde* (Minneapolis: University of Minnesota Press, 1984).

22. Matei Calinescu, *Five Faces of Modernity* (Durham: Duke University Press, 1987), 115, 119.

23. V. I. Lenin, "The State and Revolution," in *Selected Works: Two-Volume Edition,* vol. 2 (Moscow: Foreign Languages, 1947), 169.

24. Raymond Williams, *The Politics of Modernism* (London: Verso, 1989), 14.

25. Christopher Nealon, *The Matter of Capital: Poetry and Crisis in the American Century* (Cambridge, MA: Harvard University Press, 2011), 42, 43.

26. Ruth Jennison, *The Zukofsky Era: Modernity, Margins, and the Avant-Garde* (Baltimore: Johns Hopkins University Press, 2012), 5.

27. Gertrude Stein, *Writings, 1903–1932,* ed. Catharine R. Stimpson and Harriet Chessman (New York: Library of America, 1998), 377, 385. Stein's earlier book about the United States, *The Making of Americans,* was written several years before the Russian Revolution.

28. Fredric Jameson, *A Singular Modernity: Essay on the Ontology of the Present* (London: Verso, 2002). 136.

29. The films mentioned here are *Orphans of the Storm,* directed by D. W. Griffith (1921); *The Ten Commandments,* directed by Cecil B. DeMille (1923 and 1956); *King Kong,* directed by Merian C. Cooper and Ernest B. Schoedsack (1933); *Ninotchka,* directed by Ernst Lubitsch (1939); and *The Great Dictator,* directed by Charles Chaplin (1940). I owe this reading of *King Kong* to Susan Buck-Morss, *Dreamworld and Catastrophe: The Passing of Mass Utopia in East and West* (Cambridge, MA: MIT Press, 2000), 174–80.

30. Boris Groys, *The Total Art of Stalinism: Avant-Garde, Aesthetic Dictatorship, and Beyond,* trans. Charles Rougle (London: Verso, 2011), 3.

31. Buck-Morss, *Dreamworld and Catastrophe,* 61.

32. Marx, "Critique of the Gotha Program," in *The Marx-Engels Reader,* 531.

33. Lenin, "State and Revolution," 164, 219.

34. Trotsky, *The Revolution Betrayed: What Is the Soviet Union and Where Is It Going?* (Detroit, MI: Labor, 1991), 28.

35. Wallace Stevens, *Collected Poetry and Prose,* ed. Frank Kermode and Joan Richardson (New York: Library of America, 1997), 299–300.

36. Alan Filreis, *Wallace Stevens and the Actual World* (New Jersey: Princeton University Press, 1991), 159–60.

37. Stevens, *Collected Poetry and Prose,* 730.

38. Jodi Dean, *Crowds and Party* (London: Verso, 2016). Kindle edition.

39. G. W. F. Hegel, *The Phenomenology of Mind,* trans. J. B. Baillie (New York: Dover, 2003), 12.

40. Martin Puchner, *Poetry of the Revolution: Marx, Manifestos, and the Avant-Gardes* (New Jersey: Princeton University Press, 2006), 2.

41. Slavoj Žižek, *The Parallax View* (Cambridge, MA: MIT Press, 2006), 4.

42. Eric Hobsbawm, *How to Change the World: Tales of Marx and Marxism* (London: Little, Brown, 2011), 246.

43. Alex Callinicos and Justin Rosenberg, "Uneven and Combined Development: The Social-Relational Substratum of 'The International,'" *Cambridge Review of International Affairs* 21.1 (March 2008): 88.

44. Fredric Jameson, *The Political Unconscious: Narrative as a Socially Symbolic Act* (Ithaca: Cornell University Press, 1981), 39, 40.

45. Alexander Kluge and Oskar Negt, *History and Obstinacy,* trans. Richard Langston (Massachusetts: MIT Press, 2014).

46. Lenin, "Letter to American Workers," *Pravda* 178 (August 22, 1918).

47. Anthony Read, *The World on Fire: 1919 and the Battle with Bolshevism* (London: Random House, 2008), 93.

48. Carl Sandburg, *Collected Poems, Unabridged* (New York: Dover, 1994), 2.

49. Lola Ridge, *Sun-Up and Other Poems* (New York: B. W. Huebsch, 1920), 87.

50. Richard Wright, "I Have Seen Black Hands," *New Masses* 11.13 (June 26, 1933): 16.

51. Lorine Niedecker, *Collected Works,* ed. Jenny Penberthy (Berkeley: University of California Press, 2002), 88–89.

52. Rosa Luxemburg, *Socialism or Barbarism: The Selected Writings of Rosa Luxemburg,* ed. Paul le Blanc and Helen C. Scott (New York: Pluto, 2010), 119.

53. Leo Panitch and Sam Gindin, *The Making of Global Capitalism: The Political Economy of the American Empire* (London: Verso, 2012), 11.

54. This term originates with Eugene Lyons. See his *The Red Decade: The Stalinist Penetration of America* (Indianapolis: Bobbs-Merrill, 1941).

55. Michael Denning, *The Cultural Front: The Laboring of American Culture in the Twentieth Century* (London: Verso, 1997), 22.

56. The designation "Marxist noir" belongs to Alan Wald. See Graham Barnfield, "The Urban Landscape of Marxist Noir: An Interview with Alan Wald," *Crime Time,* June 26, 2002, www.crimetime.co.uk/features/marxistnoir.html.

57. Kenneth Fearing, *Selected Poems of Kenneth Fearing,* ed. Robert Polito (New York: Norton, 2004), 49.

58. This episode in cultural history is explicitly referenced in another of Fearing's poems about communist organization. From within a meeting, "Vanzetti's face shows green," looming down from "above the speaker's stand"; this image appears immediately before that poem's depiction of mass insurrection gives way to an epitaph, "scrawled large in the empty prison cell," which begins, "I have just received my sentence of death." Fearing, *Selected Poems,* 66.

59. Bruno Bosteels, *The Actuality of Communism* (London: Verso, 2014), 209.

60. Steven Lee, *The Ethnic Avant-Garde: Minority Cultures and World Revolution* (New York: Columbia University Press, 2015), 1.

61. H. H. Lewis in Nelson, *Repression and Recovery,* 48.

62. Ibid.

63. William Carlos Williams, *Something to Say: William Carlos Williams on Younger Poets,* ed. James E. B. Breslin (New York: New Directions, 1985), 69.

64. Langston Hughes, *The Collected Works of Langston Hughes,* vol. 1, ed. Arnold Rampersad (Missouri: University of Missouri Press, 2001), 224.

65. Ibid., 228.

66. James Smethurst, *The New Red Negro: The Literary Left and African American Poetry, 1930–1946* (Oxford: Oxford University Press, 1999), 94.

67. David Priestland, *Red Flag: Communism and the Making of the Modern World* (London: Penguin, 2009), 151–52.

68. E. E. Cummings in Ezra Pound, *Pound/Cummings: The Correspondence of Ezra Pound and E. E. Cummings,* ed. Barry Ahearn (Michigan: University of Michigan Press, 1996), 240.

69. Cummings, *Complete Poems: 1904–1962,* ed. George J. Firmage (New York: Liveright, 2013), 413.

70. "Uncleanliness in childhood," wrote Freud, "is often replaced in dreams by avariciousness for money: the link between the two is the word 'filthy.'" Sigmund Freud, *The Standard Edition of the Complete Psychological Works of Sigmund Freud: The Interpretation of Dreams (First Part),* trans. James Strachey with Anna Freud, Alix Strachey, and Alan Tyson (London: Vintage, 2001), 200.

71. Theodor Adorno, *Aesthetic Theory,* trans. Robert Hullot-Kentor (London: Continuum, 1997), 34, 33.

72. David Trotter, *Literature in the First Media Age: Britain between the Wars* (Cambridge, MA: Harvard University Press, 2013), 36.

73. See F. T. Marinetti, "Beyond Communism," in *Futurism: An Anthology,* ed. Lawrence Rainey, Christine Poggi, and Laura Wittman (New Haven: Yale University Press, 2009), 254–64. "The workers," he claimed in 1920, "who today are marching and waving red banners demonstrate after four years of victorious war an obscure need of their own to wage a little heroic and glorious war" (255).

74. Jameson, *The Political Unconscious,* 225.

75. T. J. Clark, *Farewell to an Idea: Episodes from a History of Modernism* (New Haven: Yale University Press, 2001), 9.

Chapter 2. Ezra Pound

1. Ezra Pound, *The Cantos of Ezra Pound* (New York: New Directions, 1996), 733; Vladimir Lenin, "Imperialism, The Highest Stage of Capitalism," in *Selected Works: Two-Volume Edition,* vol. 1 (Moscow: Foreign Languages, 1947), 643; Pound, *Literary Essays of Ezra Pound,* ed. T. S. Eliot (New York: New Directions, 1954), 86.

2. William M. Chace, *The Political Identities of Ezra Pound and T. S. Eliot* (Stanford: Stanford University Press, 1973), 31. Chace also develops this idea in "Ezra Pound and the Marxist Temptation," *American Quarterly* 22.3 (Autumn 1970): 714–25. See also W. G. Regier, "Ezra Pound, Adam Smith, Karl Marx," *Minnesota Review* 12 (Spring 1979): 72–76; Peter Nicholls, "The Quarrel with Marxism," in *Ezra Pound: Politics, Economics and Writing* (London: Macmillan, 1984), 47–59; and, for a tidy summary of the disagreement, see Douglas Mao, *Solid Objects: Modernism and the Test of Production* (New Jersey: Princeton University Press, 1998), 147. That claim should be reserved for Major C. H. Douglas and then, after 1935, for Silvio Gesell, whose influence will be discussed later. There are multiple books on Pound and economics, almost all of which explain the influence of Douglas and Gesell. In addition to the book by Nicholls, I have found the most useful of these to be Alec Marsh, *Money and Modernity: Pound, Williams, and The Spirit of Jefferson* (Tuscaloosa: University of Alabama Press, 1998), and Timothy Redman, *Ezra Pound and Italian Fascism* (Cambridge: Cambridge University Press, 1987). Additionally, for an emphasis on Pound and capitalism, see the first chapter of Christopher Nealon's book, "A Method and a Tone: Pound, Auden, and the Legacy of the Interwar Years," *The Matter of Capital: Poetry and Crisis in the American Century* (Cambridge, MA: Harvard University Press, 2011), 36–72.

3. Pound, "Atrophy of the Leninists," *New English Weekly,* July 23, 1936.

4. Hugh Kenner, *The Pound Era* (London: Faber and Faber, 1972), 360. See also Reed Way Dasenbrock, *The Literary Vorticism of Ezra Pound and Wyndham Lewis: Towards the Condition of Painting* (Baltimore: Johns Hopkins University Press, 1985).

5. Miranda B. Hickman, "Vorticism," in *Ezra Pound in Context,* ed. Ira B. Nadel (Cambridge: Cambridge University Press, 2010), 294.

6. Karl Marx, *Capital: A Critique of Political Economy,* vol. 1, *The Process of Capitalist Accumulation,* trans. Samuel Moore and Edward Aveling, ed. Friedrich Engels (Chi-

cago: Charles H. Kerr, 1906), 13. I use the outdated Moore and Aveling translation as opposed to the recent and improved translation by Ben Fowkes because the poets themselves were reading *Capital* in Moore and Aveling's words. That said, some of my language derives from Fowkes, through whom I normally read Marx; for instance, I generally use the more specific "large-scale industry" instead of "modern industry."

7. Pound, "Vortex. Pound.," *Blast* 1 (June 10, 1914): 154.

8. Kenner, *The Pound Era,* 163-73. We encounter this kind of patterning as early as Canto 2 ("Lithe turning of water"), as late as the draft of Canto 114 ("Tendrils trailing/caught in rocks under wave"), and in many poems written between them. Pound, *The Cantos,* 9, 791-92.

9. Wyndham Lewis, *Rude Assignment* (London: Hutchinson, 1950), 128.

10. Julian Murphet, *Multimedia Modernism: Literature, Media, and the Anglo-American Avant-Garde* (Cambridge: Cambridge University Press, 2009), 143.

11. Pound, "Salutation the Third," and "Come My Cantilations," *Blast* 1 (June 10, 1914): 45, 46.

12. Pound, "Before Sleep," *Blast* 1 (June 10, 1914): 46.

13. Pound, *Poems and Translations,* ed. Richard Sieburth (New York: Library of America, 2004), 1291.

14. Wallace Martin, *The New Age Under Orage* (Manchester: Manchester University Press, 1967), 5.

15. Tom Villis, *Reaction and the Avant-Garde: The Revolt Against Liberal Democracy in Early Twentieth-Century Britain* (London: I. B. Taurus, 2006), 45. It is worth remembering that this magazine owes a lot to British thought, especially to the thought of William Blake, Thomas Carlyle, John Ruskin, and Philip Morris, and that it acknowledges this debt more explicitly than its debt to Marx. For more, see Paul Jackson, *War Modernisms and the New Age Magazine* (London: Bloomsbury, 2012).

16. Herbert Read, "Sorel, Marx, and the War" *New Age* 19.6 (1916): 129.

17. Pound, "Marx and the Paddlewheel Steamer," YCAL MSS 43, Ezra Pound Papers, box 111, folder 4724, Beinecke Library, Yale University; Marx, *Capital,* 410, 411, 411n2, 470. The hydraulic turbine was designed in 1822 by French engineer Claude Burdin and first constructed in 1827 by Burdin's student, Benoit Fourneyron. However, it would not be until 1855 that James Francis's discoveries in hydrodynamics would give rise to the "Francis Turbine," which is the most commonly deployed turbine and which by the first decades of the twentieth century had already become an industrial mainstay. See Ross Thompson, *Structures of Change in the Mechanical Age: Technological Innovation in the United States, 1790-1865* (Baltimore: Johns Hopkins University Press, 2006), 177-78, and David Blackbourn, *The Conquest Of Nature: Water, Landscape, and the Making of Modern Germany* (London: Pimlico, 2007).

18. Pound, *Selected Prose, 1909-1965* (New York: New Directions, 1973), 34, 115; Marx, *Capital*, 407.

19. Pound, "Vortex. Pound.," 153.

20. Kenner, *The Pound Era,* 146.

21. Pound, "Vortex. Pound.," 154; Marx, *Capital,* 462. We might also hear an echo from Marx on the way commodities are alienated from their means of production: "The corpses of machines," he writes, "are always separate and distinct from the product they helped to turn out." Marx, *Capital*, 226.

22. F. T. Marinetti, "The New Religion-Morality of Speed" and "Let's Murder the Moonlight!," in *Futurism: An Anthology,* ed. Lawrence Rainey, Christine Poggi, and Laura Wittman (New Haven: Yale University Press, 2009), 226, 59. Marinetti's essay on symbolism deals in similar imagery. "Multicolored billboards on the green of the fields," he writes, "iron bridges gripping the hills, surgical trains piercing the blue belly of mountains, enormous turbine pipes, new muscles of the earth, may you be praised by the Futurist poets, since you destroy the old, sickly, and cooing sentimentalism of earth!" Marinetti, "We Abjure Our Symbolist Masters, the Last Lovers of the Moon," in *Futurism,* 94.

23. Terry Eagleton, "Communism: Lear or Gonzalo?" in *The Idea of Communism,* ed. Coastas Douzinas and Slavoj Žižek (London: Verso, 2010), 102.

24. Wyndham Lewis, *Blasting and Bombardiering* (London: Calder and Boyars, 1967), 34; Perry Anderson, *English Questions* (London: Verso, 1992), 44; Pound, *Literary Essays,* 87. This statement by Pound can be compared to another of his claims that is also subtended by the logic of uneven and combined developments: "It is dawn at Jerusalem while midnight hovers above the pillars of Hercules. All ages are contemporaneous. It is B.C., let us say, in Morocco. The Middle Ages are in Russia." Pound, *The Spirit of Romance* (London: Peter Owen, 1910), 8.

25. Fredric Jameson, *Representing Capital: A Reading of Volume One* (London: Verso, 2011), 33–34; Zukofsky, *"A",* 46.

26. Pound, Untitled Manuscript, YCAL MSS 43, Ezra Pound Papers, box 111, folder 4724; Pound, "Means of Distribution Exist," YCAL MSS 43, Ezra Pound Papers, box 111, folder 4732, Beinecke Library, Yale University.

27. Pound, *The Cantos,* 17.

28. Marx, *Capital,* 382, 446.

29. Ibid., 446n2.

30. In Dante's poem, the souls array "as birds, rising from the river bank," taking shape first "in a round flock," then as "innumerable sparks," and that vortical whirling is also visualized in Gustave Doré's and William Blake's celebrated illustrations for the poem. Dante Alighieri, *The Divine Comedy,* trans. C. H. Sisson (Oxford: Oxford University Press, 1980), 429–30.

31. Pound, *The Cantos,* 17.

32. Ibid., 101.

33. Marx, *Capital,* 51.

34. Pound, *Ezra Pound and the Visual Arts,* ed. Harriet Zinnes (New York: New Directions, 1980), 217.

35. Kenner, *The Pound Era,* 376, 363.

36. Beasley, "Vortorussophilia," 36. See also Richard Cork, *Vorticism and Abstract Art in the First Machine Age* (Berkeley: University of California Press, 1976).

37. Lenin, "Imperialism," 644.

38. Pound, *The Cantos,* 131.

39. Marx, "The Eighteenth Brumaire of Louis Bonaparte," in *The Marx-Engels Reader,* 2nd ed., ed. Robert C. Tucker (New York: Norton), 597.

40. Brumaire takes place between October 22 and November 20, which is the period in which Napoleon Bonaparte overthrew the French Directory in 1799. Fructidor, from August 18 to September 16, is when members of the French Directory first seized power from the Royalists in 1797. And, while Petrograd nominates a place as opposed to a time, this specific place-name is nonetheless temporal, insofar as Petrograd was only given that name from 1914 to 1924, after being St. Petersburg and before becoming Leningrad.

41. Daniel Tiffany, *Radio Corpse: Imagism and the Cryptaesthetic of Ezra Pound* (Cambridge, MA: MIT Press, 2003), 222.

42. Pound, *Selected Letters of Ezra Pound, 1907–1941* (New York: New Directions, 1971), 342.

43. Tiffany, *Radio Corpse,* 225.

44. See, e.g., Paul Morrison, *The Poetics of Fascism: Ezra Pound, T. S. Eliot, Paul de Man* (Oxford: Oxford University Press, 1996), 38, and Matthew Feldman, *Ezra Pound's Fascist Propaganda, 1935–45* (Basingstoke: Palgrave Macmillan, 2013).

45. Tiffany, *Radio Corpse,* 222.

46. Pound, *Guide to Kulchur* (New York: New Directions, 1970), 241.

47. A. David Moody, *Ezra Pound: Poet,* vol. 2, *The Epic Years* (Oxford: Oxford University Press, 2014), 103.

48. Hegel, *Hegel's Aesthetics: Lectures on Fine Art,* vol. 2, trans. T. M. Knox (Oxford: Oxford University Press, 1975), 1064, 1065.

49. Pound, *Poems and Translations,* 318.

50. Pound, *The Cantos,* 6.

51. Pound, *Guide to Kulchur,* 194.

52. Pound, *The Cantos,* 41.

53. Lawrence Rainey, *Ezra Pound and the Monument of Culture: Text, History, and the Malatesta Cantos* (Chicago: University of Chicago Press, 1991), 1.

54. Pound, *The Cantos,* 63.

55. Pound, *The Spirit of Romance,* 215

56. Pound quoted in J. J. Wilhelm, *Ezra Pound in London and Paris, 1908–1925* (Pennsylvania: Pennsylvania State University Press, 1990), 254.

57. Pound, *Poems and Translations,* 556.

58. Adele Marie Barker and Bruce Grant, eds., *The Russia Reader: History, Culture, Politics* (Durham: Duke University Press, 2010), 570.

59. Pound, *The Cantos,* 163.

60. Pound, *Jefferson and/or Mussolini: L'Idea Statale Fascism As I Have Seen It* (New York: Liveright, 1970), 51.

61. Pound, *The Cantos,* 68. For an illuminating account of Blake's poetry and thinking in relation to industrial capitalism, see Michael Ferber, *The Social Vision of William Blake* (New Jersey: Princeton University Press, 1985).

62. Pound, *Selected Letters,* 342.

63. Benjamin, *Selected Writings,* vol. 2, part 2, *1931–1934,* ed. Michael W. Jennings, Howard Eiland, and Gary Smith, trans. Rodney Livingstone and Others (Cambridge, MA: Harvard University Press, 1999), 567.

64. Pound, YCAL MSS 43 Ezra Pound Papers, box 7, folder 57, Beinecke Library, Yale.

65. Pound, *The Cantos,* 69, 70.

66. David G. Farley, *Modernist Travel Writing: Intellectuals Abroad* (Missouri: University of Missouri Press, 2010), 56.

67. Pound quoted in Tiffany, *Radio Corpse,* 40.

68. Pound, *The Cantos,* 69.

69. Ibid.,74.

70. Lenin, "Imperialism," 646–47.

71. Ibid., 647.

72. Pound, *The Cantos,* 85.

73. Redman and Chace discuss this letter at some length, but Moody is correct to identify that the editors were "over-hopeful" in publishing it under the title "Pound Joins The Revolution." Redman, *Ezra Pound and Italian Fascism,* 73; Chace, *The Political Identities of Ezra Pound and T. S. Eliot,* 30; Moody, *Ezra Pound,* 72.

74. Mary Colum quoted in Wilhelm, *Ezra Pound in London and Paris,* 317.

75. Lincoln Steffens, *The Autobiography of Lincoln Steffens* (Berkeley: Heyday, 2005), 833.

76. Pound, *The Cantos,* 86, 540, 787.

77. Walter Benn Michaels, "Lincoln Steffens and Pound," *Paideuma* 2.2 (Fall 1973): 209.

78. Steffens, *Autobiography,* 760.

79. Ibid., 761.

80. Pound, *The Cantos,* 74.

81. Steffens, *Autobiography,* 761.

82. Trotsky, *The History of the Russian Revolution,* trans. Max Eastman (London: Pluto, 1997), 300.

83. Susan Buck-Morss, *Dreamworld and Catastrophe: The Passing of Mass Utopia in East and West* (Cambridge, MA: MIT Press, 2000), 137.

84. Nikolai Nikolaevich Sukhanov, *The Russian Revolution 1917: A Personal Record by N. N. Sukhanov,* trans. Joel Carmichael (Princeton, NJ: Princeton University Press,

1984), 280. One might read this in relation to *The Waste Land,* where "the shrill sounds of contemporary life are replaced by distant thunder," or even *Finnegans Wake,* whose sonic patterning is shaped by the recurrence of "thunder words." See Juan A. Suárez, *Pop Modernism: Noise and Reinvention of the Everyday* (Urbana: University of Illinois Press, 2007), 125, and Eric McLuhan, *The Role of Thunder in Finnegans Wake* (Toronto: University of Toronto Press, 1997).

85. Theodor Adorno, *Current of Music,* trans. Robert Hullot-Kentor (Cambridge: Polity Press, 2009), 91.

86. Pound, *Exile* 4 (Autumn 1928): 6.115–16.

87. Steve Phillips, *Lenin and the Russian Revolution* (Oxford: Heinemann, 2000), 68.

88. Trotsky, *Russian Revolution,* 466, 967.

89. Steffens, *Autobiography,* 751.

90. Pound, *The Cantos,* 75.

91. Orlando Figes and Boris Kolonitskii, *Interpreting the Russian Revolution: The Language and Symbols of 1917* (New Haven: Yale University Press, 1999), 31–32. See Stevens, *Poetry and Prose,* 567–91.

92. Marshall McLuhan, *Understanding Media: The Extensions of Man* (London: Routledge, 2001), 327.

93. Buck-Morss, *Dreamworld and Catastrophe,* 137.

94. Pound, *The Cantos,* 48.

95. Daniel Albright, "Early Cantos I–XLI," in *The Cambridge Companion to Ezra Pound,* ed. Ira B. Nadel (Cambridge: Cambridge University Press, 1999), 73.

96. Pound, *The Cantos,* 75.

97. This phrase is the title of the eighth chapter in Alec Marsh, *Ezra Pound* (London: Reaktion, 2011), 135–48. See also Redman, *Ezra Pound and Italian Fascism,* 93–121.

98. Pound, *Jefferson and/or Mussolini,* 63.

99. Gessell quoted in Redman, *Ezra Pound and Italian Fascism,* 132.

100. Pound, *Jefferson and/or Mussolini,* 36.

101. Pound quoted in Redman, *Ezra Pound and Italian Fascism,* 144. See Nicholls, *Ezra Pound,* 47–59, for the best account of Pound's failure to grasp some crucial aspects of Marxism, which would develop into this kind of monetary positivism.

102. Pound, *Selected Letters,* 276.

103. Pound, *Jefferson and/or Mussolini,* vii.

104. Ibid., 127.

105. Ibid., 128.

106. Redman, *Ezra Pound and Italian Fascism,* 121.

107. John Laver, *The Modernisation of Russia, 1856–1985* (Oxford: Heinemann, 2002), 79.

108. Hegel, *Aesthetics,* 2:1059, 1060.

109. Marx, *Grundrisse: Foundations of the Critique of Political Economy,* trans. Martin

Nicolaus (London: Penguin, 1973), 11; Pound, *Selected Letters,* 239; Keston Sutherland, *Stupefaction: A Radical Anatomy of Phantoms* (London: Seagull, 2011), 46.

110. Kenner, *The Pound Era,* 202.

111. Pound, *Selected Letters,* 231.

112. Pound, *Poems and Translations,* 551–52.

113. Pound, *Selected Letters,* 112.

114. Pound, *Poems and Translations,* 552.

115. Marsh, *Ezra Pound,* 71.

116. Albright, "Early Cantos I-XLI," 57.

117. Pound, *The Cantos,* 81.

118. See Norman Polmar and Jurrien Noot, *Submarines of the Russian and Soviet Navies, 1718–1990* (Maryland: Naval Institute Press, 1991), 18.

119. Pound, *The Cantos,* 75.

120. Ibid.

121. Pound, *Selected Prose,* 222.

122. Pound, *The Cantos,* 187.

123. Ibid., 191.

124. Ibid., 191, 62.

125. Ibid., 188–89.

126. Redman, *Ezra Pound and Italian Fascism,* 100.

127. Pound, *Jefferson and/or Mussolini,* 72.

128. Ernst Mandel, *The Meaning of the Second World War* (London: Verso, 2011), 66.

129. Pound, *The Cantos,* 425, 440.

130. Patricia Cockram, "Collapse and Recall: Ezra Pound's Italian Cantos," *Journal of Modern Literature* 23.2–3 (2000): 537.

131. Pound, *The Cantos,* 432.

132. Peter Nicholls, "Bravura or Bravado? Reading Ezra Pound's *Cantos,*" in *Modernism and Masculinity,* ed. Natalya Lusty and Murphet (Cambridge: Cambridge University Press, 2014), 243.

133. Pound, *"Ezra Pound Speaking": Radio Speeches of World War II,* ed. Leonard W. Doob (Westport, CT: Greenwood, 1978), 18, 175, 350, 294. Winston Churchill and Franklin D. Roosevelt were subject to comparable criticism in the radio broadcasts. What makes Stalin different is that, until the late 1930s, Pound wanted to keep Stalin and the USSR separate from the economy of which Churchill and Roosevelt had always been a part, and so the satire directed at Stalin and the USSR attaches itself to an economy that retains some distance from capitalism, even during its integration into capitalism by way of military and political alliances. As such, Pound seems to strain harder to implicate Stalin and the USSR with capital, and satire is his means of doing so.

134. Pound, *"Ezra Pound Speaking,"* 356, 13, 11.

135. Žižek, "Stalinism," *Lacan Dot Com,* 2007, www.lacan.com/zizstalin.htm. "Under Stalin," writes Ben Lewis, "a large and distinctive new group of jokes emerged that reflected not only the new social conditions of Stalinism but also the new mood of the people." Ben Lewis, *Hammer and Tickle: The Story of Communism Told Through Communist Jokes* (London: Weidenfeld and Nicolson, 2008), 55.

136. Lewis, *Hammer and Tickle,* 51–92. See also Karen L. Ryan, *Stalin in Russian Satire, 1917–1991* (Wisconsin: University of Wisconsin Press, 2009).

137. Bush, "Modernism, Fascism, and the Composition of Ezra Pound's *Pisan Cantos,*" *Modernism/modernity* 2.3 (1995), 76.

138. Pound, *The Cantos,* 445.

139. Bush, "Modernism," 80.

140. Marx, "Eighteenth Brumaire," 594.

141. Pound, *Selected Prose,* 187.

142. Pound, *The Cantos,* 63.

143. Ibid., 445.

144. Pound, "Augment of the Novel," *New Directions in Prose and Poetry* 6 (1941): 709, 707.

145. Farley, *Modernist Travel Writing,* 53.

146. Pound, *Radio Speeches,* 44.

147. Pound, *The Cantos,* 465.

148. Frederick Winslow Taylor, *Scientific Management: The Early Sociology of Management and Organizations,* vol. 1 (London: Routledge, 2004), 40.

149. Antonio Gramsci, *Prison Notebooks,* vol. 2, ed. and trans. Joseph A. Buttigieg (New York: Columbia University Press, 1996), 200, 216.

150. For a good account of this period in Stalin's life, see Isaac Deutscher, *Stalin: A Political Biography* (Oxford: Oxford University Press, 1950), 27–48.

151. Sutherland, *Stupefaction,* 63.

152. Pound, *The Cantos,* 446.

153. Pound, *Radio Speeches,* 197.

154. Ibid., 449; Pound, *Selected Prose,* 314.

155. Pound, *The Cantos,* 449.

156. Terrell, *A Companion to The Cantos of Ezra Pound* (Berkeley: University of California Press, 1984), 369.

157. Pound, "Canto LXXIV," YCAL MSS 183 Pisan Cantos Manuscripts, box 1, folder 12, Beinecke Library, Yale University.

158. Lenin, "The State and Revolution," 167.

159. Pound, *The Cantos,* 461.

160. Pound, "Canto LXXIV," Beinecke Library, Yale University.

161. Pound, *The Cantos,* 497.

Chapter 3. William Carlos Williams

1. Paul Mariani, *William Carlos Williams: A New World Naked* (New York: Norton, 1990), 186.

2. Walter Benn Michaels, *Our America: Nativism, Modernism, and Pluralism* (Durham: Duke University Press, 1995), 85. While I take a definition of nativism from this book, it is worth recalling the controversy surrounding its publication, which finds its clearest articulation in the dossier of articles arranged for it in the third issue of *Modernism/modernity* for 1996. The discussants (Marjorie Perloff, Robert von Hallberg, and Charles Altieri) all seem to agree that Benn Michaels's conception of "nativist modernism is much more nativist than modernist." While there is critical value in Benn Michaels's characterization of Williams as a nativist modernist, I endorse it here with two serious reservations. First, as von Hallberg points out, rather than locating a "revolutionary dimension of artistic expression," Benn Michaels "excavates a spirit of realism and conformity instead, or a neat fit between political history and artistic expression," 115. Second, as Altieri comments, "Williams's nativism is of a distinctly metaphoric kind, more involved with the republic of letters than with actual citizenship," 107. Robert von Hallberg, Marjorie Perloff, Charles Altieri, and Walter Benn Michaels, "*Our America* and Nativist Modernism: A Panel," *Modernism/modernity* 3.3 (September 1996): 97–125.

3. Fredric Jameson, *The Modernist Papers* (London: Verso, 2007), 7.

4. William Carlos Williams, *Paterson,* ed. Christopher McGowan (New York: New Directions, 1992), xiii. See pp. 6–7, 9–10, and 27, where Williams incorporates material from his 1927 poem "Paterson."

5. Charles Bernstein, *Attack of the Difficult Poems* (Chicago: University of Chicago Press, 2011), 174. For a good, sustained engagement with localism as the dialectical antipode of cosmopolitanism, see Eric White, *Transatlantic Avant-Gardes: Little Magazines and Localist Modernism* (Edinburgh: Edinburgh University Press, 2013).

6. Williams, *Spring and All,* in *Imaginations,* ed. Webster Schott (New York: New Directions, 1970), 89.

7. Ibid., 133–34.

8. Perloff, *The Poetics of Indeterminacy: Rimbaud to Cage* (Illinois: Northwestern University Press, 1981), 129; Henry M. Sayre, "Avant-Garde Dispositions: Placing *Spring and All* in Context," *William Carlos Williams Review* 10 (Fall 1984): 18; and J. Hillis Miller, "Williams's *Spring and All* and the Progress of Poetry," *Daedalus* 99 (1970): 419.

9. Samuel Taylor Coleridge, *Biographia Literaria: The Collected Works of Samuel Taylor Coleridge, Biographical Sketches of My Literary Life and Opinions,* ed. James Engell and Jackson Bate (New Jersey: Princeton University Press, 1983), 304.

10. Ralph Waldo Emerson, *Essays and Poems,* ed. Peter Norberg (New York: Barnes and Noble, 2004), 211.

11. Williams, *Spring and All,* 112–13. If Whitman is the key expositor of the imagination, then nativism itself finds its first major articulation in Edgar Allan Poe. Williams hails Poe as "the first American poet" because his work embodied a break with the European tradition, and because Williams recognized that the reality of Poe's national context had manifested in the necessity for imaginative negotiation. "Poe could not have written a word without the violence of expulsive emotion combined with the indriving force of a crudely repressive environment. Between the two his imagination was forced into being" (111).

12. Karl Marx, *Capital: A Critique of Political Economy,* vol. 1, *The Process of Capitalist Accumulation,* trans. Samuel Moore and Edward Aveling, ed. Friedrich Engels (Chicago: Charles H. Kerr, 1906), 198.

13. Williams, *Spring and All,* 98. Similarly, in an unpublished poem from the period, Williams compares poetic labor to the way bees carry honey between pollen pots. Williams, "By Dint of Labor," PCMS-0024 William Carlos Williams Collection, box 1, Microform A309, Poetry Collection, State University of New York at Buffalo.

14. Leon Trotsky, *Lenin: Forming a Government,* 1925, www.marxists.org/archive/trotsky/1925/lenin/06.htm.

15. Williams, *Spring and All,* 120. Here "words" might be a typo or misprint, as it would make more sense to read "worlds," but this edition as well as the facsimile reprint have it as "words."

16. Ibid., 135; Marx and Engels, "Manifesto of the Communist Party," in *The Marx-Engels Reader,* 2nd ed., ed. Robert C. Tucker (New York: Norton, 1978), 473–74.

17. Mariani, *William Carlos Williams,* 173.

18. Williams, *Spring and All,* 90.

19. Ibid.

20. Williams, *The Autobiography of William Carlos Williams* (New York: New Directions, 1967), 146.

21. Williams had previously written that, when it came to form, Eliot "was looking backward; I was looking forward. He was a conformist, with wit, learning which I did not possess. He knew French, Latin, Arabic, god knows what." Williams, *I Wanted to Write a Poem,* 30.

22. Williams, *Spring and All,* 90.

23. Marianne Moore, *Complete Poems* (London: Faber and Faber, 1956), 46.

24. Williams, *Spring and All,* 95–96. Unless indicated otherwise, all subsequent quotations in this paragraph derive from the same pages.

25. I say "destination" instead of "location" because the poem's speaker is located on the road to the hospital but not in or at the hospital itself; if we can assume the speaker and Williams are similar, then this might be a poem spoken by a traveling doctor who writes verse on the way to appointments and from behind the wheel of a car. As such, there is already a shape of labor in this poem, where the roadside nearby

the hospital might serve as a locus for the intersection between paid and poetic work. The car will return at the end of this chapter.

26. Philip Bufithis, "William Carlos Williams Writing Against *The Waste Land,*" *Sagetreib* 8.1–2 (Spring-Fall 1989): 219. That Pound and Eliot particularly appreciated this poem was an evident source of disappointment to Williams. In a damning phrase, he suggests that it had only been "praised by the conventional boys for its form." Williams, *I Wanted to Write a Poem,* 37.

27. Richard R. Frye argues this point in "Seeing the Signs: Objectivist Premonitions in Williams's *Spring and All,*" *Sagetrieb* 8.3 (Winter 1989): 77–95.

28. Williams, *Spring and All,* 127.

29. Ibid., 127–28.

30. Williams, *Collected Poems of William Carlos Williams,* vol. 1, *1939–1962,* ed. Christopher MacGowan (New York: New Directions, 1991), 41.

31. Marya Zaturenska, "A Russian Easter—Russian Peasants," *Poetry* 16.1 (April 1920): 24–25.

32. Zukofsky in Williams, *The Correspondence of William Carlos Williams and Louis Zukofsky,* ed. Barry Ahearn (Middletown, CT: Wesleyan University Press, 2003), 38.

33. Julian Murphet, *Multimedia Modernism: Literature, Media, and the Anglo-American Avant-Garde* (Cambridge: Cambridge University Press, 2009), 187–88.

34. Jameson, "Reification and Utopia in Mass Culture," *Social Text* 1 (Winter 1979): 144.

35. Richard Parker, "'Baseball over Tea-Cakes': Major League Baseball in American Avant-Garde Poetry from Imagism to L=A=N=G=U=A=G=E," *NINE: A Journal of Baseball History and Culture* 20.2 (2012): 87.

36. Williams, *Spring and All,* 147–49. Unless indicated otherwise, all further quotations in this paragraph derive from the same pages.

37. Ezra Pound, *A Memoir of Gaudier-Brzeska* (New York: New Direction, 1974), 89.

38. For a clear elucidation of the "variable foot," which is an altogether vague concept in Williams's theoretical armature, see the entry on it by Stephen Cushman in Roland Greene, Stephen Cushman, Clare Cavanagh, Jahan Ramazani, and Paul Rouzer, *The Princeton Encyclopedia of Poetry and Poetics,* 4th ed. (New Jersey: Princeton University Press, 2012), 1503.

39. Williams, *I Wanted to Write a Poem,* 15.

40. Schott in Williams, *Imaginations,* iv.

41. Williams, *Selected Letters of William Carlos Williams,* ed. John C. Thirlwall (New York: New Directions, 1957), 135.

42. Williams, "America, Whitman, and the Art of Poetry," *Poetry Journal* 8.1 (November 1917): 78.

43. Eliot, *To Criticize the Critic* (London: Faber and Faber, 1965), 183.

44. Williams, *Spring and All,* 235.

45. Kenner, *The Pound Era* (London: Faber and Faber, 1972), 386.

46. Anna M. Lawton and Herbert Eagle, *Words in Revolution: Russian Futurist Manifestoes, 1912–1928* (Washington: Cornell University Press, 2004), 13.

47. Williams, *Autobiography,* 163. The poem's correct title is "Black and White."

48. Vladimir Mayakovsky, "How Are Verses Made?" in *Poetry in Theory: An Anthology, 1900–2000,* ed. Jon Cook (Malden, MA: Wiley-Blackwell, 2004), 147, 146.

49. This ownership was thrown into dispute during the Depression, when Europe ceased importing agricultural produce from the United States: "The economic impact of collapsing farm prices severely affected farmers, who began to default on equipment loans, tax payments, and mortgages." Cynthia Clark Northrop, *The American Economy: Essays and Primary Source Documents* (Santa Barbara: ABC-CLIO, 2003), 328.

50. Joel Nickels, *Poetry of the Possible: Spontaneity, Modernism, and the Multitude* (Minnesota: University of Minnesota Press, 2012), 50.

51. Theodor Adorno and Max Horkheimer, *Dialectic of Enlightenment,* trans. John Cumming (London: Verso, 1997), 121.

52. From that biographical knowledge alone we might begin to speculate on the poem's motivations, given that it is written for and about a working-class counterpart to Eliot's petit-bourgeois typist. Unless indicated otherwise, all quotations in the following paragraphs derive from Williams, *Spring and All,* 131–33.

53. Louis Zukofsky, *Prepositions: The Collected Critical Essays of Louis Zukofsky* (Berkeley: University of California Press, 1981), 150.

54. Thomas Whitaker, "Open to the Weather," in *Modern American Poetry,* ed. Harold Bloom (New York: Chelsea House, 2005), 103.

55. Adorno and Horkheimer, *Dialectic of Enlightenment,* 120.

56. Giorgio Agamben, *The End of the Poem,* trans. Daniel Heller-Roazen (Stanford: Stanford University Press, 1999), 112.

57. Williams, *Spring and All,* 133.

58. Emerson, *Essays and Poems,* 225.

59. Williams, *Spring and All,* 133.

60. Williams, *Collected Poems,* 1:42; Raymond Williams, *The Country and the City* (Oxford: Oxford University Press, 1973), 302.

61. Williams, *Collected Poems,* 1:49.

62. Ibid.

63. Ibid., 384–85.

64. Williams, *Spring and All,* 132.

65. For an excellent and necessary account of gender and sexuality in Williams's verse, see Linda A. Kinnahan, *Authority and Literary Tradition in William Carlos Williams, Mina Loy, Denise Levertov, and Kathleen Fraser* (Cambridge: Cambridge University Press, 1994). In his reading of *Paterson,* Jameson argues that in its "classic patriarchal" view of women, who are invariably seen from a male perspective, "the poem

faithfully represents the imbalance of its own historical period, and that it also marks that imbalance structurally by way of the visible deconstruction of this allegory," which he rightly concedes "may not be a particularly satisfying defense." Jameson, *Modernist Papers,* 13.

66. Williams, *Collected Poems,* 1:540, 2:126–27.

67. Williams, *Paterson,* xiv.

68. Numerous critics have identified the importance of the visual arts to Williams's poetry, and several studies have explored his borrowings from portraiture and photography. Charles Altieri's two books on painting and poetry remain the best resources here: *Painterly Abstraction in Modernist Poetry: The Contemporaneity of Modernism* (Cambridge: Cambridge University Press, 1989) and *The Art of Twentieth-Century American Poetry: Modernism and After* (Malden, MA: Blackwell, 2006). Peter Halter connects Williams's interest in the visual arts, including photography, to his social thinking in *The Revolution in the Visual Arts and the Poetry of William Carlos Williams* (Cambridge: Cambridge University Press, 1994). Bram Dijkstra writes about Williams and photography in *Cubism, Stieglitz, and the Early Poetry of William Carlos Williams* (New Jersey: Princeton University Press, 1969).

69. Walter Benjamin, *The Work of Art in the Age of Its Technological Reproducibility and Other Writings on Media,* ed. Michael W. Jennings, Brigid Doherty, and Thomas Y. Levin (Cambridge, MA: Harvard University Press, 2008), 27.

70. Ibid., 24.

71. Marx and Engels, "Manifesto," 468.

72. Theodor Adorno, *Minima Moralia: Reflections on a Damaged Life* (London: Verso, 2005), 17.

73. Leon Trotsky, *Literature and Revolution,* trans. William Keach (Chicago: Haymarket, 2005), 191.

74. Vladimir Mayakovsky, *Selected Works in Three Volumes,* vol. 2, trans. Dorian Rottenberg (Moscow: Raduga, 1986), 196.

75. William Stott, *Documentary Expression and Thirties America* (Chicago: University of Chicago Press, 1986), 227.

76. Williams, "The Descent of Winter," in *Imaginations,* 249.

77. Ibid.

78. Kazimir Malevich quoted in T. J. Clark, *Farewell to an Idea: Episodes from a History of Modernism* (New Haven: Yale University Press, 2001), 252.

79. Williams, *Collected Poems,* 1:278.

80. Marx and Engels, "German Ideology," in *The Marx-Engels Reader,* 2nd ed., ed. Robert C. Tucker (New York: Norton), 160.

81. Williams, "The Descent of Winter," 303–4.

82. Slavoj Žižek, *In Defense of Lost Causes* (London: Verso, 2008), 194.

83. Marx and Engels, "Manifesto," 484.

84. Williams, "The Descent of Winter," 253.

85. Ibid., 250.

86. Georg Lukács, *History and Class Consciousness: Studies in Marxist Dialectics,* trans. Rodney Livingstone (London: Merlin, 1971), 315.

87. Brian A. Bremen, *William Carlos Williams and the Diagnostics of Culture* (Oxford: Oxford University Press, 1993), 71, 252. In 1933, Williams developed this sentiment into a poem that cautions against walking "on the delicate parts/of necessary mechanisms," or else "you will pretty soon have/neither food, clothing, nor/even Communism itself." Williams, *Collected Poems,* 1:370.

88. Williams, "The Descent of Winter," 250.

89. Ibid., 251.

90. Jodi Dean, *The Communist Horizon* (London: Verso, 2012), 192.

91. Bremen, *William Carlos Williams and the Diagnostics of Culture,* 71.

92. Marx and Engels, "German Ideology," 160.

93. Williams, "The Descent of Winter," 251.

94. Ibid., 252.

95. Williams, *Collected Poems,* 1:517.

96. Williams, "The Descent of Winter," 253.

97. See Williams, "Introduction to Charles Sheeler—Paintings—Drawings—Photographs," in Williams, *Selected Essays* (New York: New Directions, 1969), 231–34.

98. Williams, *Collected Poems,* 2:12.

99. Williams, "The Descent of Winter," 254.

100. Ibid., 253.

101. Trotsky, *Literature and Revolution,* 197.

102. Williams, "The Descent of Winter," 253.

103. Ibid., 254.

104. Williams, *The Correspondence of William Carlos Williams and Louis Zukofsky,* 308.

105. Mariani, *William Carlos Williams,* 522.

106. Williams, *Collected Poems,* 2:473.

107. Ibid., 2:144.

108. The suggestion that this image is a photograph or perhaps even a postcard is strengthened by the drafts of "Russia," where it is referred to as one of multiple inexpensive reproductions. "Russia," PCMS-0024, William Carlos Williams Collection, box 1, Microform A288, Poetry Collection, State University of New York at Buffalo.

109. Mark Solomon, *The Cry Was Unity: Communists and African Americans, 1917–1936* (Jackson: University Press of Mississippi, 1998), xvii. For a useful account of Williams's engagements with African American language and culture, see Michael North, *The Dialectic of Modernism: Race, Language, and Twentieth-Century Literature* (Oxford: Oxford University Press, 1998), 147–74.

110. For the lines themselves, see Louis Zukofsky, *"A"* (New York: New Directions, 2011), 32. For a brilliantly detailed reading of them, see Ruth Jennison, *The*

Zukofsky Era: Modernity, Margins, and the Avant-Garde (Baltimore: Johns Hopkins University Press, 2012), 35–36.

111. Another poem by Williams, "Choral: The Pink Church," from 1949, uses the church setting as an allegory for multiple ideologies, including communism. In Cohen's fine reading of this poem, the erotic pink ("the nipples of/a woman") doubles as an evocation of the ubiquitous epithet "pinko," for which Williams had expressed admiration in a letter to Babette Deutsch: "I am *not red.* I sympathize strongly with the blood, the thing that makes a communist whatever good he is capable of being. The 'pink' of life, of a pink cheek." The poem ends with a depiction of "Milton, the unrhymer," who is "singing among/the rest . . .//like a Communist." Williams, *Collected Poems,* 2:177–80, 477; Cohen, 214–16.

112. Williams, *Collected Poems,* 2:144.

113. Hegel, *Aesthetics,* 2:1128–29.

114. Williams, *Collected Poems,* 2:145.

115. Ibid, 2:145–46.

116. Clare Cavanagh, "Whitman, Mayakovsky, and the Body Politic," in *Rereading Russian Poetry,* ed. Stephanie Sandler (New Haven: Yale University Press, 1999), 205.

117. Williams, *Collected Poems,* 2:146.

118. Hegel, *Aesthetics,* 2:865.

119. Williams, *Collected Poems,* 2:147.

120. White describes the field in these terms: "Yet recently, scholars have been drawn to analyzing the historical avant-garde's contrapuntal focus on localism—the specificities of place, time, nationality, region and milieu—that emerged as a component of (rather than a trend opposed to) the transnationalism generally taken to characterize literary modernism." White, *Transatlantic Avant-Gardes,* 1.

121. Williams, *Something to Say,* 77.

122. Jacques Rancière, *Aisthesis: Scenes from the Aesthetic Regime of Art,* trans. Zakir Paul (London: Verso, 2013), 63–64.

123. Quoted in Mariani, *William Carlos Williams,* 268.

124. Williams, *Autobiography,* 392.

125. Jameson, *Modernist Papers,* 12.

126. Those otherwise muted Cold-War sentiments are readily apparent in Williams's "Song," from 1949, a short lyric that concludes with these lines: "The world / will realign itself—ex- / cluding Russia / and the U.S.A." Williams, *Collected Poems,* 2:197.

127. Michael Denning, *The Cultural Front: The Laboring of American Culture in the Twentieth Century* (London: Verso, 1997), 3–4.

128. Williams, *Collected Poems,* 1:31.

129. Ibid., 112.

130. Williams, *The Autobiography,* 61.

131. Williams, "Comment," *Contact* 1.3 (October 1932): 131.

132. This *Blast* is not to be confused with the *Blast* we encountered in chapter 2,

which was based in London and edited by Wyndham Lewis. For a critical history of the New York *Blast,* see Peter Marks, "The Left in the 1930s: *The Modern Quarterly* (1929–33, became *The Modern Monthly,* 1933–40); *Blast: A Magazine of Proletarian Short Stories* (1933–4); and *The Windsor Quarterly* (1933–5)," in *The Oxford Critical and Cultural History of Modernist Magazines,* vol. 2, *North America 1894–1960,* ed. Peter Brooker and Andrew Thacker (Oxford: Oxford University Press, 2012), 881–902.

133. William Carlos Williams, "Art and Politics: The Editorship of BLAST," in *A Recognizable Image: William Carlos Williams on Art and Artists,* ed. Bram Dijkstra (London: New Directions, 1978), 75. See also, within the same collection, "A Letter to the Comintern Upon Censorship in the Arts."

134. Williams, "Art and Politics," 79. "Red Front" also refers to Louis Aragorn's poem by that title, which was translated into English by E. E. Cummings in 1933.

135. Williams, "Art and Politics," 79. The interjections belong to Dijkstra, whose transcription is slightly different from the manuscript, which is housed in Buffalo.

136. Ibid., 78.

137. Williams, *Paterson,* 2.

138. Ibid., 4, 8. Jameson reads this gendering as part of a distinctly American strain of naturalism: "There is a Sister Carrie note to this evocation of the women from the back country [. . .] who gradually drift down into the small city to live out their frustrations and unsatisfied desires." Jameson, *Modernist Papers,* 13.

139. Williams, *Paterson,* 6.

140. Ibid., 36.

141. James E. B. Breslin, *William Carlos Williams: An American Artist* (Chicago: University of Chicago Press, 1985), 170–71.

142. Ibid., Williams, *Paterson,* 2, 99.

143. Ibid., 57–58.

144. David Kadlec, "Early Soviet Cinema and American Poetry," *Modernism/modernity,* 11.2 (April 2004): 319.

145. André Bazin, *What is Cinema?,* vol. 1, ed. and trans. Hugh Gray (Berkeley: University of California Press, 1967), 44.

146. Williams, *Paterson,* 55.

147. Ibid., 62.

148. Ibid., 33–34.

149. Ibid.

150. Ibid, 40.

151. Williams, *Paterson,* 239.

152. Williams, *Collected Poems,* 2:198.

153. Ibid., 62, 99.

154. Ibid., 159–60.

155. Williams quoted in Mike Weaver, *William Carlos Williams and the American Background* (Cambridge: Cambridge University Press, 1971), 120.

156. Georg Lukács, *The Theory of the Novel,* trans. Anna Bostock (Cambridge, MA: MIT Press, 1971). 50.

157. Ibid., 50–51.

158. Williams, *Collected Poems,* 1:28.

159. Williams, *Selected Essays*, 282.

160. William Carlos Williams in Ezra Pound, *Pound/Williams: Selected Letters of Ezra Pound and William Carlos Williams,* ed. Hugh Witemeyer (New York: New Directions, 1996), 236.

161. Williams, "The Attack on Credit Monopoly from a Cultural Viewpoint," in *A Recognizable Image, 97–118.* For why this stance is counterfactual, see Jodi Dean: "The communist subject is not an ensemble or assemblage of individuals but a force opposed to such an individualism and its attachments." Dean, *The Communist Horizon,* 192–93.

162. Williams, "The Attack on Credit Monopoly from a Cultural Viewpoint," 115.

163. Ibid.

164. Jameson, *Modernist Papers,* 42.

165. Williams, *Paterson,* 181, 180, and 290n180.

166. Ibid., 22.

167. Walter Benjamin, *Selected Writings,* vol. 4, *1938–1940,* ed. Michael W. Jennings and Howard Eiland (Cambridge, MA: Harvard University Press, 2003), 395.

168. Marx, *Capital,* 837.

169. For an account of Hamilton's economic thinking in relation to Pound and Williams which stresses the similarities between Hamilton's sense of finance and Douglas's Social Credit, see the chapter on "Jeffersonian Economics" in Marsh, *Money and Modernity,* 11–41.

170. Williams, *Paterson,* 10, 70.

171. Dennis Gilbert, *The American Class Structure in an Age of Growing Inequality* (London: Sage, 2015), 3.

172. Williams, *Paterson,* 46.

173. James E. Miller Jr., "William Carlos Williams's 'Paterson,'" in *Modern American Poetry,* 213.

174. Williams, *Paterson,* 44.

175. Williams, *Selected Letters,* 258–59.

176. Williams, *Paterson,* 80.

177. Marx, *Capital,* 836–37.

178. Williams, *Paterson,* 81.

Chapter 4. Louis Zukofsky

1. Vladimir Il'ich Lenin, "The State and Revolution," in *Selected Works: Two-Volume Edition,* vol. 2 (Moscow: Foreign Languages Publishing House, 1947), 142.

2. Ibid., 225.

3. Louis Zukofsky, *Prepositions: The Collected Critical Essays of Louis Zukofsky* (Berkeley: University of California Press, 1981), 215.

4. Mark Scroggins, ed., *Upper Limit Music: The Writing of Louis Zukofsky* (Tuscaloosa: University of Alabama Press, 1997), 49.

5. For critical work on this belatedness, see Charles Bernstein, "Objectivist Blues: Scoring Speech in Second Wave Modernist Poetry and Poetics," in *Attack of the Difficult Poems* (Chicago: University of Chicago Press, 2011), 131–58, and Andrew Crozier, "Zukofsky's List," in *The Objectivist Nexus: Essays in Cultural Poetics,* ed. Rachael Blau DuPlessis and Peter Quartermain (Tuscaloosa: University of Alabama Press, 1999), 275–85.

6. Louis Zukofsky, *Anew: Complete Shorter Poetry,* ed. Robert Creeley (New York: New Directions, 2011), 16.

7. Ibid., 8.

8. Zukofsky, *Prepositions,* 77.

9. Norman Finkelstein, *The Utopian Moment in Contemporary American Poetry* (London: Associated Universities Press, 1993), 37.

10. Luke Carson, *Consumption and Depression in Gertrude Stein, Louis Zukofsky, and Ezra Pound* (New York: St. Martin's Press, 1999), 225.

11. Finkelstein, *The Utopian Moment,* 37.

12. Fredric Jameson, *Archaeologies of the Future: The Desire Called Utopia and Other Science Fictions* (London: Verso, 2005), xiii.

13. Louis Zukofsky, *"A"* (New York: New Directions, 2011), 30–31.

14. Lenin quoted in Clara Zetkin, "Lenin on the Women's Question," www.marxists .org/archive/zetkin/1920/lenin/zetkin1.htm.

15. Alexandra Kollontai, *Selected Articles and Speeches* (New York: International, 1984), 130.

16. For a detailed history of these events, see Hans Schmidt, *The United States Occupation of Haiti, 1915–1934* (New Jersey: Rutgers University Press, 1995).

17. Georg Lukács, *Theory of the Novel, trans. Anna Bostock* (Cambridge, MA: MIT Press, 1971), 29.

18. Louis Zukofsky, *Anew: Complete Shorter Poetry,* 8, 20.

19. Ibid., 21.

20. Mark Scroggins, *The Poem of a Life: A Biography of Louis Zukofsky* (Washington: Shoemaker and Hoard, 2007), 51.

21. Alfred Tennyson, *Selected Poetry* (New York: Broadview, 2014), 89.

22. Ruth Jennison, *The Zukofsky Era: Modernity, Margins, and the Avant-Garde* (Baltimore: Johns Hopkins University Press, 2012), 34.

23. Zukofsky, *Anew: Complete Shorter Poetry,* 21.

24. Williams, *Selected Letters of William Carlos Williams,* ed. John C. Thirlwall (New York: New Directions, 1957), 102.

25. Scroggins bases an excellent chapter on Zukofsky and politics around this phrase, "the revolutionary word," which derives from Zukofsky's claim that the "revolutionary word if it must revolve cannot escape having a reference." See Scroggins, " 'The Revolutionary Word': Zukofsky, the Political Radical," in *Louis Zukofsky and the Poetry of Knowledge* (Alabama: Alabama University Press, 1998), 140–61.

26. Jameson, *Archaeologies,* xv.

27. Theodor W. Adorno, *Aesthetic Theory,* trans. Robert Hullot-Kentor (London: Continuum, 1997), 32.

28. Clara Zetkin, *Reminiscences of Lenin* (Moscow: International, 1924).

29. Zukofsky, *"A",* 90.

30. Lenin, "A Letter to A. M. Gorky," November 25, 1908, www.marxists.org/archive/lenin/works/1908/feb/25.htm; Zukofsky, "A", 53.

31. Lenin, "A Letter to A. M. Gorky."

32. Zukofsky, *Prepositions,* 4.

33. Louis Auguste Blanqui, "Eternity by the Stars: *L'éternité par les astres,*" trans. Matthew H. Henderson, *New Centennial Review* 93 (2010): 58.

34. Walter Benjamin, *The Arcades Project,* trans. Howard Eiland and Kevin McLaughlin (Cambridge, MA: Harvard University Press, 2002), 111, 343.

35. Osip Mandelstam quoted in Marshall Berman, *All That Is Solid Melts Into Air: The Experience of Modernity* (London: Penguin, 1982), 272–73.

36. Lenin quoted in Susan Buck-Morss, *Dreamworld and Catastrophe: The Passing of Mass Utopia in East and West* (Cambridge, MA: MIT Press, 2000), 44. This anecdote is quoted from Maxim Gorky, for whom the words "the earthly limit" are attributed directly to Lenin.

37. Joseph MacLeod, *The Eclyptic* (London: Faber, 1930), 23.

38. Louis Zukofsky in Pound, *Selected Letters of Ezra Pound and Louis Zukofsky,* ed. Barry Ahearn (New York: New Directions, 1987), 82–83.

39. Charles Reznikoff, *The Poems of Charles Reznikoff, 1918–1975,* ed. Seamus Cooney (Boston: Black Sparrow, 2005), 114.

40. Ibid.

41. Zukofsky quoted in Scroggins, *The Poem of a Life,* 37.

42. Jennison, *The Zukofsky Era,* 41.

43. This phrase emerged from John Quincy Adams's first annual address to Congress, on December 6, 1825, in which he implored the government to improve basic operations of production, including agriculture, commerce, and manufacture, and in which he asked for greater support to the arts and sciences, including the construction of observatories, which he called "lighthouses of the sky." For a lively narration of this speech, see Harlow Giles Under, *John Quincy: A Life* (Philadelphia: Da Capo, 2012), 229–59.

44. Zukofsky, *"A",* 72.

45. John Quincy Adams, *Memoirs of John Quincy Adams, Comprising Portions of His*

Diary From 1795 to 1848, vol. 10, ed. Charles Francis Adams (Philadelphia: J. B. Lippincott, 1876), 38.

46. William Butler Yeats, *The Collected Poems of W. B. Yeats,* ed. Richard J. Fineran (New York: Simon and Schuster, 1996), 180.

47. Zukofsky, *"A",* 72.

48. Carson, *Consumption,* 274n15.

49. Trotsky, *The Permanent Revolution and Results and Prospects* (Seattle: Red Letter Press, 2010), 50.

50. Zukofsky, *"A",* 80–1.

51. Ibid., 81–82.

52. Walter Benjamin, *Selected Writings,* vol. 2, part 1, 1927–1930, ed. Michael W. Jennings, Howard Eiland, and Gary Smith, trans. Rodney Livingstone et al. (Cambridge, MA: Harvard University Press, 1999), 36.

53. Lenin, "Our Foreign and Domestic Position and Party Tasks: Speech Delivered To The Moscow Gubernia Conference Of The R.C.P. (B.)," November 21, 1920, www.marxists.org/archive/lenin/works/1920/nov/21.htm.

54. Henry Adams, *The Education of Henry Adams,* ed. Ernest Samuels (Boston: Houghton Mifflin, 1973), 410.

55. Zukofsky, *"A",* 68–69. All remaining quotations in this paragraph are from the same two pages.

56. Ibid., 69.

57. T. S. Eliot, "The Metaphysical Poets," in *The Annotated Waste Land and Eliot's Contemporary Prose,* ed. Lawrence Rainey (New Haven: Yale University Press, 2005), 198.

58. Zukofsky, *Anew: Complete Shorter Poetry,* 171. Part fourteen of *"A"* begins with a rocket launch and soon arrives at a lunar thematic, describing a "paddle satellite" caught in "solar winds," 315.

59. Zukofsky, *"A",* 60.

60. "Topics of The Times," *New York Times* (January 23, 1935).

61. Jameson, *Archaeologies,* 60.

62. Zukofsky, *"A",* 43.

63. Donna Haraway, "A Cyborg Manifesto: Science, Technology, and Socialist-Feminism in the Late Twentieth Century," in *The Cybercultures Reader,* ed. David Bell and Barbara M. Kennedy (London: Routledge, 2000), 291; N. Katherine Hayles, *How We Became Posthuman: Virtual Bodies in Cybernetics, Literature, and Informatics* (Chicago: University of Chicago Press, 1999), 2. McKenzie Wark has written a useful account of the relationships between Marx, Haraway, and Soviet sci-fi writers Alexander Bogdanov and Andrey Patonov. McKenzie Wark, *Molecular Red: Theory for the Anthropocene* (London: Verso, 2015).

64. Andrei Platonov quoted in Buck-Morss, *Dreamworld and Catastrophe,* 77.

65. Zukofsky, *Anew: Complete Shorter Poetry,* 40.

66. Trotsky, *Literature and Revolution,* 207.

67. Mayakovsky, *The Bedbug and Selected Poetry,* ed. Patricia Blake, trans. Max Hayward and George Reavey (Bloomington: Indiana University Press, 1960), 35.

68. Alexander Rodchenko quoted in Buck-Morss, *Dreamworld and Catastrophe,* 55.

69. Jameson, *Archaeologies,* 64.

70. Zukofsky, *"A",* 58; Marx, *Capital: A Critique of Political Economy,* vol. 1, *The Process of Capitalist Accumulation,* trans. Samuel Moore and Edward Aveling, ed. Friedrich Engels (Chicago: Charles H. Kerr, 1906), 406n2, 223.

71. Zukofsky, *"A",* 45–46.

72. Marx quoted in Lenin, "State and Revolution," 204. Early drafts of these lines include the phrase "bourgeois right," which has been excised from the published text. Zukofsky, "A", 1–12, TXRC98-A11 Louis Zukofsky Collection, series 1, box 1, folders 6–9, Harry Ransom Center, University of Texas at Austin.

73. Leo Panitch and Sam Gindin, *The Making of Global Capitalism: The Political Economy of the American Empire* (London: Verso, 2012), 52.

74. Lenin, "State and Revolution," 203–6.

75. Zukofsky, *"A",* 46.

76. Marx, *Capital,* 332–34n2.

77. Ibid., 837n1.

78. Lenin, "May Day Action by the Revolutionary Proletariat," *Sotsial-Demokrat* 31 (June 15, 1913), www.marxists.org/archive/lenin/works/1913/jun/15.htm.

79. Zukofsky, *"A",* 48. This rhetoric is echoed in part 7, in which there are "no diggers," and where "the graves were turfed and the horses grassed" (p. 40), and it appears verbatim in the poem's final installment (p. 718), as well as in a shorter poem, "The Immediate Aim." Zukofsky, *Anew: Complete Shorter Poetry,* 56.

80. Zukofsky, *"A",* 48. That these lines are channeling not just *Capital* but also its quotations from the *Manifesto* is implied by what follows. "To this end," read the lines subsequent to the chorus, "Communists assembled in London / Sketched the Manifesto of the party itself." Zukofsky, *"A",* 49.

81. Marx, "Marx on the History of his Opinions (Preface to A Contribution to the Critique of Political Economy," in *The Marx-Engels Reader,* 2nd ed., ed. Robert C. Tucker (New York: Norton, 1978), 5.

82. Zukofsky, *"A",* 61.

83. Ibid., 57.

84. Zukofsky, *Prepositions,* 63.

85. Zukofsky, *"A",* 88.

86. Marx, *Capital,* 51. The carbuncles might also recall Eliot's paradigmatic depiction of the technological colonization of organic bodies: that miserable tryst between a "young man carbuncular" and a female typist, whose postcoital "brain" famously "allows one half-formed thought to pass." Eliot, *Poems and Plays,* 68–69.

87. Zukofsky, *"A",* 74–75.

88. Marx, "Letters of Marx and Engels: 1863," https://www.marxists.org/archive/marx/works/1863/letters/index.htm.

89. Marx, *Capital,* 416–17.

90. Zukofsky, *"A",* 32.

91. Lenin, "State and Revolution," 205.

92. Stalin in Mark R. Beissinger, *Scientific Management, Socialist Discipline and Soviet Power* (London: I. B. Taurus, 1988), 5.

93. Lenin, "Telegram to Comrades Kuraev, Bosh, Minkin, and other Penza communists," August 11, 1918, https://www.marxists.org/archive/lenin/works/1918/aug/11c.htm.

94. Zukofsky, *"A",* 32.

95. Lenin in Paul R. Josephson, *Would Trotsky Wear a Bluetooth? Technological Utopianism Under Socialism, 1917–1989* (Baltimore: Johns Hopkins University Press, 2010), 29.

96. Jennison, *The Zukofsky Era,* 35.

97. Zukofsky, *"A",* 34.

98. Zukofsky, "A", 1–12, TXRC98-A11 Louis Zukofsky Collection, series 1, box 1, folders 6–9, Harry Ransom Center, University of Texas at Austin.

99. Zukofsky, *"A",* 25.

100. "Ford Defends Life in Industrial Age; Declares in Interview on 67th Birthday Machine Era Will Develop Culture," *New York Times,* July 31, 1930.

101. Panitch and Gindin, *The Making of Global Capitalism,* 30.

102. Zukofsky, *"A",* 26.

103. Benjamin, *The Work of Art in the Age of Its Technological Reproducibility and Other Writings on Media,* ed. Michael W. Jennings, Brigid Doherty, and Thomas Y. Levin (Cambridge, MA: Harvard University Press, 2008), 21.

104. Zukofsky, *"A",* 26.

105. Ibid., 27.

106. Zukofsky, *Prepositions,* 77.

107. This is Lenin's original text, which Zukofsky alters only slightly. Zukofsky, "Matter That Thinks: Or Notion Towards Action," TXRC98-A11 Louis Zukofsky Collection, series 1, box 14, folders 9, Harry Ransom Center, University of Texas at Austin.

108. In A. Preminger, C. Scott, and D. Caplan, "Sestina," in *The Princeton Encyclopedia of Poetry and Poetics,* 1297.

109. David Caplan, *Questions of Possibility: Contemporary Poetry and Poetic Form* (Oxford: Oxford University Press, 2005), 23.

110. Zukofsky, *Anew: Complete Shorter Poetry,* 69.

111. In A. Preminger, C. Scott, and D. Caplan, "Sestina," in *The Princeton Encyclopedia of Poetry and Poetics,* 1297.

112. Michael Davidson, *Ghostlier Demarcations: Modern Poetry and the Material*

Word (Berkeley: University of California Press, 1997), 119; Zukofsky, *Anew: Complete Shorter Poetry,* 70, 72.

113. Zukofsky, *Anew: Complete Shorter Poetry,* 66.

114. Quoted and discussed at length in Michael Golston, "Petalbent Devils: Louis Zukofsky, Lorine Niedecker, and the Surrealist Praying Mantis," *Modernism/modernity* 13.2 (2006): 332.

115. Zukofsky, *Anew: Complete Shorter Poetry,* 70.

116. Zukofsky, *"A",* 42.

117. Scroggins, *Poem of a Life,* 180.

118. Zukofsky, *"A",* 51–52.

119. Emily Dickinson, *The Complete Poems,* ed. Thomas H. Johnson (London: Faber and Faber, 1975), 1082.

120. The final line's naming of the *Manifesto* seems to confirm a palpable shift away from the programmatic statements of Marx's critiques and back toward the more impulsive, political rhetoric that underwrites his critical thinking on technology.

121. Marx, "Critique of the Gotha Program," in *The Marx-Engels Reader,* 2nd ed., ed. Robert C. Tucker (New York: Norton, 1978), 531.

122. This observation belongs to Peter Quartermain, and he makes it in *Disjunctive Poetics: From Gertrude Stein and Louis Zukofsky to Susan Howe* (Cambridge: Cambridge University Press, 1992), 76.

123. Zukofsky, *"A",* 103–5.

124. See J. G. Fucilla and C. Kleinhenz, "Canzone" in *The Princeton Encyclopedia of Poetry and Poetics,* 190–91.

125. Pound, *Literary Essays of Ezra Pound,* ed. T. S. Eliot (New York: New Directions, 1954), 168, 149.

126. Zukofsky, *Prepositions,* 241.

127. Adorno, *Aesthetic Theory,* 212–13.

128. Zukofsky, *"A",* 106.

129. Jennison, *The Zukofsky Era,* 127.

Epilogue

1. Eric Hobsbawm, *Age of Extremes: The Short Twentieth Century, 1914–1991* (London: Abacus, 1994), 393.

2. Basil Bunting quoted in John Seed, "Irrelevant Objects: Basil Bunting's Poetry in the 1930s," in DuPlessis and Quartermain, *The Objectivist Nexus,* 135.

3. Leszek Kołakowski, *Main Currents of Marxism,* trans. P. S. Falla (New York: Norton, 2008), 495.

4. Žižek, *In Defense of Lost Causes,* 176.

5. Zukofsky, *"A",* 35.

6. Charles Olson, *The Collected Poems of Charles Olson,* ed. George F. Butterick

(Berkeley: University of California Press, 1997), 87. For a useful account of the source material quoted in these lines, see Ralph Maud, *What Does Not Change: The Significance of Charles Olson's "The Kingfishers"* (Plainsboro, NJ: Associated University Press, 1998), 38–41.

7. Olson, *Collected Poems,* 91.

8. Anderson, *The Origins of Postmodernity* (London: Verso, 1998), 12.

9. Allen Ginsberg, *The Essential Ginsberg,* ed. Michael Schumacher (London: Penguin, 2015), 30.

10. Robert Duncan, *The Collected Early Poetry and Plays,* ed. Peter Quartermain (Berkeley: University of California Press, 2012), 362.

11. Ginsberg, *The Essential Ginsberg,* 161.

12. Ibid.

13. Anderson, *The Origins of Postmodernity,* 12.

Index